CREATIVE MARKETING FOR NEW PRODUCT AND NEW BUSINESS DEVELOPMENT

CREATIVE MARKETING FOR NEW PRODUCT AND NEW BUSINESS DEVELOPMENT

Editors

Akira Ishikawa
Aoyama Gakuin University, Japan

Atsushi Tsujimoto
University of Tokyo, Japan

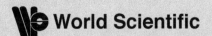

World Scientific

NEW JERSEY · LONDON · SINGAPORE · BEIJING · SHANGHAI · HONG KONG · TAIPEI · CHENNAI

Published by

World Scientific Publishing Co. Pte. Ltd.

5 Toh Tuck Link, Singapore 596224

USA office: 27 Warren Street, Suite 401-402, Hackensack, NJ 07601

UK office: 57 Shelton Street, Covent Garden, London WC2H 9HE

British Library Cataloguing-in-Publication Data
A catalogue record for this book is available from the British Library.

Originally published in Japan in 2006 by Japan Productivity Center for
Socio-Economic Development (http://www.jpc-sed.or.jp/eng/index.html)

Translation by Raj Mahtani/TranNet KK, Japan

**CREATIVE MARKETING FOR NEW PRODUCT AND NEW BUSINESS
DEVELOPMENT**

ISBN-13 978-981-277-218-3
ISBN-10 981-277-218-9

Typeset by Stallion Press
Email: enquiries@stallionpress.com

Printed in Singapore.

Foreword

Japan, as you may very well know, is a resource-poor nation with an extremely small landmass. Despite this, one in five people is above 65 years old, and what is more, its population exceeds 120 million. To survive, this nation has no other choice but to secure a permanent intellectual edge that goes beyond military strength. Toward this end, participation of senior citizens, whose experience and insight are unsurpassable, is indispensable.

With this intellectual edge, which has its source in creativity, a nation can achieve affluence and even go on to help bring about happiness for humankind, such as using new ideas to create something out of nothing, or adding new value by reinventing existing products. As a matter of fact, this intellectual edge is the *raison d'être* of any organization, whether we are talking about a company or the government.

After World War II, Japan saw a rise in the affluence of its people as it went on to become the world's second largest economic power. While excellent product services realized through diligent work habits certainly helped, it would be no exaggeration to say that creativity played a supportive role.

In an organizational attempt toward supporting this creativity, the Japan Institute of Invention and Innovation has been contributing toward spreading the industrial property rights system and toward realizing the advancement of science and technology for more than a hundred years since its inception in 1904, and has been carrying out official commendations for inventions nationwide through the presentation of nine special awards, including The Prime Minister Invention Award; The Minister of Education, Culture, Sports, Science and Technology Invention Award; The Minister of Economy, Trade and Industry Invention Award; and the Commissioner of Patents Award.

Meanwhile, the Japan Society for the Advancement of Inventions, a foundation engaged in activities to promote and propagate inventions by mainstay small to medium-sized enterprises, has been subsidizing research fellowships for 27 years and has been supporting the cultivation of creativity among young people for many years by establishing "invention classrooms" for elementary- to middle-school students.

Non-profit institutions also exist, such as the Hatsumeigakkai (Invention Society), and the Japan Creativity Society, a registered association of the Science Council of Japan, which has scholars, researchers, teachers, and businessmen as members. Furthermore, to develop creative potential, international intellectual competitions have been held for mainly high-school students, such as the International Mathematics Olympics, the International Chemistry Olympics, the International Biology Olympics, and additionally, the International Information Olympics.

Where the World Creativity Forum is concerned, in 2006 alone, there were many conferences held, including the American Creativity Association International Conference (America), the 4th Creativity European Association Conference, the 17th International Conference on Creativity in Colleges and Universities (America), the 1st International Conference on Knowledge, Information and Creativity Support Systems (Thailand), the 12th Annual International Creativity Conference in Africa (South Africa), and the 11th International Creativity Conference (Latvia), and many others. How many

Japanese will actually have participated in these international conferences by the end of this year? Is creativity education being adequately carried out in kindergartens, elementary and middle schools, and institutions of higher learning such as universities and graduate schools?

This book is about this creativity and is written by primarily eight individuals, including young, frontline scholars, researchers, and talented businesspeople as a text for university students, while also targeting business entrepreneurs, administrators, and additionally, people who intend to start a business in the future.

Its origin can be traced back to the Japan-US Product Development Conference, where I had the opportunity to serve as co-chairman. This conference was held for five years throughout the mid-1970s. Based on presentation materials and reports gathered from this period, I went on to hold lectures and seminars across Europe and Japan, and in 1988 I published *The Q&A Primer to Information Searching for Developing New Products and New Businesses* (Dobunkan). This book was a compilation of my answers to important questions posed to me at those lectures and seminars. I made use of the compilation at private and governmental seminars and found them to be highly valuable. However, nearly 20 years have already come to pass, and with the concern of assuring the succession of my intellectual property, I gathered a team of young scholars, researchers, and adept businesspeople to publish this new book.

Compared to its earlier version, this book has seen considerable revisions in both format and content and has been further enriched. Firstly, the Q&A format has been discontinued and replaced by the normal text format. This is due to the fact that we have made it a top priority to see the book serve as a textbook for university students. Nevertheless, it is written not only for students, but, as previously mentioned, for businesspeople, researchers, and educators as well.

If you are a reader who is studying the fields of research and development, new product development, and new business development for the first time, then I recommend that you read the book sequentially from the Introduction. If you are a manager or researcher who is in a position to advocate the necessity of R&D, or if you are in charge of the R&D department or product development department and concerned about the gaps found between management strategy, R&D, and product development, I particularly recommend that you carefully read Chapters 2 through 5, where you will find thorough discussions of viewpoints dealing with such topics as the "Darwinian Sea" (the phenomena which refers to the fact that business projects generally fail to materialize soon, even after having goals of commercialization in sight), product development and R&D engineering that deals with the "Death Valley" phenomena (which arises from the gap found between basic research/invention and applied research/product development), marketing research for product development, and furthermore, R&D alliances and outsourcing.

For readers concerned with matters of how to go about planning, selecting, and evaluating R&D projects, they should refer to Chapter 3, where the decision making process is introduced. Based on a broad perspective, this process includes the criteria for determining whether to continue (extend) projects, and for determining when to abort them. Interspersed with illustrative examples, it particularly delves into discussions on terminating difficult and unsuccessful projects. Furthermore, regarding the ideal evaluation system, it asserts that judgments should be made in light of the importance of corporate policies and general societal norms.

This book attaches great importance to the new ways information is being systematized and turned into assets, and recognizes these very ways as the key basis for R&D, new product development, and new business development. For this reason, Chapter 4 has been intended for managers and CIOs (executives in charge of information) who experience great pains in handling the strategic management of development information, and additionally, for those in charge of information development and management.

In Chapter 5, with respect to advancing R&D, new product development, and new business development, we discuss thoroughly how to link sources of information with basic research and sources of information with applied research, in addition to discussing the management of personnel training. We then go on to consider a shortcut to the successful development of information as an asset, which is a thorny issue for CIOs and those in charge of development. The chapter concludes with the assertion that "the foundation for this must lie strictly in the solid training of personnel in the concerned field."

This book is divided into two parts: Part 1 is introductory and includes many illustrative examples, and Part 2 is the case example section. Readers who are already well-versed with the contents of Part 1 will do well to begin from Chapter 6's case example on Coca Cola Japan's "Karada Meguri Cha™" (a health-oriented tea whose Japanese name literally translates to Body Circulation Tea). There, you will find an extremely elaborate record of a time-consuming search for information carried out by the person in charge. This record lays down the core philosophy behind new product development, builds its basic strategy, and emphasizes that the design phase is the very phase you should apply your time, passion, and resources. There is adequate recognition of the lesson that compared to the cost of withdrawing a product due to an undesirable sales performance stemming from a lack of preparation before the product's release, it is overwhelmingly cheaper to call off a product from the market after spending an ample amount of developmental cost and time prior to its release. This case is considered to be crucial and offers plenty of suggestions for heads of R&D and research workers.

As a third large feature, in addition to the noteworthy case example of the product recommendation website equipped with the Web recommendation engine in Chapter 7, I have included in Chapter 8 robot development case examples, which is something that Japan prides itself on. According to the Chairman of the Board of Yaskawa Electric Corporation, Mr. Shin Nakayama, who claims that the 21st century is the "age of robots," Japan once had 200 robot business-related companies, but as a result of excessive competition, there are approximately only 50 companies surviving today, with only two in Europe and one in the US. With regard to industrial robots, he adds that Japan overwhelmingly leads the world.

However, I must point out that this book does not touch upon the subject of robots for military use. I am hoping that readers interested in this field will proceed with their own research, even though there are many facets of it that remain undisclosed. I encourage this because there is an undeniable possibility that research in military-use robots will spur the advance of civilian-use robots in the same way research in the military use of the Internet had contributed towards spreading the civilian use of the Internet in the past.

Additionally as a fourth feature, while the primary theme of this book is concerned with new product and new business development, cases on management and maintenance have also been added to prompt discussion on how to protect developed products and product materials in crisis situations. After all, new products and new service businesses also need to take into account the significance of remaining sustainable in the market after undergoing their R&D and market entry.

This is why even risk management personnel are also considered as this book's target readers. Furthermore, it will become clear through these cases that those in charge of Corporate Social Responsibility (CSR) affairs have an important role to fulfill in this field as well and are far from being unrelated to it.

Finally, as a special feature, readers will find not only spectacular stories of successful new products and businesses, but also stories of failure and chance (and even stories of how a failure can lead to success) sprinkled here and there throughout the book. The king of inventions, Thomas Edison, once responded to a newspaper reporter, "Genius is one percent inspiration and ninety-nine percent perspiration." This quote is well-known, but on a separate occasion, he commented that he had never achieved anything of value through mere coincidences and that his various inventions were not brought about by chance at all, but were created by dint of sheer work. This is important to note as well. While simple, the remark has its feet on the ground and I believe it will become a motto for creative undertakings.

It would make me happy if this book is found to be helpful by readers who are enthusiastic about such activities.

Akira Ishikawa
November 2006

Contents

Chapter 1

Introduction

According to what I learned from anthropology over a half-century ago, the first humans to appear were the Peking man and the Java man about 100,000–150,000 years ago. Even if these figures were allowed a wide margin of error, the commonly held view then was that they would not exceed one million years.

However, currently, the origin of humankind (*pithecanthropus*) is said to date back to five million years ago, which differs from the previous estimate by an entire digit. Furthermore, today, humankind is said to be subdivided into the categories of *pithecanthropus*, proto-man, paleo-man, and neo-man. Still, compared to the origin of life, which is estimated to have emerged approximately 3.6 billion years ago, the birth of humankind differs by three digits and can be seen to be extremely recent.

In this way, it can be seen that as times change, it becomes necessary to make drastic changes to the text of knowledge as well, as the anthropological example above demonstrates. In other words, discoveries and inspections of remains have the ability to change what we should be studying to a substantial degree, and in some cases, they may change them on a fundamental level. Inventions and discoveries, which are subjects that lie at the heart of this book, are testaments to humanity's right and obligation to progress. Seen from a certain perspective, they can be considered as the greatest privilege offered to the primate known as human.

This teaches us not to be too captive to preconceived ideas. For example, regarding human civilizations five to six thousand years ago, if you look at the arts and cultures of places like Crete and Santorini, where Egyptian civilization and the Aegean Sea played central roles, and additionally, if you look at the lost articles of Troy, it becomes clear that their levels of art and technology were highly advanced already. Generally speaking, it is not impossible to suppose that considerable cultural exchanges had been taking place between civilizations back then. Consequently, if excavations of ruins around such regions continue, the world history of civilization itself, including the hypothesis of Atlantis, may see drastic alterations.

Relative to such a long-term, macroscopic observation, this book concentrates on an extremely short-term and microscopic perspective. Even when the phrase "long-term" is used, I will be referring to units of several decades at most. Additionally, while handling ultra short time frames, such as the microsecond, nanosecond, and the picosecond (which is one-trillionth of a second), I will also make unfazed use of supplementary units of extremely gigantic memory capacities, such as mega, giga, tera, and peta (10^{15} times). With such frames of reference in mind, let us proceed by beginning with a contextual understanding of the times, which is necessary to have in order to carry out R&D, new product development, and new business development.

1.1   From the Age of Information to the Age of Information Communication (Network)[1]

In the first edition of this book, I pointed out that if I began to mention waves of change that surged as we headed towards the

---

[1] While David Moschler foresees a contents-centric era during the period from 2020 through 2030 subsequent to the arrival of an (information) network-centric era, there are books such as Masakazu Kobayashi's *The Disappearance of Content* (Kobunsha), which warn otherwise. So it can be seen that the future is in no way set in stone.

21st century, such as the liberalization of communication, financial deregulation, sudden fluctuations in the exchanges and stock prices, relaxation of regulations, and agricultural liberalization, there would be too many examples to mention in their entirety. Moreover, I mentioned that they were merely the first waves and were going to change shape and surge again as second and third waves.

As a solution for reinforcing your organization and improving your personal life, I also emphasized that you had no choice but to detect these waves beforehand and not only ride them out successfully, but at the same time, acquire, process, assess, and interpret relevant information from an enormous amount of data or obtain a small amount of information (which are nevertheless crucially important), from the most appropriate information media or information provider.[1]

To this end, I pointed out that it all depended on having a sufficient grasp of the characteristics of the information age, which occupies a fundamental place in the context of the times, and on how you go about preparing and reinforcing your organizational or personal information management system.

Even as we find ourselves headlong into the first ten years of the 21st century today, such observations continue to remain relevant. Even so, I did not foresee that the wave of the commercial internet, which was not that strongly anticipated in the 1980s, would have had as large an impact as it has today on our business activities and day-to-day living through the development of communication equipment and communications technology as represented by PC networks and cellular phones.

According to the Computer Industry Almanac, September 2004 figures showed that the number of global Internet users exceeded 930 million, and at present (as of October 2006), it is by no means off the mark to claim that on average, one out of every five to six people in the world is estimated to be an Internet user.

In fact, it is believed that this is an extremely conservative estimate. Among these users, the number of Internet users in Japan is 77.3 million (December 2004 survey on telecommunication usage trends conducted by the Ministry of Public Management, Home Affairs, Posts and Telecommunications), and surprisingly, this translates to the fact that more than one out of two of the total population is making use of the Internet.[3]

On the other hand, the number of cellular phone Internet users is nearly the same, surpassing 71.93 million (June 2004 data from the Ministry of Public Management, Home Affairs, Posts and Telecommunications). This research is performed every month, and shows the total number of users of the cellular phone enterprises, i-mode, EZWeb, and Vodafone (now Softbank). However, users who are not accessing the web are also counted. If we take these figures and the prediction that the number of personal computers will easily exceed one billion in 2007, it becomes clear that the first half of the 21st century cannot merely be described as the age of information — that would be an insufficient description. Instead, it would be more appropriate to describe it as a period seeing a transition into the age of information communication, which encompasses information networks and functions.

In the *White Paper on Computerization* (2005 edition),[2] the government reexamines the former "e-Japan" strategy, which had as its aim "the realization of Japan as the most advanced information technology nation in the world by 2005," and presents a future image of a ubiquitous network society dubbed "u-Japan," where a free flow of information will be realized through a network that can be accessed "at anytime, from anywhere, by anything, and by anybody." The paper also explains what policies are needed to realize such an aim.

The idea behind this u-Japan is conveyed by the following four words that begin with the letter U: ubiquitous, indicating a time when communication plays a vital role in every aspect, linking every person and every object together; universal, indicating ease of use regardless of age or handicap; user-centric, indicating the merger of the user viewpoint; and unique, indicating the blossoming of individuality to help express higher creativity. At the heart of u-Japan, however, is "ubiquitous," emphasizing that it is about a society where communication takes place easily between not only people, but also between people and objects and between objects themselves.

So what kind of presence should organizations and companies have in such a ubiquitous age? How should they act? Furthermore, how should they go about fulfilling their roles? I would like to attend to these questions in the next section.

1.2   A Course of Action for Companies in the Ubiquitous Age

To clarify the ideal role and conduct for companies existing in an ubiquitous society, which is a society that exists in a highly complex information communication age, we must first of all grasp the characteristics of an ubiquitous society.

Firstly, in the advanced age of information, the quantity of information transmitted in a given period of time is extremely large. Just as more and more expressions used to indicate sums of money are seen to be going from the trillion-yen unit, as seen in the gross national wealth figure of 1,400-cho yen (1,400 trillion yen or 1.4 quadrillion yen), to the ten-quadrillion yen unit, the expressions used to indicate memory capacity and information storage capacity, such as the megabyte and gigabyte, are seen to be increasingly giving way to the general adoption of expressions such as the terabyte, the petabyte, and even exabyte, in fields that handle high capacities of data like business intelligence analysis.

Secondly, there is an increase in the number and types of information means and media available for transmitting these large quantities of data. The main public and private information media include the newspaper, magazine, book, telephone, and radio, in addition to

CATV, fax, electronic bulletin board, blog, electronic conferencing system facilitated through computer and television networks, online shopping spaces made available through personal computer networks and cellular phones, and countless databases and knowledge-bases, including home banking, travel information and game networks. Activities closely associated with day-to-day living and work, such as placing orders, invoicing, carrying out payments, and requesting materials, are designed to be reliant on brand new electronic intelligence media that are being rapidly developed one after another.

In particular, in the age of information communication, it is expected that services such as non-contact IC cards, GPS functions, services using electronic tags, music delivery, and home security services will become even more widespread in the form of new "information-service media" or as services that help to make use of such media. These services will help to promote efficiency in work, while also reducing workload and saving time. Furthermore, in terms of day-to-day living, these services will also heighten the sense of security and help to de-stress and raise satisfaction levels.

However, as a third point, we must also turn our attention to the flip side of all this and touch upon the points of information security and its limits. This is because there have been no end to the damages incurred and abuses committed due to leakages of governmental and corporate information, and additionally, the private information of individuals. Consequently, instances have occurred where societal functions and security functions became paralyzed, which is a situation that was unimaginable during times when information networks were not that advanced yet.

Currently, we have entered into a situation that demands our constant vigilance, as cases of computer viruses have become outnumbered by cases of the even more malicious spyware programs. For this reason, companies are making considerable investments in computer security and adopting defensive policies, but it remains difficult to say that the situation has seen any improvement. This is because there is a vicious circle in place that sees the tit-for-tat development of new, highly advanced viruses and spyware for every new, highly advanced security measure adopted.

Moreover, with the problem of information leakage and information tampering being basically a matter concerned with issues of ethics, morality, and a sense of mission, information managers cannot possibly be expected to be in complete control, since that would mean that they would have to be in control of the feelings of people in the company as well. This is a major setback.

Despite this dark, forbidding situation, on the whole, the emergence of the age of information communication and the ubiquitous society in particular have blessed companies with many opportunities as well, and depending on your point of view, it can be considered as indicative of the arrival of a time when we will see the fulfillment of important roles that could not have been anticipated in the past. I would like to address these points as follows.

Firstly, while duties such as new product and new business development and R&D had been previously assigned to only a limited number of those in charge, when the nature of ubiquity begins to spread within a company and the duties within the company become seamless with the advancement of networks, it will become very likely that interest in such tasks will be shared by all employees.

Currently, as internal networks increase, more and more formal, or perhaps informal, intra-company communities are seen to be emerging and evolving. With such communities, the setup often allows for a quick understanding of "who the most experienced and informed people regarding a certain development project are." If this setup is designed correctly, improvements and upgrades will continue to be made, room is made for presenting value-added ideas, and fantastic projects could be completed over an even shorter space of time, which should in turn help to bring about the success of new product and new business developments.

Secondly, the strength of such intra-company communities lies in their ability to help increase opportunities whereby participants can freely discuss what is on their mind, or in other words, their tacit knowledge. Tacit knowledge refers to the type of knowledge that people consider to be still half-baked or the type of knowledge people are reluctant to make known at times, as opposed to explicit knowledge, which refers to knowledge that is already out in the open. However, in communities that function on a virtual level, going beyond time and space, the clash of ideas (fusion) occurs more readily, which drastically increases the chances of paving the way to unexpected new products and new businesses.

Thirdly, the characteristic of going beyond time and space means that all R&D approaches on the face of this earth will become ongoing and multilevel. In other words, a project that progresses to some extent within an eight-hour workday will be inherited by the staff located in the next time zone where the workday is about to begin, and when the workday ends in this time zone, the project will be inherited by the staff in the next time zone where the workday is about to begin, and thus the project will never be stopped. What's more, if a three-shift schedule is adopted within the same region, then it will be possible to maintain continuity within that region alone. Furthermore, if the same or related projects are advanced in parallel with several teams, then the multilevel nature can be increasingly amplified. In addition, with the sharing of knowledge, we can hope for a rise in value-added ideas created through exchanges among experts of diverse areas.

In this way, at least theoretically, it will not be surprising at all to see a dramatic rise in the speed it would take for R&D projects to link to new product and business developments, and, on the whole, make it possible for the ubiquitous society to continue to churn out unprecedented new products and new businesses. In fact, whenever we are not able to create new products and businesses through collaborations or whenever we find the creative output to be infrequent, we should be questioning whether there are any flaws in the system.

Since business intelligence (BI) information systems are being increasingly adopted as one of the key means to enlarge these structures, I would like to end this introduction by touching upon such systems.

1.3 Development and Deployment of Three Business-Intelligence (BI) Type Information (Management) Systems

A bird's eye view of how information systems have developed up to the present reveals that the 1950s and the 1960s were the time that saw the development of the task-oriented, localized information systems. For example, information systems geared towards production management/process control were at the heart of those systems. Subsequently, the 1970s arrived and saw the development of finance-centric information systems at first, accompanied by improvements in computer functions. Then, towards the latter half of the 1970s, the development of task-integration or companywide types followed. This writer has also participated in this type of project in the US from the end of the 1960s through the 1970s.[4]

Upon entering the 1980s, the fifth-generation computer project[5,6] was started in earnest as one of the national projects and came into global prominence. On a parallel track with this, information systems based on Artificial Intelligence (AI) models, Expert System (ES)[7] models, and additionally, the Fuzzy Expert System (FES)[8-11] models came into the limelight as well.

Furthermore, interest was raised in information systems for acquiring, applying, and assessing strategic information and for developing strategic information systems that carried out strategic applications of information. Consequently, these systems became buzzwords during the 1980s and the 1990s. The phrase "strategic information" (or knowledge information) became synonymous with the word "intelligence." In other words, strategic information became key information concerned with the existential success or failure of an organization or company, and therefore became a buzzword no one could afford to disregard, irrespective of how information systems had developed.[12]

There was a sense, though, that such a forward-looking phrase was forgotten during the economic slump of the 1990s. The impact of the commercial Internet during this time was substantial and as personal computers saw improvements in performance and their networks began to spread, information systems that could be described as decentralized information communication network models, which were, in a static sense, dependent on workstations, were developed, and consequently, the phrase "strategic information" came to be forgotten.

With the arrival of the 21st century, the movement to grasp in a more positive light the significance of information systems built on information-communication networks became more active, and the term "intelligence" was restored to replace "strategic information" and "knowledge information." In particular, people became convinced of the appropriateness of business intelligence in the domain of the private enterprise, and consequently, business intelligence type (BI-type) information systems appeared. Along with increases in books and products,[13−15] the concept is beginning to come into prominence.

The first characteristic of the BI-model information system is that, by definition of being an information system, it fundamentally inherits the concept of strategic and confidential information. In that respect, it can be considered to be an improved version of the Strategic Information System model.

But just what about this is different from the strategic information system that had come into prominence in the 1980s? In terms of computer systems, the first difference is undoubtedly the development of systems and techniques that made it possible to immediately perform information processing analysis of high-volume data such as those in the terabyte range. We cannot overlook the point that it had become possible to make effective uses of ultra-large volumes of data that had accumulated to date.

However, accumulating ultra-large volumes of data is an entirely different story from detecting and acquiring truly valuable information, and we must be wary of this difference. No matter how abundant the amount of information gathered may be, it must not be forgotten that there is no other type of information easier to gather than the useless kind.

Generally speaking, this is because the more valuable the information becomes, organizations will raise their level of confidential classification and toughen their guard by taking encryption measures to assure such data does not get out, and even if there is a leak, they will see to it that decoding is rendered difficult.

Secondly, tools that realize BI are often categorized as knowledge types, simulation types, or automatic types (AI-augmented types).[16] The knowledge type attempts to incorporate ideas and techniques of areas that pursue information value and information sharing by including fields of knowledge that had attracted attention since 2000, such as knowledge engineering and knowledge management.

On the other hand, the simulation type makes use of data warehouses and data marts, integrates metadata through the application of ETL tools, and aims to generate and use BI through recursive, multilevel analysis by adopting such measures as OLAP.

The automatic type attempts to systematize and automate types that used to carry out decision-making by automating the decision rules that were formerly set by AI and ES types. Towards this end, the automatic type attempts to make such types apply to business rules and a typical example of the automatic type is the Business Rule Automation.

The third characteristic of the BI-type information system is that it is closely tied to groupware such as Lotus's Notes/Domino, Hitachi's Groupmax, and additionally, GroupSystem,[17] which was developed at the University of Arizona. Such groupware realize their worth when they function as a means for facilitating group collaborations. By making use of such groupware, it becomes possible to carry out idea-generation sessions and productivity evaluations of meetings, which are ends that could not be achieved through features of the communication network alone.

The BI-type information system, which is seeing a penetration into the World Bank and NASA, is apparently also penetrating into most companies in Japan as well in one way or another, but mainly to companies in the service sector, such as trading companies, supermarkets, and convenience stores. For the future, I should like to hope for the development and maintenance of systems endowed with more strategic capabilities, demonstrable competitiveness, and a high level of creativity.

This therefore concludes my brief coverage of BI-type strategic information systems for civilian enterprises with a focus on their aspects of computer technology. As for strategic information systems concerned with aspects of national strategy and military strategy, and additionally, competitive strategy, space limitations have prevented me from touching upon them at all. Readers interested in these subjects are advised to refer to the references found at the end of the chapter.[18-20]

This book clarifies the answers to the following questions to help you realize successful R&D undertakings, and in particular, new product and business developments. Firstly, how should you view the R&D environment from the present onwards?

Secondly, what forms should strategic plans and the management of R&D developments take in light of the fact that they are integral to the survival and growth of organizations and companies? Thirdly, what are the types of plans and methods of selection and assessment available for R&D projects that arise from such management? And fourthly, how can you attain the systematization and assetization of information, which will form the basis for such methods and lead R&D programs to success? In the latter half, this book aims to deepen the reader's understanding on an even more comprehensive level by introducing case examples.

References

1. Akira Ishikawa, *The Q&A Primer to Information Searching for Developing New Products and New Businesses*, Dobunkan, 1988, p. 1.
2. Japan Information Processing Development Corporation, *2005 White Paper on Computerization: Trust and Accountability in the IT Society — Support for Compliance*, Computer Age Corporation, 2005, p. 331.
3. Ministry of Public Management, Home Affairs, Posts and Telecommunications, *2005 White Paper on Telecommunications*, 2005, p. 3.
4. Akira Ishikawa, *Corporate Planning and Control Model Systems*, New York University Press, 1975.
5. Akira Ishikawa, *Future Computer and Information Systems*, Praeger, New York, 1986.
6. Akira Ishikawa, *Fifth-Generation Computers and Enterprise Management*, Yuuhikaku Anthology, 1988.
7. Akira Ishikawa, *The Business Expert System Explained*, Yuuhikaku New Book, 1988.
8. Akira Ishikawa, *Fuzzy Research Strategy*, Ohmsha, 1991.
9. Akira Ishikawa, Hiroshi Mieno, *Introduction to Fuzzy Management*, Chuokeizai-sha, 1991.
10. Akira Ishikawa (editor), *Fuzzy Thinking for Social Studies and the Humanities*, Ohmsha, 1993.
11. Akira Ishikawa, *et al.*, *Analysis and Evaluation of Fuzzy Systems*, Kluwer Academic Publishers, Boston, 1995.
12. Akira Ishikawa, *Introduction to Strategic Information Systems (New Edition)*, Nihon Keizai Shimbun, 1997.
13. Bernard Liautaud, Hayashi Sakawa (translator), *Business Intelligence*, Shoeisha, 2002.
14. Joerg Reinschmidt, Allison Francoise, Kayoko Sugawara (supervising translator), *Business Intelligence Official Guide*, Pearson Education, 2002.
15. Benjamin Gilad, Tamar Gilad (authors), Juro Nakagawa, Taizo Omoto, Kazuaki Katori (translators), *The Business Intelligence System: Intelligence Organization Strategies for Global Enterprises*, Elco K.K., 1996.
16. Monthly Task Software News Editorial Department, *Business Intelligence*, Task System Promotion, 1999, pp. 23–25.

17. Akira Ishikawa, Masahiro Horiuchi, *The Electronic Conference Revolution — Digital Conferences Will Change the Office*, Sanno University Press, 1997.
18. Kensuke Ehata, *Information and the State — Pitfalls of Collecting, Analyzing, and Evaluating*, Kodansha Gendaishinsho, 2004.
19. Yoshio Omori, *The State and Information — Protecting the National Interests of Japan*, WAC Bunko, 2006.
20. Yoshio Omori, *et al.*, *The Total Picture of the American Information Agency*, Japan Military Review, 2006.

Part 1

GENERAL OUTLINE SECTION

Chapter 2

Strategic Planning and R&D Management

While pointing out that modern corporations tend to cut back on R&D expenditures as they shift towards the adoption of a business approach that prioritizes investors, this chapter shows that we should be demanding the promotion of R&D activities that can lead to profitability. And in order to promote effective R&D activities, this chapter points out that it is necessary to promote tie-ups between the R&D department and other operating departments through the determination of clear management strategies.

2.1 The Modern Enterprise and R&D

2.1.1 The necessity of R&D

In the US during the 1950s and 1960s, consumer durable goods such as automobiles and household electrical appliances rapidly achieved diffusion due to economies of large scale and brought about affluent living for the people. J.K. Galbraith proved that stable economic growth could be attempted through the control of consumer demand by the technological group made up of technical experts and the managerial class of major corporations, known as the technostructure, and the bureaucratic organization of the government.[1]

Subsequently, the major corporations went on to stimulate consumer desire for their mass-produced products through the full use of advertising and sales techniques. Galbraith called this phenomenon of private business-led expansion of consumption the "dependence effect" and showed that consumers may be passive, but they nevertheless carry out consumption to attain satisfaction.[2]

In contrast to the production-to-order method adopted for the traditional craft manufacturing system, the mass production system, with its use of machines, required the adoption of the production-to-stock method, which called for carrying out production on the basis of predictions made for quantity demanded by consumers. Amid such a historical backdrop, Japan's R&D made use of the results of basic research conducted by mainly other countries and carried out product developments which made industrialization and commercialization practicable. And the produced products were sold by applying push-sales techniques.

From the 1970s through the 1980s, a shareholder counterrevolution occurred in the US and demands were made to sell or reorganize unprofitable operations that had become uncontrollable by the management of major corporations, which had become excessively large. Additionally, demands were also made to curb investments in R&D that were carried out for the mere purpose of realizing scale expansion. As a result, since around the 1980s in the US, research expenditure for cultivating technological seeds within companies and development expenses for connecting those seeds with consumer needs began to see cutbacks, and outsourcing of R&D came to be promoted.

However, in terms of the efficiency of R&D activity, it gradually became clear that it was difficult to justify from an economic standpoint, which aims to realize maximum output from minimum input. Research activities, whose investment effects are difficult to measure, and development activities that require considerable time to confirm profitability, became impediments to achieving high-share price management, which pursues short-term upward swings in stock prices and excessive dividends. This fact led to the demand to have the quarterly results of R&D activities reported.

Consequently, to carry out effective R&D activity, it is necessary for executive officers to devise long-term strategies and help make researchers aware that they are members of the organization as well. And it is also necessary for managers to sufficiently persuade shareholders and creditors to acknowledge the importance of carrying out R&D activity over a long period of time.

Traditionally, most of Japan's major corporations have been indirectly financed through the main banking system, rather than directly through shareholders and bondholders. As a result, there was a rollover, or in other words, an abundant amount of money was provided through continual refunding. For this reason, it was rare to be inquired on the results of R&D undertakings in any strict fashion. However, currently, it has become necessary for individual researchers to consider how R&D can lead to profitability by confirming the direction of the organization as a whole, while attempting tie-ups with other operating departments, including the marketing department.

Michael J. Piore and Charles F. Sabel in *The Second Industrial Divide* indicated that from the 1980s onwards the "flexible specialization system" had arrived as an industrial structure superseding the declining, private business-led mass production system.[1],3

The craft element, which was supposed to have been rejected by the technological system of mass production, is seeing a possible revival in such places as the Toyota Production System in Japan and in industrial clusters of the various communities of Europe. In this chapter's first section, we will point out that the efficiency of R&D has been deteriorating in recent years, and in the second section, we will attempt to investigate the relevance between management strategy and R&D, while taking into account the Management of Technology (MOT) in order to arrive at a measure for overcoming the deterioration.

---

[1] Here, Piore and Sabel raise the emergence of mass production, which began around 1800, as the first industrial divide and consider it to have been established mainly in America around the 1890s.

2.1.2 *International comparison of R&D investment*

As seen in Figures 2-1 and 2-2, compared to other developed nations, a high percentage of the total R&D amount in Japan is made up by expenditures from private enterprises that are chiefly channeled into applied research in engineering. On the other hand, regarding basic research in the science, Japan's percentage is low, and this fact is contributing towards weakening such areas as Japan's chemical industry.

Meanwhile, in Germany and France, the proportion of basic research and governmental expenditure is high. And in recent years

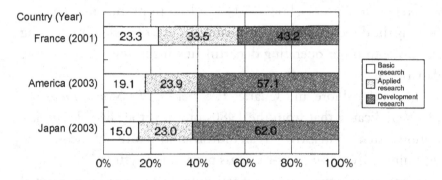

Figure 2-1:   Research Expenditure by Characteristic
Source: *2005 White Paper on Science and Technology*, p. 123.

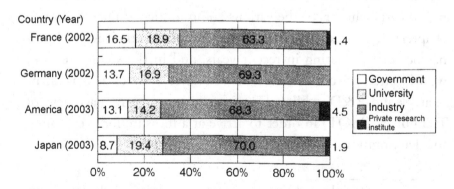

Figure 2-2:   Major Country Usage Ratios of Research Funds by Organization
Source: *2005 White Paper on Science and Technology*, p. 116.

in the US, industry-university tie-ups that are seeing collaborations between private enterprises and universities have been flourishing (especially in the physical sciences area), and the fruits of their collaborations have been appearing in such sectors as the petrochemical industry and the bioindustry. Japanese enterprises, on the other hand, have been paying attention to applicable technologies that can lead to the creation of products, such as radios, desktop calculators, or flat-screen TVs, instead of focusing on deepening basic technology like transistor technology and liquid crystal technology, which had been invented through basic research in the US.

Since the 1980s, the US has been seeing reductions in R&D spending. This trend is largely attributable to the impact made by the strengthening of the shareholder's voice.

According to Lester and Piore, science and technology policies of the past had inclined towards analytical initiatives, where results were already known and clearly definable. For this reason, engineers had been bound by an existing sense of values and had been carrying out rational decision-making that involved grappling with problems that were givens, while feeling the pressures of global competition. Consequently, towards discovering and understanding problems from now on, they suggest that it is necessary to promote an interpretive approach that goes beyond the boundaries of the organization.[4]

In recent years, within major industries of the US such as the chemical and semiconductor industries, the promotion of basic research areas has become essential, and active promotion of industry-university cooperation is being carried out. These basic research areas are not premised on any requirement to realize businesses, but are instead geared towards the accumulation of technological seeds. Upon promoting the interpretive approach, which attempts the integration of a diversity of knowledge, the industry-university cooperation activates new exchanges between universities and business enterprises, which are two absolutely disparate entities.

Consequently, such cooperation can be said to be offering the opportunity for businesses to reexamine their management practices.

2.1.3   *International comparison of product architecture*

As indicated on the previous page, a substantial discrepancy can be seen between the US and Japan in terms of how they weigh their R&D investments. To explain the cause of this, we can start by looking at differences in product architecture.

When Japanese companies seek to procure raw materials and parts, they have not been doing so through the market, but instead through taking advantage of long-term transactions with specific business connections. In areas such as automobiles and household electrical appliances, which are Japanese companies' fields of expertise, the assembling manufacturer cannot complete a component before product design is carried out, since close coordination is required between components. For this reason, there have been many cases where such manufacturers have carried out product development and production in sync with relevant companies. This type of product architecture is referred to as integral architecture. As the phrase suggests, it is a design that is an integrated whole and it is reached through bouncing ideas off each member of a group.

On the other hand, with US companies, after creating new technologies through industry-university tie-ups for basic research or through tie-ups between technology-led venture businesses and major corporations for development purposes, a modular form of product design is promoted.[5] This approach entails division of labor by component processes and goes beyond the framework of the company in terms of even business creation and productization. The merit of the modular architecture is that it lets companies procure components from extensive companies and helps build more open-ended relationships between them. On the other hand, in the case of the integral architecture, the relationship between companies will necessarily become closed-ended.

The desktop PC is a typical example of the modular architecture. With this approach, standardized interfaces for linking components (such as USB and SCSI) are pre-established, making it possible for companies to realize *ex post facto* combinations of their components with even those components designed by makers who do not closely cooperate, as long as the specifications meet the standards. For this reason, it also becomes possible to promote the outsourcing of not only the R&D department, but also the production department. Additionally, if the production of components can be carried out at a comparatively low technical level, it becomes possible to put together components that have been manufactured in developing countries, and, as a result, realize sales at low prices.

Therefore, whereas US companies lead in the production of desktop PCs, for which the modular architecture approach is easy to apply, when it comes to the production of small-scale and lightweight notebook PCs, which require close coordination between components, the market share of Japanese companies is relatively high, thanks to their expertise in integral architecture.

2.1.4 *Innovation and economic progress*

Technological innovation is one of the causes of economic growth. Inventions drawn from new technologies and their rapid commercialization are bringing about a material richness in the lives of people.

The 50-year business cycles, as conceived by Kondratiev, helped to explain the periodic phenomenon of the discoveries, inventions and technological innovations of epoch-making new technologies that emerged after the Industrial Revolution. However, to make the results of basic research lead to commercialization and industrialization, the ability for the entrepreneur to innovate started to become necessary. The Austrian economist, Schumpeter, while depending on Kondratiev's business cycles, paid attention to simply the difference between invention and innovation, and pointed out that entrepreneurial features were indispensable to the realization of innovation.[6] To promote economic progress, a company should not just hope for spontaneous evolution to take its course, but instead it should take note that "new combinations" of management resources are needed.[2]

For this reason, in recent years, to contribute to economic progress, a switch from the Keynesian, government-led financial and fiscal policy to Schumpeterian ideas is being demanded to help foster new industries and entrepreneurs and to support the creation of innovation. For example, in the revival of the American economy, the contribution from R&D-oriented venture companies were substantial and helped to supplement activities designed to foster innovation for major companies, whose R&D investments were declining. On the other hand, Japanese venture companies may find it difficult to follow the same road traveled by their American counterparts, since such Japanese companies are mainly Internet-based concerns that have relatively low start-up costs and are a combination of information and financial services, which can readily be listed on the stock exchange. Moreover, there is a lack of talent who can start companies through creating spin offs from major corporations.

When carrying out big-business centered innovation policies that accord with Japan's existing set of circumstances, referring to Drucker's ideas can prove helpful. While pointing out that the high-tech industry did not lead to rapid employment creation, despite the fact that it supports America's economic growth, Drucker had indicated that organizational innovation coming from within the

---

[2] As cases of "new combinations," Schumpeter raises the following: 1) development of new products; 2) introduction of new production techniques; 3) cultivation of new markets; 4) acquisition of new sources of supply for raw materials; and 5) organizational reform.

company helps to shorten long-term business cycles, and that this innovation does not stop short at technological inventions, pointing out the significance of the role of management.[7] Drucker inherits Schumpeter's concept that considers the entrepreneurial function to be the leading factor driving economic progress, and is thought to be suggesting an ideal form of R&D activity for the business organization.

The prosperity of Japan's economy in the future hinges on the business organization's ability to innovate in order to create technologies indispensable to society and then have such creations lead to industrialization.

2.1.5 *Governmental policy on technology*

An examination of the scope of governmental budgets related to science and technology reveals that Japan's governmental budget is around 3.4 trillion yen, whereas America's budget rises to around 11 trillion yen (90.9 billion dollars). A salient distinction of the Bush Administration can be seen in the fact that it had attempted the expansion of the energy supply through means such as drilling for natural gas and petroleum by having strongly promoted the National Energy Policy (NEP), which was chiefly advocated by Vice President Cheney.

A distinction of the previous Clinton Administration, on the other hand, can be seen in the fact that it had helped to increase investments in basic research and the building of the information infrastructure by having promoted cooperation between businesses and universities in the IT sector through the administration's adoption of its science and technology policy, which had been mainly championed by Vice President Gore.[8] Both of these administrations focused their attention on industries considered to be America's forte and carried out concentrated investments in them.

Additionally, the role private think tanks and nonprofit research institutions or foundations play in the determination or assessment of American policy on technology is large. They carry out assessments regarding the merits and impact of various researches, consider which fields should receive concentrated budget allocations, and offer regular assessments after the allocations are made.

Meanwhile, in the case of the Japanese government, while they put forward the importance of facing the challenges of technology, they rarely commit to offer any active support, and in most cases, strictly remain at the level of offering lateral support (such as grants).

Since 1996, the Japanese government has been formulating a basic plan for science and technology once every five years. In the second basic plan set by the Cabinet in 2001, the following three points were made: a nation that can contribute to the world through the creation and application of intelligence; a nation that is internationally competitive and can continue to develop permanently; and a nation with security and high standards of living. The plan went on to confirm "life science," "information communication," "the environment," "nanotechnology materials," and other such primary fields as areas for key policy considerations, while proposing to expand investment in basic research, carry out third-party assessments of research themes, and implement reforms in industry-academe-government cooperation in an attempt to make Japan's science and technology policy approach closer to America's science and technology policy. However, it cannot be denied that the government still tends to be oriented towards product development (see Figure 2-3).

2.1.6   *R&D challenges facing the Japanese company*

Since the 1970s through the 1980s, the management approach of Japanese companies, which attached great importance to commercialization, achieved great results. The companies were able to realize a high level of productivity and profitability by specializing

- Strategic prioritization of science and technology
  1. Promotion of basic research
  2. R&D that responds to national and societal challenges
     Examples: Nanotechnology, life science, etc.
  3. Apt response for fields showing the potential for rapid development
     Examples: Bioinformatics, nanobiology, etc.
- Promotion of the internationalization of science and technology activities
  1. Promotion of independent international collaborations
  2. Reinforcement of the capability to internationally transmit information
  3. Internationalization of the domestic research environment
- Reform of the science and technology system to realize superior achievements and applications
  1. Reform of the R&D system
     Examples: Redoubling of competitive funds, reform of evaluation systems for making
               appropriate resource allocations
  2. Reinforcement of industrial technology and reform of the industry-government-academia setup for
     cooperation
  3. Arrangement of conditions for the promotion of science and technology in local communities
  4. Training of superior science and technology talent and reform of education regarding science and
     technology
  5. Promotion of study related to science and technology, building of channels to society
  6. Ethics and social responsibility related to science and technology
  7. Maintenance of foundations for promoting science and technology
     Example: Maintenance of facilities such as universities

Figure 2-3: Key Policies of the Science and Technology Basic Plan
Source: Cabinet Office's science and technology policy website
(http://www8.cao.go.jp/cstp/kihonkeikaku/point.pdf).

in the development of products that were particularly easy to mass produce and improve in terms of quality, and by practicing a bottom-up style of management that actively paid attention to the voices of employees at the manufacturing floor.

However, according to the concept of Abernathy's "Productivity Dilemma," industries that have reached their mature phase experience a decline in productivity, and the conventional management approach starts to become incompatible. The infancy of an industry is the period that sees the birth of many product innovations. Thereafter a dominant design within the industry gets established, and when the industry reaches its growth stage, process innovation, which pursues efficient production approaches based on this design, occurs one after the other. Furthermore, when it reaches its mature phase, innovation activities see a decline[9] (see Figure 2-4).

After the 1990s, many of Japan's globally competitive industries, such as the automotive industry and the consumer electronics industry, saw a decline in innovation activities and became exposed to the surge of price competition. As a result, the scalpel of reform had pierced R&D departments, which has traditionally been considered to be sacrosanct in Japanese companies. This caused concerns that the motivation of researchers might deteriorate.

However, even in the consumer electronics industry, where many of its sectors are believed to have reached their mature phase, room to develop popular products such as the videodisc recorder still remains in many cases. By having made good use of the hard disk's inherently beneficial capability to store recorded content within its own framework, the videodisc recorder, which became a hit, responded to the user's reluctance toward having to frequently swap media for storage purposes and went on to trigger active competition over developments that aimed to improve performance. Makers who neglected R&D suddenly found themselves in a predicament and were compelled to engage in price competition to recapture their

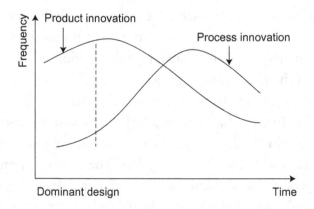

Figure 2-4:   The Dilemma of Productivity
Source: Adapted from Abernathy (1978, Figure 4.1).

market share. Additionally, even in the home appliances sector, where products may not be low priced at all, such as the popular washing machine with a built-in dryer, there is scope for realizing profit, just as long as a substantial number of customers who recognize the value of such a product exists.

Consequently, with future prospects for attaining profitability through product development becoming difficult, the leadership of managers will be called to account when attempting the invention of new technologies and their effective use. Specifically, the top level will be asked to harmonize the orientation of members through the development of clear management strategies, instead of overly relying on bottom-up inputs from the work front. Concurrently, at the middle level, project leaders of R&D departments will be expected to help their members assert their independence, while coordinating with corporate-wide policies at the same time.

2.2 Management Strategy and Its Relationships with R&D and Product Development Management

2.2.1 *Requirements for the Management of Technology (MOT)*

Throughout the 1990s, Japanese corporations saw the efficiency of R&D gradually deteriorate. For the future, it became necessary not to reduce R&D expenses, but pursue how R&D could lead to profitability. Toward this end, the need arose to bury the perception of distance between executive officers, who carry out corporate operations, and the R&D department.

Consequently, Japanese corporations recognized that original product development was indispensable to long-term progress and began to pay attention to the Management of Technology (MOT) concept from around 2000 as a management technique that could make sufficient use of the talents of the engineer. Riding this trend, the "technological management consortium" led by the Ministry of Economy, Trade and Industry, was established in 2003 with the aim of cultivating experts in the management of technology through cooperation between industry, government, and the academic community.

The idea of technological management resulted from the pursuit of efficient R&D in the American manufacturing industry from about the 1970s, and in the academic world, it has been treated as a part of the industrial engineering discipline. The context that gave rise to the general adoption of the name of MOT can be found in the fact that there was a need to integrate with the field of business administration to primarily realize R&D activities that led to industrialization and profitability. For this reason, in American graduate schools today, curriculums oriented toward the management of technology are established in not only engineering schools, but also business schools.

Even in Japan, MOT courses are seeing a trend of being set up in mainly engineering-oriented graduate schools. In the future, even the engineer will be expected to acquire the kind of sophisticated knowledge that is comprised of not only the knowledge of technology, but also of the management field.

2.2.2   Corporate strategy and R&D

When promoting cooperation between R&D and business, settling on a long-term corporate strategy becomes initially necessary. In management strategy theory, it is common to distinguish between corporate strategy and competitive strategy (business strategy). The corporate strategy focuses on the corporation as a whole and helps to select the relevant business domain and determine the method of allocating management resources, such as people, objects, and money. The competitive strategy helps to analyze competitive relations with other companies in terms of business and product.

To have corporate strategy decisions reflect MOT principles, the concept of "core competence" as conceived by Prahalad and Hamel will prove helpful.

They have built a resource-based theory of corporate strategy that explains that the way to secure long-term competitiveness is through the accumulation of proprietary management resources held by the corporation.[10] The administration recognizes the corporation's technological expertise, and by devising a corporate strategy that places this at its core, the business domain becomes established, making it possible to precisely give direction without diffusing the activities of employees, including engineers.

Therefore, the engineer will be sought to accomplish the accumulation of technological seeds by taking future commercialization and productization into consideration and carrying out R&D in alignment with the corporation's expertise. By having the R&D department adopt an attitude that favors cooperation with other business departments, it will be able to move toward ridding itself of the "sanctuary" image, which will in turn lead to the prevention of curtailing R&D expenses.

The idea of "core competence" aims at fostering the ability to innovate, which ties to the realization of long-term and stable profitability. It is not merely something that is maker-centric and product-oriented. Certainly, much technological accumulation in Japanese companies until now was made possible through an ample R&D budget procured through the stable supply of funds made available from banks. Consequently, many businesses were developed in a bottom-up fashion, which involved carrying out product developments that incorporated new technologies and functions created through such R&D. However, from now on, companies need to recognize the necessity of securing future profitability not through research for research's sake, but through carrying out R&D that reflects the overall corporate strategy.

2.2.3   *Competitive strategy and R&D*

In competitive strategy, since offering products with originality becomes key in staying ahead of the competition, the relevance of product development in particular to R&D activity becomes a focal point. While it cannot be denied that research activities remain to this day seeds-oriented for the purpose of accumulating technology for the future, when it comes to product development activities, we need to link them directly to business success by making them needs-oriented, as it is necessary to be able to respond to customers. The problem that arises here are the various obstacles that stand in the way of fostering the ability to innovate, such as those known as the "Death Valley" and "Darwinian Sea."

"Death Valley" points to the large gulf that occurs between basic research/invention and applied research/product development. This shows that it is not easy to adjust the technological seeds accumulated in a corporation to meet the needs of customers and turn them into useful technology. A typical precedent of overcoming the "Death Valley" obstacle is the case of the DNA chip, which gauges genes that could cause illnesses. The US government recognized the "Death Valley" gap existing in the development of this chip and overcame it by supplying funds for its industrialization.

The "Darwinian Sea," on the other hand, points to the fact that prospects for manufacturing a product do not necessarily lead to commercialization at once, even if applied research shows such prospects to be good, since there are the issues of building production facilities and distribution channels to contend with. As concrete examples for this type of obstacle, the cases of the next-generation DVD standard (HD-DVD system and Blu-ray Disc system) and the next-generation TV panel technology (the SED system) can be cited.

Toward clearing these two obstacles, the development of a clear competitive business strategy is demanded. As representative types of such a strategy, cost leadership strategy, differentiation strategy, and segmentation strategy[3] can be cited, but the one with a strong relevance to R&D activity is the differentiation strategy.[11] If a corporation only adopts the cost leadership strategy, which aims to drop the selling price by holding down personnel and distribution costs, there is the danger of seeing a rapid decline in profitability once other companies begin to imitate. For this reason, it is necessary to promote a differentiation strategy and aim for the establishment of a long-term competitive advantage. In such a case, the R&D department will have to bear the heavy responsibility of overcoming both the Death Valley and Darwinian Sea obstacles at the same time. Toward this end, the department will have to recognize the product functions and level of quality demanded by customers with precision and thereby promote the type of product development that helps to prevent imitation.

2.2.4 *Product strategy and R&D engineering*

To make R&D relevant to product strategy, it is necessary to ascertain the required technology by sufficiently grasping the product's life cycle (PLC).

In the introduction stage, companies need to allow the developed product to create a new market for itself. At this stage, since significant cost build-up occurs for the development of new technology, interest in the new product runs extremely high among principal customers, the targets who are enthusiastic innovators and do not mind the high price tag.

Subsequently, when consumers gradually start to recognize the product as it enters its growth stage, the market expands and a battle against rival firms for market share unfolds as a performance upgrade

---

[3] Regarding segmentation strategy, Porter defines it as one that concentrates management resources on 1) specific buyer groups, 2) product types, and 3) specific regional markets in order to aim for cost reduction and differentiation via narrowing down targets.

is attempted. At this stage, it is necessary to carry out product development that meets the needs of opinion leaders who possess extensive knowledge and whose will to consume are comparatively high. Everett M. Rogers, in his landmark work *Diffusion of Innovations*, asserts that these very opinion leaders have substantial influence in achieving diffusion among general consumers and that they determine the merits of competing in a business.[12]

In the maturity stage, since product diffusion extends up to general consumers, companies will not be able to anticipate any further market expansion. However, they will be securing stable profitability by deploying an unmatchable differentiation strategy made possible through process innovation in production.

Furthermore, during the decline stage, although market growth comes to an absolute stop, companies that had succeeded in the mature phase with their differentiation strategy do not necessarily have to withdraw. In fact, they can anticipate even more profitability through further process innovation.

When seen in the light of the life cycle concept, many business sectors in Japan's manufacturing industry are facing the maturity stage or the decline stage and need to reexamine their existing state of technology-development competition that pursues all-out performance enhancements, which had proved beneficial in bringing about success in the past. The product development strategies of Japanese companies had tended to lapse into becoming product-centric out of a sense of rivalry against competitors, and often ignored customers in the process. From now on, it is demanded that product development adequately takes customer viewpoints into account.

For example, the succession of hit products appearing in the household appliance sector in recent years such as washing machines and vacuum cleaners can be said to be offering a large hint for generating substantial profitability during the maturity and decline stages for companies that have survived competition in the course of the life cycle process.

2.2.5 *Marketing research for new product development*

While Japanese companies switch from a seller's market to a customer-centric one, they need to extend and tie the idea of marketing to the product development stage. Traditionally, it could not be said that cooperation between the R&D department and the marketing department was sufficiently attempted. Since the search for target customers had been entrusted to the marketing department, in the event a product did not lead to viable sales after it had overcome technical difficulties to reach the stage of production, the chances the R&D department was held responsible was close to none. However, from now on, the department will be required to try to maintain interaction with customers and demonstrate the imagination to carry out developments that take the user's viewpoint into account.

However, it should be noted that this measure by no means downplays the importance of technological improvement. The R&D department, with the cooperation of the marketing department, needs to have the ability to access their repository of technological seeds and extract appropriate technology that suits product functions that respond to user needs.

With existing products, to make improvements for the purpose of securing sustained profitability through high value-added production, we need to accurately grasp the needs of target customers. By incorporating marketing ideas into the R&D field, it will become possible to switch from the technology-push paradigm, which only requires packing in numerous features that correspond to price, to the demand-pull paradigm. As a solution, companies can narrow down their technologies to those that can turn into products and propose them as an answer to the problems troubling customers, persuading the importance of their necessity.

The need to connect with marketing ideas is necessary not only for existing products, but for building new business domains as well. Toward this end, companies will have to carry out marketing research for the purpose of aligning their core technologies with market trends. However, with new businesses, investigating the needs of future customers is not easy, and more often than not, there will be a risk involved in promoting its commercialization and industrialization.

The idea of the "co-creation" of value by Prahalad and Ramaswamy offers a hint toward a solution.[13] In the present age, when it has become and possible to convey opinions on purchased products at blogs and websites, consumers can reach the decision to make a purchase not only via advertisements, but via word-of-mouth as well. For this reason, certain company-led marketing activities are beginning to show their limitations; specifically, activities that aim to control demand by relying on ads that help consumers recognize the features and image of a product (see Figure 2-5).

As a result of companies aggressively pursuing cost-cutting competition and business process improvements, the market is overflowing with products that incorporate diverse functions and those that have realized low prices. However, just offering an increased number of choices will not satisfy customers. To acquire customers who can support the continuation and progress of a corporation on a long-term basis, the imagination to build a solutions-oriented business is demanded. What buyers seek is not simply the possession of a product. From now on, it will become crucial to be able to answer to problems troubling customers through the very use of the products themselves.

	Until now	In the future
Bearer	Business led	Customers and businesses
Basis	Products and services	Co-creative experience
Result	Consumer demand management	Problem solving for customers

Figure 2-5: Framework of Value Creation
Source: Adapted from Prahalad and Ramaswamy (2004).

2.2.6 *R&D alliances and outsourcing*

As can be drawn from the ideas expressed in the preceding paragraph, it could be seen that companies would face difficulty if they were to assume risks on their own. When a firm is not able to advance developments with its internal management resources alone, it is supposed that there will be many occasions when the use of external technological expertise becomes necessary. We believe this can be attributed to budgetary and time constraints that accompany the need to carry out R&D with speed and sophistication. Depending on the situation, there may be times when carrying out technological cooperation with rival firms is preferable.

Regarding alliances with other companies, many of them are carried out to conduct long-term R&D oriented toward the creation of future customers, and in the case of outsourcing, many of them are carried out when rapid industrialization is required once the opportunity arrives to expand market share and realize profits.

An examination of the forms of alliances forged between companies reveals that within companies of different business types, they take the form of complimentary alliances. Namely, in some cases, they involve companies carrying out industrialization/commercialization through mutual technology contributions, or in other cases, they involve cooperation between companies without the capacity to produce and companies with distribution channels ready. Within companies of the same business type, joint-development alliances are promoted to aim for the industrialization of next-generation technologies.

A typical case of outsourcing can be seen when a maker of finished products entrusts the production of electronic parts for such products as personal computers and digital cameras. In the case of digital appliances, demand trends are hard to grasp, and despite investing large sums of money to cover development and production costs, there is a possibility of not being able to acquire sufficient profit. So finished-product makers outsource production to Electronics Manufacturing Service (EMS) companies and attempt risk reduction.

EMS companies can readily reduce production costs, even if all the orders they receive are small in scale, as such orders help to enlarge their total volume of orders in the end, since they undertake orders from many companies. On the other hand, businesses hiring EMS companies are able to heighten the added value of the whole product by being able to specialize in production processes that require advanced technological expertise. Whereas outsourcing is realized in fields where modular architecture is carried out, in fields where integral architecture is carried out, production is still accomplished in most cases through long-term, vertical relationships with affiliated subcontractors. However, in recent years, even in the home appliance industry, which had been adopting the integral approach to product design, the movement to introduce an outsourcing system that makes effective use of EMS companies is gaining ground.

However, since there are demerits to outsourcing that can be considered, careful judgment becomes necessary. As indicated previously, there is little hope of acquiring customers through just reducing the production cost. Additionally, if a corporation fails to sufficiently recognize the core technology it possesses, a loss in long-term competitiveness may result due to the disappearance of its technological advantage.

Furthermore, in the case of alliances, due to disparities in bargaining power or conflicts of interest arising from differences in objectives, a tie-up may cease to make progress. Therefore, companies need to reevaluate the suitability of their alliances on a retroactive basis. As measures, non-disclosure contracts can be concluded or cross licensing that sees both parties acknowledging the implementation of patented technologies can be carried out. By adopting such measures, companies can promote the active application of their respective proprietary technologies, while attempting intellectual-property protection.

Therefore, businesses need to make good use of technologies accumulated internally, and reexamine the appropriateness of the balance they maintain between development activities that could be completed within the corporation and activities that make use of external resources. To gain a grasp of management resources within the corporation and appropriately apply stakeholder knowledge, the formulation of a clear corporate strategy is required. Toward this end, it can be said that the ability to lead executive officers is a sought-after talent.

Junpei Nakagawa

References

1. J.K. Galbraith, *The New Industrial State*, 3rd edition, Houghton Mifflin, 1978, Chapters 6 and 28.
2. J.K. Galbraith, *The Affluent Society*, 4th edition, Houghton Mifflin, 1984, Chapter 11.
3. M.J. Piore, C.F. Sabel, *The Second Industrial Divide*, Basic Books, 1984, Chapter 1.
4. R.K. Lester, M.J. Piore, *Innovation: The Missing Dimension*, Harvard University Press, 2004, Preface and Chapter 2.
5. Takahiro Fujimoto, *Akitekucha no sangyo ron* (transl. "The industrial theory of architecture"), edited by Takahiro Fujimoto, Akira Takeishi, and Yaichi Aoshima, *Business Architecture*, Yuhikaku Publishing, 2001, Chapter 1.
6. J.A. Schumpeter, *The Theory of Economic Development: An Inquiry into Profits, Capital, Credit, Interest and the Business Cycle*, Harvard University Press, 1934, Chapter 2.
7. P.F. Drucker, *Innovation and Entrepreneurship*, Harper & Row, 1985, Prologue.
8. The Research Center of Technology Trends of the National Institute of Science and Technology Policy of the Ministry of Education, Culture, Sports, Science and Technology, *Technology Trends*, June 2001 issue, Chapter 4 (http://www.nistep.go.jp/achiev/ftx/jpn/stfc/stt003j/index.html).
9. W.J. Abernathy, *The Productivity Dilemma: Roadblock to Innovation in the Automobile Industry*, The Johns Hopkins University Press, 1978.
10. G. Hamel, C.K. Prahalad, *Competing for the Future*, Harvard Business School Press, 1994, Chapter 9.
11. M.E. Porter, *Competitive Strategy*, Free Press, 1980, Chapter 2.
12. E.M. Rogers, *Diffusion of Innovations*, 3rd edition, Free Press, 1983.
13. C.K. Prahalad, V. Ramaswamy, *The Future of Competition*, Harvard Business School Press, 2004, Chapter 1.

Chapter 3

R&D Project Planning, Selection, and Evaluation

In this chapter, I will show the key concepts you will need to be aware of in order to plan and implement new products and businesses. First of all, I will indicate the necessity of gaining an understanding of your internal and external circumstances and then of reexamining your own company to discover new themes in extended areas of your business or in completely new domains. I will then discuss how you could start prioritizing those discovered themes and then turning them into projects. Additionally, I will discuss the structure of management that needs to be in place for implementing the projects, the principles of appropriately making decisions for continuing or terminating them, and finally, the perspective of realizing standard products/businesses at the time of success.

3.1   Planning and Selecting R&D Projects

3.1.1   *Recognition of existing product/business circumstances*

First of all, when launching new products and businesses, it is necessary to have a grasp of the present conditions of existing products and businesses. When I say "existing," I am largely referring to only two viewpoints. They are as follows:

- Internal environment (existing products and businesses of your own company), and
- External environment (market conditions and other companies' existing products and businesses).

With regard to the external environment, I will elaborate not only from the perspective of other companies' competing products and businesses, but also from the perspective of the marketplace.

1)   *Understanding the present conditions of the internal environment (your own company's existing products and businesses)*

When attempting to grasp present conditions, it is necessary to see the lineup of the products of your company in a new light. In particular, it is necessary to recognize new such points as the quantity, quality, and sales period of existing products. Generally speaking, new businesses that readily achieve success are the ones that involve products that are positioned as extensions of your company's lineup. This is because their bottom lines are clear, and it is easy to understand how to promote their growth.

However, products have life cycles as those described in Figure 3-1, and depending on their stage of market development, the worth of releasing a new product can be determined.

For example, during the period of the growth phase of your company's product, the development of a new, augmentable product that is peripheral or related to the existing product will not only serve to support the existing product, but will also raise the possibility of success for itself.

When an existing product enters its mature and waning phases, in response to the trends of the times, there may be a need to see this product make a paradigm shift toward a new domain, where

	Introductory phase	Growth phase	Mature phase	Waning phase
Marketing objective	Recognition of product and promotion of trial	Acquisition of market share	Maximizing profits while protecting share	Reap profits
Product	Basic product	Product extension, offering of services and warranties	Diversification of product lineup	Gradual phasing-out of weak models
Price	Cost build-up approach	Market penetration price	Price equals or exceeds competitor's price	Price reduction
Channel	Selective	Channel cultivation	Channel cultivation	Elimination of routes with low profitability
Promotion	• Advertisement for initial adopters and dealers • Large-scale sales promotion aimed at promoting trials	• Advertisement aimed at arousing recognition and interest in the mainstream market • Scaling down sales promotion costs	• Advertisement that emphasizes factors of differentiation and merits • Enlargement of sales promotion costs to push forward the switchover of customers from other companies	• Level of advertisement necessary for maintaining key customers • Minimum sales promotion costs

Figure 3-1: Product Life Cycle and Marketing Strategy

new products can be created. However, if you have a product that is in its introductory phase, you should refrain from launching a new product in a similar domain, since doing so will raise the possibility of competition among products of your own company. Furthermore, in the event that one of the products fails to become a hit, there is always the possibility of bringing about mutual ruin.

On the other hand, there are cases of launching new products that are not extensions of your company's lineup, as described above. This applies to situations of moving into separate domains in terms of the corporate strategy and does not involve taking your company's products into account. Instead, this involves taking the entire market and existing products of other companies into account.

The above-mentioned viewpoints do not only apply to new products but to new businesses as well, so it is also equally important to have an accurate grasp of the life cycle of existing businesses. Therefore, to assure that conflicts of interest within the company do not occur, it is necessary to ascertain the domain of new businesses. In this case, domain mainly refers to target customers and product categories.

2) *Understanding the present conditions of the external environment (markets and other companies' existing products and businesses)*

Next, it is necessary to understand other companies' products and businesses as elements of the external environment. In the case of products, such elements include all companies that have launched competing products. In the case of businesses, likewise. In other words, it is appropriate to gain a comprehensive overview of the market of the product line you wish to introduce and the peripheral environment of products and businesses as well. To obtain such a comprehensive view of a market requires considerable effort.

Therefore, you need to be able to examine a market from all possible perspectives, such as the following:

- Market trends
- Market scale
- Principal companies
- Situation of competitors and new entrants
- Technological trends
- Product and service attributes
- Channel attributes
- Customer attributes.

When launching a product upon examining a market as a whole, it is necessary to clarify the 4Ps of marketing (Product, Price, Place, and Promotion) and the 4Ps of other sales points (Positioning, People/Person, Partnership, and Packaging) along with targets. However, in order to first of all understand present conditions, you would do well to adopt the above-mentioned perspectives, which take the marketing factors into account.

Market trends

Market trends are the vogues of the entire market itself, while products and businesses are matters that depend on the support of customers. Therefore, trends can occur when customers become influenced by economic conditions or seasonal vogues. For example, customers tended to "save" during the period after the burst of the economic bubble, and goods that are related to events that take place once every four years, such as the Olympics and the Soccer World Cup, become popular when they occur. It is necessary to recognize these trends and if a response to these trends have already been made by another company, the decision to have your own company do the same or not needs to be made carefully. Trends can be fleeting or they can last up to several years. If you fail to understand them properly, there is always the possibility that your product or business will turn out to be outdated when launched.

In addition, current trends can also be said to be "creations of companies." Favorite sports of the Japanese, such as baseball and volleyball, can become ideal trends. For example, there were the festive events of the World Baseball Classic (WBC), which caused a sensation in Japan when the country's national team became champions, and the World Cup of volleyball. In particular, world tournaments held within Japan can become one single trend. Creating trends with the use of mass media through such tournaments and elements of entertainment is a characteristic of the modern age.

Even deregulation can turn into a trend and help broaden the scope for market entry in the process. In the past, many companies made their entry when the liberalization of communications took effect and, in recent times, in addition to the liberalizations of finance and electricity, the convergence of broadcasting and communications can be mentioned as a case in point.

Market scale

Market scale is crucial in helping companies find room for entry. As can be inferred from the often-used description, "X % market share," we see a market in terms of units of companies that offer products and services. This indicates how much of the total market is secured at a given time, and while it depends on the definition of the market, in markets where a state of oligopoly has advanced to some extent, no matter how good a product or business you intend to launch may be, if the market is insular, making an entry may prove difficult at times.

In many cases, market scale varies in accordance with the passage of time. While fluctuations in basic necessities, such as food, clothing, and shelter, are small, the scale naturally changes in accordance with the state of the economy. In markets where fluctuations are intense, such as the information and communication market, the scale tends to repeatedly increase suddenly within a short period of time or become stagnant all at once.

Principal companies

The subject of principal companies is precisely about the situation of competitors. If certain new products or new businesses are an extension of an existing product or business, then they represent your present competitors. In fact, it is highly likely that you may have already been monitoring them, so it may be easy to recognize them. However, in the case of entering into a new domain, it is necessary to see whether there is any company or companies dominating the market or whether your firm has the opportunity to dominate it after making an entry.

In addition, it is also necessary to take note of the financial situations of these companies themselves. This is because in the event your product starts to engage in price competition, you will be able to clarify how much cost you will be able to bear. At times, companies strategically rush their products or businesses into price competition in a bid to prevent other companies from following. A good example of this is SOFTBANK, which released its ADSL service at a bargain price from the very beginning in the broadband market. At first they managed to create a situation whereby it became difficult for existing communication carries to flex their muscles. They accomplished this through distributing modems for free through parasol promotions (street-side sales promotions), making other companies hesitate to make their market entry. Ultimately, various companies made their entries and competition became fierce, but they nevertheless repeated such techniques and developed into the No. 1 company in the broadband market.

It is necessary to accurately recognize major companies that dominate within such markets. While existing major companies can be recognized easily through general information, in order to grasp whether a company has the potential to become one, supplementary and detailed corporate analysis and research becomes necessary.

Situation of competitors and new entrants

Time must factor into the discussion of the situation of competitors and new entrants. In other words, competitors must be considered as not only the present ones, but also those who are planning to enter the market. Specifically, it may be necessary to recognize market entrants as not only companies that have expressed their intent to enter, but companies that can readily enter from related markets (even if they belong to a different sector), companies that can possibly offer substitute products or businesses, and even individuals who can possibly start up a spin-off venture business, as has been happening in recent times. If you underestimate these emerging powers, your company may be caught off guard by an unconventional approach, and end up becoming a case study of a "conservative company in decline."

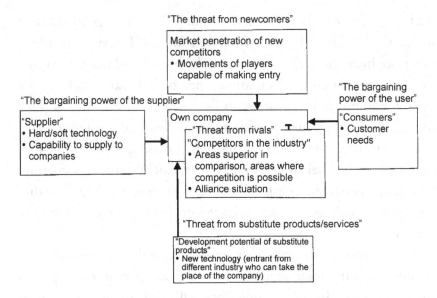

Figure 3-2:   A Summary of the Five Forces Analysis
Source: This author's summary of Michael E Porter's *Competitive Strategy*.

In sectors where market entry is easy, competition is intense. Obstacles to entry include not having the necessary capital, staff, technology, and sales channels, in addition to regulatory restrictions. It must be taken into account that these hurdles are being relaxed through the recent deregulations, rise in the availability of information, the development of outsourcing, mobility of the workforce, and, in addition, injection of capital from foreign companies.

Such a situation of competitors and new entrants can be subjected to a Five Force Analysis, as illustrated in Figure 3-2, for example.

Technological trends
When examining a market, while it is necessary to not only look at seeds-oriented approaches that focus on such issues as technology, but also at needs-oriented approaches that take customer viewpoints into account, technological trends are nevertheless crucial. Though there seems to be no point in considering products and businesses

that are technically incompatible, if you consider only compatible ones on the other hand, you may find that a new product you release into the market after completing its development is obsolete and no longer competitively viable, since its technology may have become outdated. For such a reason, keeping a check on these trends becomes crucial.

Furthermore, technology is concerned with not only products, but with many other aspects, ranging from the procurement of raw materials to factory production, distribution, inventory management, and the process of gathering information for upgrading products. For example, if a real-time system excelling in inventory management can be created, it will become possible to realize efficient delivery of products, and you will be able to avoid carrying unnecessary stocks, which will in turn lead to cost reduction. In effect, this will lead to improving your product and the plant equipment required to make the product, making it easier to produce new products. Technological development plays a significant role in such a positive, upward spiral.

Among the technological trends seen in recent times, you should pay particular attention to patent-related issues. Even when it is possible to swiftly adopt and develop cutting-edge technology, another company may be holding the rights to it. The present age is considered to be the age of intellectual property, and if you think little of intellectual property management, you may have to pay a hefty price in the end. Previously, Japanese companies had failed to heed this point, and had to pay sums of money that amounted in the billions of yen to US firms as compensation. In societies such as the US, where patents are highly valued, there are companies that rely on them for a large part of their revenue stream, with the number of staff working in some companies' intellectual property divisions totaling in the hundreds. In these internationalized times, even if a company only targets domestic markets in Japan, international issues are certain to arise. Consequently, it is important to properly recognize the technology patent systems of such aspects as the technology of other countries.

Furthermore, recently, there have been intra-company lawsuits taking place. For example, the inventor and former employee of Nichia Kagaku Kogyo, Mr. Shuji Nakamura (presently a professor of the University of California in Santa Barbara), filed a suit against the company over the invention of the blue-light emitting diode, and the company eventually was made to pay a substantial sum of money to him. In effect, the company had the carpet pulled from under its feet by a former employee, a researcher demanding compensation for the value of an invention. From the inventor's point of view, it is natural to be rewarded for the invention, but for Japanese companies so far, such as Nichia Kagaku Kogyo, such a matter apparently does not merit serious consideration. Perhaps for the corporation, this day and age will prove difficult to navigate, but it can be clearly seen that the management of technological intellectual property is becoming vital.

Product and service attributes

Needless to say, it is important to recognize product and service attributes. It is necessary to understand from the beginning such matters as whether a product is one whose costs can be easily recovered after carrying out mass production for it or whether development services and marketing services cannot be separated from each other. In other words, no matter how much expense you decide to tolerate in the development stage, if you can generalize it, you will receive enough change afterwards. On the other hand, no matter how much cost you manage to reduce in the development of a product, if there is a need to make use of very expensive human resources and locations in order to offer it, realizing a profit will not be easy. It is necessary to have a sufficient understanding of such characteristics, and in particular, if you are attempting to offer a new product or service by carving out a market that is different from an existing one, you will need to do your research well, since there are no precedents you can refer to for guidance.

<u>Channel attributes</u>
When investing in a product, channels are important, along with the pricing strategy. The channels you need to recognize have the attributes of width and depth. The matter of the channel width of other companies is a matter of how extensive their coverage is. In other words, to put it simply, it is a matter of whether the coverage comprises Japan and/or overseas. Channel depth, on the other hand, is a matter of whether a company interacts with customers through brick and mortar stores or through a virtual means such as the Internet. By recognizing these corporate channels existing within markets, a company will begin to understand where to sell its goods and where its deficiencies lie.

For example, there are some companies that have a nationwide coverage of retail outlets, but do not provide Internet channels. This is because they wish to avoid giving a negative impression to their sales agents, who serve as their existing distribution channels, even when the Internet route is clearly cheaper and will allow them to hold down the price of their product. After all, using the Internet will mean that they will be able to sell directly at bargain prices. But this would cause a conflict of interest with the existing channel companies, who will certainly put up a fierce rebellion against the company. A famous precedent is the case of Matsushita Electric and the Panashop stores located in various places nationwide. Matsushita Electric was seen to be refraining from selling through the Internet, since doing so at bargain prices could lead to the annihilation of the Panashops, which had been contributing nationwide to date.

In terms of understanding existing circumstances of channel attributes, it therefore can be said that if another company has a nationwide coverage through its channels, your company may find it difficult to develop new products and businesses, and may refrain from doing just that. On the other hand, this same situation could also make the development of your company's Internet sales easier and even help your company to make use of the Internet in an offensive fashion.

Customer attributes

Though I touch on this subject here at the end, explanations of it have appeared before. Products must be designed with the customers of a relevant target segment in mind. It is the customer who buys the product and if you do not reach an understanding of such an individual who exists in the market, new R&D projects will be impossible to carry out.

To grasp customer attributes of the target market, you need to recognize variables of market segment elements, such as the following:

A) Behavior attribute types
   Behavior variables

   (1) According to usage rate: Frequency of visiting stores, etc.
   (2) According to expectation level: Benefits sought after, etc.
   (3) According to customer satisfaction level: Satisfaction levels by the service, next-time purchase intentions, etc.

   Psychological variables

   (4) According to personality: According to how interested one is in new things/how conservative one is, etc.
   (5) According to lifestyle: By TV viewing frequency, by favorite sport, by frequency of travel, etc.

B) Basic attribute types
   Population dynamics variables

   (1) According to inherent attributes: By gender and age, etc.

(2) According to change (growth) attributes: By educational background, annual income, occupation, ownership of house/rented property, household number [alone/more than two (presence of minors–age of the head of household (under or over 60 years old))], etc.

Geographical variables

(3) According to the area: By metropolis, districts, and municipalities, etc.
(4) According to environment: By climate (warm/cold districts), etc.
(5) According to scale: By population density (cities/municipalities designated by government ordinance), etc.

An understanding of the above points to a certain extent will give you sufficient preparation for initiating an R&D project. If your understanding becomes too detailed however, you may fail to see the forest for the trees. It goes without saying that it is important to recognize customer attributes for any project.

3) *Importance of recognizing existing circumstances*

Up to now, I have been stating the necessity of understanding internal and external circumstances, or in other words, the existing circumstances of your own company's and other companies' existing products and businesses, and of the market as a whole, from all angles. From now on, having such a multifaceted understanding will serve as an extremely important preliminary step toward initiating and promoting R&D projects in the future. Without recognition of existing circumstances, it will be impossible to make new developments.

In concrete terms, all of this boils down to the 3Cs (Customer, Company, and Competitor), which should be monitored when drafting a marketing strategy. Among these 3Cs, while you must certainly recognize the Customer aspect, if you fail to recognize the Company and Competitor aspects as well, even if you initiate a new R&D project, not only will it fail to lead to absolute success, but the question of whether it will even take off will remain doubtful.

It should be noted that these are confidential matters that can lead to the creation of new products and businesses, and therefore should be mainly researched by your company on its own. One method, as seen in recent times, is to collect information through Internet searches, conducting interviews with experts, and making use of research firms and consultancies. Incidentally, this writer served as one of the consultants in the initial stages of the development of Chapter 6's "Karada Meguri Cha" and proposed the keywords, "Chinese medicine," to allude to the fact that the product is a distinctively Chinese health tea. The proposal was made by taking existing circumstances into account.

3.1.2 *The search for new product and new business themes*

Next, I will discuss how you can go about creatively finding new product and new business themes. As mentioned above, you should take into account existing circumstances, and upon looking at their strengths and weaknesses, you should ascertain what opportunities (and threats) there are for you to consider. However, you should not only carry out a SWOT analysis that simply looks into strengths, weaknesses, opportunities, and threats, but you should also include other perspectives to facilitate your search for themes. In the following section, we shall examine several methods of searching for new product and new business themes.

1)   *Cross between SWOT analysis and value-chain analysis*

Figure 3-3 shows how SWOT analysis can be combined with the analysis of a product's value chain. In this case, the diagram shows how a company, whose brand appeal is strong in the AV (audio and visual) and PC (personal computer) sectors, can attempt to launch

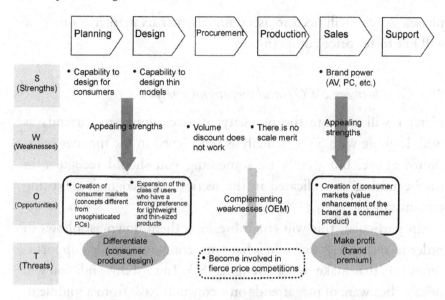

Figure 3-3:   Examples of SWOT Analysis and Value-Chain Analysis

a different product targeting the consumers in the same sectors. In effect, by combining value-chain and SWOT analyses, you will be able to ascertain where to attempt differentiation and where you may generate profit, discovering new product and new business themes in the process.

While the above explanation is abstract, it advocates the idea of having your company discover opportunities that make use of its several fortes, instead of competing in the market with its weaknesses. In other words, the above explanation promotes the concept of a product that takes threats into account. Such products can have a premium appeal and may not be suitable as consumer-oriented, general-purpose items. Since a premium product does not lend itself to mass production/mass selling, it is not profitable in an explosive sense. However, it is reflective of a business strategy that aims to profit through unit-by-unit sales. But a product such as this, as mentioned previously, will also necessarily pass through the life cycle of "the introductory phase → growth phase → mature phase → waning phase," so you will need to ascertain whether its market is one that will not foster price competition.

2)   *Cross between SWOT and megatrend analyses*

Here, I will indicate the necessity of ascertaining megatrends as well. Linking with SWOT analysis is achieved in the manner mentioned above, but trends are something you should recognize in the beginning, as indicated in the section on recognizing existing circumstances.

In particular, this will entail breaking them down as follows in order to ultimately ascertain what your company can do (opportunities ⟨O⟩ that make use of strengths ⟨S⟩). Toward this end, you will need to be aware of megatrends on a constant basis from a middle to long-term perspective.

Step 1: State a megatrend (social currents, innovations, deregulation).

Step 2: Assume what will happen from there (change, creation, termination).

Step 3: Assume new circumstances and needs that will arise due to this.

Step 4: Consider what can be accomplished by applying your firm's resources (technology, customer base, brand, distribution channels, etc.).

An example of these steps is illustrated in Figure 3-4. The figure shows the flow of a company's search for what responses it can make in the area of highly functional medical treatments in light of the fact that society is aging while experiencing a low birth rate.

Megatrends do not change suddenly, but generally change when they lose the weight of layers that decline after other layers increase. For example, in the case of the auto industry, as indicated in Figure 3-5, differentiation has no longer become possible on the

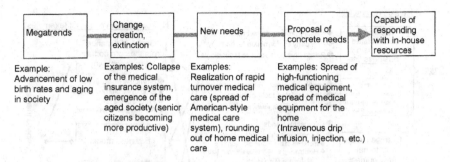

Figure 3-4:   Step Examples of Megatrend Analysis

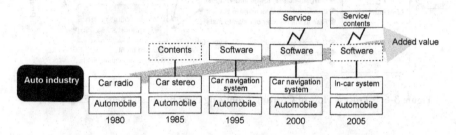

Figure 3-5:   Megatrends of the Auto Industry

grounds of appealing the object of the car itself. Instead, as seen in recent times, the addition of contents to services has become a requirement, and toward this end, telematics has been attracting attention. In addition, the auto industry itself has been transforming into one form of an advertising media as well.

3)   *Matching needs with seeds*

Where searching for themes in domains that are extensions of your firm's existing product or business is concerned, carrying out a search for new product and new business themes by incorporating SWOT analysis should become a common practice. However, in the case of examining beyond such domains, the use of such an approach only will prove insufficient and difficult. So, as mentioned in the section on recognizing existing circumstances, you will need to have a broad view of the "consumer needs" found mainly in the

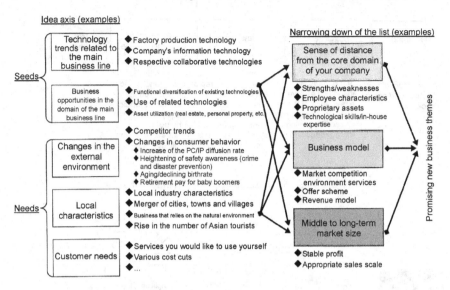

Figure 3-6:   Process Flow of Creating Promising New Business Themes (Examples)

external environment. Then by matching these needs with seeds, you will, in effect, be able to search for new business opportunities or opportunities to make product offers.

For example, as seen in Figure 3-6, you need to enumerate items that relate to seeds and needs prior to determining themes. These in turn can be narrowed down by applying such criteria as the relevance with your firm's core domain, business model, and middle to long-term market scale. The results then can be established as themes for promising new businesses (and opportunities to offer new products).

To derive ideas, you need to carry out brainstorming sessions after determining items such as those mentioned above. Once you have the ideas, you can group them and apply such methods as the KJ technique to further accelerate inspiration and create a long list of potential themes. This list in turn could be narrowed down into a short list.

Incidentally, the KJ method is a technique for developing creativity (or for creative problem solving) and was conceived by the cultural anthropologist and former professor at the Tokyo Institute of Technology, Mr. Jiro Kawakita. The name of the technique is derived from the initials of his name. A short description of the technique follows.

Write down brainstormed ideas and opinions, and miscellaneous information collected from research on small cards, using one for each item. From among these cards, sort out the ones that you feel are closely related to each other and group them into stacks of two to three. Then go on to assemble them into medium-sized and larger groups. Through such a process, you will be able to find clues and inspiration that will help you to settle on themes.

Brainstorming methods other than the KJ technique will be mentioned later, but to come up with new ideas, it is easier to merge different ideas, or in other words, to cross-fertilize or hybridize ideas and improve upon them. Such combinations are considered to be as follows:[1]

1) Technology fusion (such as a new material created through the fusion of multiple materials);
2) Business fusion (such as the fusion of communication and broadcasting, which is characteristic of the Internet society);
3) Industry fusion (such as the ATM found in a convenience store, which represents a fusion between the banking and distribution industries);
4) Social system fusion (such as the ITS, which represents a fusion between the traffic infrastructure and technological innovation);
5) Policy fusion (such as welfare medical care, aviation, and space, which are areas that receive the regulatory cooperation of relevant authorities).

Create a long list of your new business (and new product) themes by making use of your understanding of seeds and needs and external and internal environments as key concepts, while also cross-fertilizing ideas. And then gradually narrow down your list into a short list by ascertaining the utility of your business model, whether the market is medium-term or long-term, and what the SWOT analysis of your firm is in order to eventually determine your new business (and new product) themes.

4)   *Searching for themes with the revised key-needs method*

In the last part of this discussion on searching for new product and new business themes, I will be presenting a simple outline of how to search for themes with the revised key-needs method.

The original key-needs method was created by marketing business consultant Mr. Nobuyoshi Umezawa (PhD in business administration, and former marketing research manager of Sunstar Inc. and of Johnson Corporation). At the time it was developed, there was no other method available that could facilitate the development of product concepts responding to consumer needs. Over time, it has gone through improvements and has evolved into a systematic process.

The method I explain here shares the same objective and almost the same approach of the original, but it is a more simplified version of it. Basically, it requires an investigation into latent needs, questioning what needs there are from a customer's (consumer's) perspective (what would they find to be beneficial if they were to have it?). Designed to promote the discovery of such insights, the method can be further explained through the following outline.

First of all, to put it simply, the proceeds generated by a product or business depend upon the following 3 factors:

- *The appeal of the product or business*: The idea behind them, etc.

×

- *Selling power*: Power of the sales outlet, price appeal, etc.

×

- *Advertisement power*: Recognition~usage promotion.

Toward assuring the fulfillment of these three factors, the method involves repeating action steps 1 through 4 stated below:

1) Make a list of needs. Are the needs enumerated truly the needs of the many? (o : yes or X : no)

   Take note that needs could vary in the following ways:

Existential needs (... would like to live..., ... would like to become...) [Basic needs]
↑
Action needs (I want to (do)...)
↑
Target/ownership needs (I want...)

2) Do the needs from action step 1 require a novel product or is there an existing product that already responds to them? (o : novel product or X : existing product)
3) If the above is X, is there a defect in the existing product?
4) Show the needs that respond to the defect → Go to ✿ (repeat until the answer to ✿ becomes o).

Needs that finally become o in ✿ will fall under the category of Figure 3-7's "Genius." However, they need to be translated into a business through the creation of themes that can be parlayed into products with the available technology (see Figure 3-8).

And so this concludes the discussion on the steps that need to be taken into account when creating new products or businesses. The distinctive characteristic of this approach lies in its emphasis on arriving at novel products (and businesses) by focusing on consumer needs first. While I discussed in the beginning the necessity of incorporating all perspectives, creating thoroughly from the basis of needs can possibly help to narrow down variables and ultimately make the process easier to carry out. It is believed that similar approaches to this one are being adopted at various product development scenes.

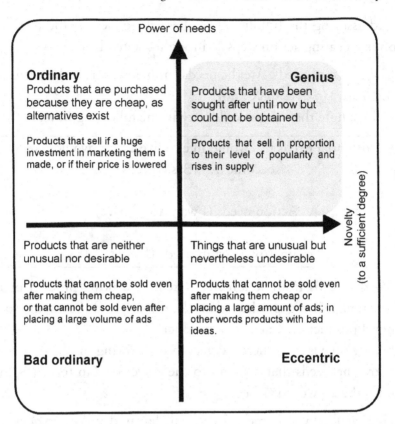

Figure 3-7:   Needs and Categories of Novelty

Needs	Yes/No	Novelty	Yes/No
	(O/×)	(BUT--existing drawbacks)	(O/×)
(1) Would like to un-clutter the wiring of office automation equipment	O	(2) Company K's product A BUT (3) Cannot be used in cramped rooms	×
(1) ...			
(1) Would like to have uncluttered wiring that could accommodate cramped rooms	O	(2) There are no drawbacks.	O

Figure 3-8:   A Summary of the Main Method's Creation Steps

3.1.3 *Prioritization of new product and new business themes and selection of R&D projects*

Next, I would like to elaborate on how to prioritize searched themes for new products and new businesses, and on the flow of parlaying them into R&D projects.

The question is how should you go about narrowing down the themes you have derived from the above methods? In other words, how should you prioritize them? To gain approval within the company, and for the sake of future developments, this is something you need to do.

To put it briefly, you should carry out R&D by prioritizing themes that correspond to the category I of Figure 3-9. The themes in this I category are highly effective while being highly feasible at the same time.

With regard to the effects themes can produce, there are various kinds of them, but in terms of future growth, the effect of market scale should be examined. In addition, if you neglect to carry out an earnings and expenses simulation to calculate a rough estimate of the market, you will not be able to know the extent of your product or business's positioning and market share. In other words, to understand the effect, you will need to have a rough estimate of revenues as well. Furthermore, qualitative effects, which are difficult to show numerically, such as synergy effects with your firm's existing products or businesses, can also help to further your understanding.

You must take the criterion of feasibility into account as well. No matter how effective a certain product or business theme may seem to be, if you cannot materialize its effect, investing in it will not be worthwhile. To judge the feasibility of a theme, you can look at how suitable and compatible it is with your firm's product or business. The higher these qualities are, the more likely the product or business of a theme in question will be an extension of your existing product or business, and therefore the higher its feasibility will

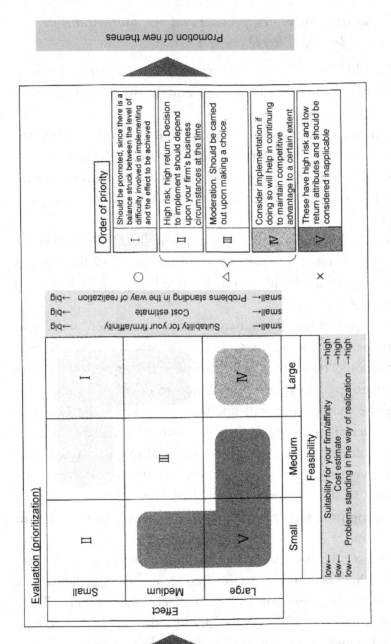

Figure 3-9:   Evaluation of Promising New Business Themes (Prioritization)

be. In addition, the rough estimate of expenses calculated in the simulation of earnings and expenses is naturally important to consider as well, and if this were high, feasibility would be low. Feasibility would also become low with the existence of many other problems that would need to be addressed before a product or business could be realized.

So when you are contemplating which theme to start working on, you must take such feasibility factors into account. If you clearly arrange your themes in an organizational framework as the one shown in Figure 3-9 for your reference, your understanding will be facilitated.

The figure clearly shows that you should begin with the items that fall under the oI category, which are items that rate the highest in terms of effect and feasibility, and then go on to carry out the items in categories II, III, and IV (as indicated by the Δ symbol) in their respective order. As for items that fall under category xV, there is no use in taking them up, since they are low return items while being high risk as well. And so this concludes the discussion on how you should prioritize and select your R&D projects.

3.1.4 *Preparations for R&D projects*

In the last part of this chapter, I will explain how to go about turning the prioritized themes of new products and new businesses into projects.

First of all, in order to research and develop the recommended themes, you will need to prepare an intra-company circular to obtain approval. This circular will have to be approved by a committee set up for promoting new businesses or by holding management conferences. Furthermore, if the value of investment is substantial, then you will have to gain approval from the board of directors. To obtain this approval, you will need to prepare a proposal that includes particulars such as the following:

- Background details (for completed themes)
- Corporate objectives and strategies (according to the theme)
- Return on investment (ROI) assumption
- Issues that need to be resolved for implementation
- Implementation strategy (including methodology)
- Implementation schedule and procedure.

Failure to specify such points will preclude official investment and prevent you from beginning your R&D project in an official capacity. That is the way the corporate world works.

If you incorporate your present assumptions into the strategies to be included in the above-mentioned proposal, you will become more persuasive. These assumptions could be on matters such as the following:[2]

- New market creation (become a market pioneer)
- Single-focus strategy (aim for the domination of a niche market)
- Guerrilla strategy (also aim for surrounding niche markets after experiencing growth)
- No. 1 strategy (aim to become No. 1 in regions)
- Fake/decoy strategy (to help other products/businesses)
- Others (brand use, every possible form of full-fledged attacks).

These are new product/new business entry strategies for securing a competitive advantage, and need to be clarified not only in the preparatory stages, but also after development projects are initiated.

While such strategies need to be included in your proposal, you will also need a driving force. Toward this end, you should organize in-house groups or teams that do not require to be profitable, labeling them with names such as Project Team X or Preparation Room Y. At times, such organizations are set up to begin vetting proposals, while in other cases, preparatory groups come into being only after a cross-departmental project team vets proposals.

For example, when Square (currently Square Enix) was about to begin an Internet-based game business, the management, who planned the project, set up a new project team named PlayOnline and then went on to establish a preparatory room for this project. On the other hand, when Rakuten was contemplating to launch a finance business on its own, it did not set up a project team, but instead established a preparatory office as a distinct organization of the company. In the end, Rakuten launched its new finance business by buying the credit card company (Kokunai Shinpan, the current Rakuten KC).

So in this way it becomes a chicken or egg question, but in order to carry out new businesses or sell new products, an appropriate driving force becomes necessary, and the larger the scale of a project becomes, the organization of such a force becomes all the more necessary even in the preparatory phase.

3.2 Operational Management and Evaluation of R&D Projects

3.2.1 *Framework for starting and implementing projects*

First of all, in the case of beginning an R&D project for a new product or new business after obtaining approval from management, you will need to undergo the preparations mentioned previously and build a framework by forming an official organization. If you already have a preparatory organization or a project team, then all you need to do is to inherit such setups. However, there may be many times also when you will need to newly build them. In addition, even when you already have a preparatory organization, if there is a need to expand further, you will need to recruit people from another organization or from outside.

When you look at corporate trends, it becomes evident that companies that succeed in cultivating themes into new businesses from

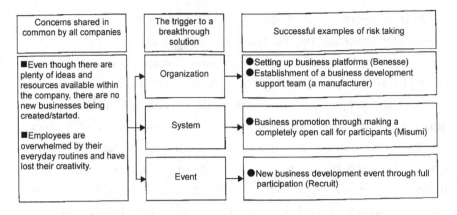

Figure 3-10:   Successful Cases of Triggers and Risk Taking

the time they start an R&D project are the ones that have used either "organizations," "systems," or "events." To cultivate a new business systematically, the setup of a "trigger" is mandatory. However, these are strictly speaking only "triggers" and nothing more. In order to continuously maintain and activate an organization or a system, it is necessary to actually carry out the business and accumulate successes. Figure 3-10 shows precedents of successes that were ushered by triggers.

As evidenced by the precedents, from now on, the types of organizations that invite people to join or request their voluntary participation will also help to revitalize operations within the company. Therefore, when recruiting personnel for a particular group, it would be desirable to recruit or request participation from within the company. At one time, Sony was extremely famous for recruiting in-house. This system of invitational recruitment allowed for employees to readily apply since the superiors of the departments they belonged to were not informed until the last minute. Meanwhile, departments suffered as they kept losing capable people, but the practice persisted nevertheless and was justified on the grounds that the department head was the one who was ultimately responsible for the operation of the department. It has been said that this practice had become a major problem for organizations with existing operations.

In the case there are no personnel or experts available within the company, you will need to consider recruiting from outside. In such an event, you will need to recruit through headhunters and the company website, but you will not be able to recruit immediately in such a case. In fact, you will require a minimum of around three months, and if you factor in the current occupation of the potential recruit, it becomes highly probable that you will require half a year. Therefore, it is ideal to have the essentials of an R&D project in order during its preparatory phase, and be prepared to begin recruiting once authorization is obtained.

The staff to be recruited will require the following attributes. These attributes also apply to people recruited from within the company:

- Familiar with the subject of new businesses and new products (is an expert)
- Has motivation for developing new businesses and new products
- Feels responsible for seeing the project through to its end
- Not afraid to see the project fail
- Understands how to handle workloads by applying such methods as setting milestones
- Has the stamina to endure overtime duties required in achieving milestones
- Able to cooperate with existing staff
- Able to reason with the existing organization whenever a conflict occurs
- Able to take action on the basis of numerical evidence
- Able to adapt to circumstances as the occasion demands.

And so this is how you should prepare a setup of talented people prior to initiating your project. The required staff, whether they are from within the organization or employed from outside, need to have an environmental arrangement that allows them the freedom of mobility.

If the people from the inside are allowed to show their strengths in coordinating with internal or existing business parties, and those from the outside are allowed to hook up with outside parties or make use of their expertise, they will be able to have a favorable impact on the promotion of future R&D projects. Often, people from the inside become dependent on being able to return to their former group in the event they fail. And, in the case of people from the outside, there are times they become suppressed by the resistance from conservative groups or individuals within the organization. When such a situation arises, much effort in searching for and carrying out promising new business or new product themes will be in vain. Consequently, the very survival of the company will be threatened, along with the decline of existing businesses and products, and the opposing conservative groups and individuals may not even remain in the company, causing consternation for everyone else in the process.

For example, Square (currently Square Enix), which launched its network-based business, "PlayOnline," not only attempted to become a pioneer for a new business domain, but also attempted to start a business that would generate a regular cash flow from a line that was different from the company's one to date. Specifically, the PlayOnline business began to offer "Final Fantasy," a formerly boxed game, on the Internet. By charging monthly fees, the business aimed to secure a stable revenue stream. (On PlayOnline, Final Fantasy 11 is being offered.) However, at the outset, the conservative group, who were accustomed to the transient nature of the boxed game business, became skeptical and uncooperative, questioning, "why new members will attempt something like that?" For this reason, the company had to go through a series of trials and tribulations before they were able to launch the business. Furthermore, Square found it difficult to invest in PlayOnline after having failed in their movie business, which had been launched several years prior to this one — they had even turned to Sony Computer Entertainment (SCE) for a capital increase of 15 billion yen to rescue them. The upshot of this was that they ended up making a smaller investment than they had originally planned for PlayOnline. And due to the conflict between the members of the preparatory room and the conservative group, all of the members resigned eventually, and the launch of the business itself was delayed. With a lack of talented staff, the scope for the development of the project became narrowed further. (However, in terms of business objectives, the business is a medium- to long-term success, having grown into one with an annual turnover exceeding 15 billion yen at present.)

The lesson to be learned from this precedent is firstly that it is possible to become influenced by the trends of other businesses, new or existing. And depending on the changes in the staff entrusted with the implementation of the project, there will be times when it will not be possible to carry out the strategy as originally intended at the outset. In the end, due to these factors, the speed of the development of a new business declines. In addition, the project could lose direction; it may become unclear as to who the new business is for, lessening the motivation of the concerned members in the process. Once again, drawing from the above-mentioned precedent, you can also see the importance of having a setup for implementing a new business and the difficulties associated with it.

3.2.2 Continuing projects (delaying and extending): Criteria for termination

Next, after initiating a project, you will need to consider how to continue it. If it stays according to schedule within the original budget, then there is no reason to terminate it in particular. Still, at this point, it is necessary to establish a more or less clear set of procedures (operational plan)[3] for determining whether to continue or terminate a project:

- Does the project show a deficit *vis-à-vis* the budget?
- Even if the project shows a deficit, is it strategically justified (in line with the initial objective) to continue it?
- Is it possible to stop the project midway and deploy elsewhere the tangible/intangible assets acquired until now?
- Instead of terminating the project at the present point, would it be preferable to terminate it when a deficit is incurred?
- Will termination have an impact on other businesses?
- If you terminate the project, will it be possible to reshuffle the personnel related to this business?

So, as a matter of corporate policy, it is necessary to determine at the outset the criteria for deciding up to what point it would be okay to continue a project, taking into account the above-mentioned requirements and procedures. These criteria should be adopted to determine the pros and cons of continuing, even when the project is experiencing a delay as it is being carried out and after it has been carried out as well. If the above observations are plotted out, they will form a flowchart as indicated in Figure 3-11.

However, there are cases when you should not even start a project, let alone continue it, even if there is no deficit shown at the outset as mentioned above. This applies to cases when deducting the investment amount from the Net Present Value (NPV), which is the future cash flow of properties converted into its present value, results in a negative figure. However, insofar as the project is in progress, investments have already been made until that point and so decisions on future investment amounts should be made on the basis of the value of the present value of the future cash flow of properties. In other words, you must look toward termination if the sum of investments (made up to the present) and the NPV yields

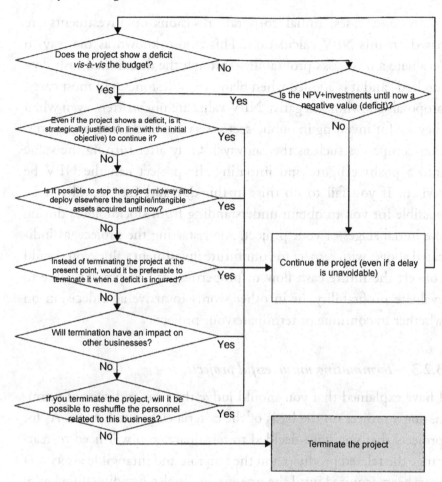

Figure 3-11: Flowchart of the Process Leading Up to the Termination of a Project

a negative figure, and there are no other factors that offer justification for continuing. In other words, to a certain extent, this assessment is considered to be similar to the above-mentioned first step of asking, "does the project show a deficit?" Figure 3-11 also reflects these points in the right-hand flow sequence. As it can be seen, you will do well to follow this procedure and regularly repeat the steps in the flowchart when deciding whether to continue or terminate a project.

In most cases, initial corporate decisions on investments are based on this NPV calculation. This is also known as the way to "evaluate a business's profitability through the discounted cash flow method" and it is applied when planning milestones.[2] In most cases, proposals showing a negative NPV value are not written, even when they are for investing in public-sector services (including transportation companies such as the railways). Only after turning the value into a positive figure and initiating the project can the NPV be revised. If you fail to do this, in this day and age, it will not be possible for you to obtain understanding from stockholders during the initial stages of your project. After starting the project, as indicated above, with respect to your future investment value, you should convert the future cash flow of properties into its present value to evaluate profitability, or in other words to arrive at a decision on whether to continue or terminate your project.

3.2.3   *Terminating unsuccessful projects*

I have explained that you should judge the pros and cons of terminating a project on the basis of the criteria elaborated above. As for projects that you have decided to terminate, you will need to rearrange the related products and the tangible and intangible assets that have been acquired until the present, while also deciding on what to do next about the related staff.

When you terminate your project though, you will have to take action immediately, since expenses will continue to accumulate one after another, such as the remunerations and costs related to staff and facilities belonging to your company or to your subcontractors, and the costs related to employee benefits.

At this point, I would like to elaborate on a project that suffered substantial loss because it was not terminated.

The previously mentioned Square (currently Square Enix) had carried out a business that specialized in the production of full

CG (computer graphics) movies. This involved establishing a subsidiary called Square Pictures in Hawaii and filming the popular RPG game "Final Fantasy" without using live-action cinematography. The business took an investment of around 16.5 billion yen altogether and generated only 3 billion yen in box-office proceeds, registering a drastic loss for the company. Despite showing earnings, the figure included earnings of distribution companies as well, so the actual share for the company was more or less zero in the end.

Why didn't the company terminate the project? The answer lies in a number of factors as pointed out below:

- As a business, the movie business needs to be well-rounded or else it will not be possible to repurpose it in other ways.
- Having no experience in film production, the company had no understanding of the bottom line until the end.
- For the company, this was the first attempt of using CG, a very costly technology.
- The project became a sanctuary for especially the top executives of the Development Division, who enjoyed a high status within the organization. Consequently, there was a lack of management oversight and while the project continued to stall during the course of production, no one was able to suspend it partway.
- The President at the time had indicated that under the best case scenario the project will be profitable, under the medium case scenario, the project will break even, and under the worst-case scenario, the project will be unprofitable, but nevertheless generate publicity. When the cost rose, he foresaw the outcome would be the worst-case scenario, but this warning did not serve as a reason to suspend the project.
- The product ended up becoming seller-centric rather than consumer-centric and was made to dance to the tune of the advertising agency.

While they may have been clear about their strategic intent to continue even in the face of being burdened with a deficit, the scale of the project's required investment was substantially large and the issues mentioned were all matters that needed careful deliberation. For such reasons, it would perhaps have been a good idea to take a longer look at the company and its implications as a business listed in the First Section of the stock exchange.

Incidentally, it was generally assessed that the project had failed because of the film's full-fledged CG graphics; it had helped to produce a photo-realistic effect that did not diverge from live-action photography in a substantial way. So the question arises of why they avoided shooting the film as a live-action one in the first place if, visually speaking, there was not to be much of a difference. Additionally, what mattered to viewers in the end, in spite of the initial fascination with the special effects technology, were the film's story and characters, just as the story and characters of a live-action film would matter. Furthermore, the story should have been given more priority, but as it turned out, it was amateurish.

Upon experiencing this failure, they turned to SCE for 15 billion yen in financing, and then went on to merge with Enix. Furthermore, Square Pictures, the subsidiary set up to handle the movie business, was dissolved, and the creators and technicians who had been gathered from all over the world were all let go.

3.2.4 *Evaluation of a project's success/failure, and the evaluation system*

First of all, let us consider how to go about evaluating a project's success or failure. Firstly, one criterion is the number of years a product or business will take for it to be in black for a single month to a single year on the basis of its special characteristics. If the business fails to show a positive balance for even a single month, it will clearly be a failed project. However, in showing a positive balance for a single month, even though in the case of a heavy industry company, taking over five years may not be an issue, in the case of the modern Internet business, if it fails to show a positive balance within one to three years, it is considered a failure, since success after that time cannot be anticipated. On the other hand, in the case of an Internet-based business, in the event it fails, it is easy to launch a different project, since it takes only a short time to start it up, and since the required investment is small compared to the amount required for a heavy industry company.

Next is the matter of the number of years it will take for the product or business to achieve an accumulated positive balance. If you take the NPV into account, merely showing an accumulated positive balance is of no use. The project can only be called a success when the value of the past investment and the value of the present, in which results can be seen, and the value of the future put together exceeds the investment. In other words, it can be called a success when earnings exceed the amount of investment with annual interest rates added to it. So the sooner the project attains a single positive balance, the sooner it will attain an accumulated positive balance. In other words, in the case of an Internet business, achieving an accumulated positive balance is apt to be fast, while in the case of a heavy industry business, it is apt to be slow. For example, in the railway industry, even in the case of related businesses (businesses other than the railway business), approximately ten years seems to be one benchmark. Many of these businesses are real estate like operations making use of their existing assets. When considering that they are offsetting their construction costs from the income earned through monthly rent payments, the length of around ten years makes general sense. Even though this is extremely long when compared to the period for a regular business, it is nevertheless tolerated as a special characteristic of a public enterprise.

Now, regarding the system/organization set up for the purpose of evaluating, as long as a project can output clear figures on a product-specific or business-specific basis, it may be all right to do without a particular setup. In other words, these figures will directly factor into management's evaluation. However, if this is not possible, then the following three alternatives in particular are considered to be ideal:[3]

- An organization set up to scrutinize the very contents of an R&D project and evaluate whether they are truly aligned with the aims of the middle- to long-term management plan and the R&D program;
- An organization set up to consider the methods of managing the operations of an R&D project and evaluate whether human, material, and information resources are being put to full use;
- An organization set up to analyze an R&D project's investment (cost) *vis-à-vis* its effect (sales profit) and evaluate whether sufficient benefits or results are being secured for the investment effort being made.

In any case, it is necessary to have an organization apart from the one that carries out the research and development for a new business or a new product; one that will be able to carry out objective and neutral evaluations. This organization will not only be responsible for evaluating just figures, but also for evaluating such factors as whether any synergy exists between the R&D project and other projects, whether there are any strategic results, and whether the motivation of its own company's employees or that of the employees of related firms was raised.

In major companies these days, there are groups set up specifically for the purpose of examining only the launch of new businesses and new products. After considering and forming plans for such projects, they entrust their actual development to the business unit. In such a setup, it will not do to just evaluate the organization set up to consider new businesses, but instead evaluations should be made on a more overall level; they should be made on the performance of such a business unit as well and they should be made at a stage when the activities of planning, launching, and achieving a track record have been completed to a certain extent. In that case, the investment amount needs to straddle both groups and care should be taken when contrasting it with results. To evaluate these points accurately, the managerial accounting of products and services has to be made transparent. By doing so, an indirect department such as an evaluation group can stay small, and since costs associated with an indirect group need not be included in new businesses and new products, the probability of success rises. While these techniques may amount to nothing more than cheap tricks, avoiding unnecessary costs such as these may be one factor that can contribute toward the success of new businesses and new products.

On the other hand, there is a line of thinking that advises that R&D for new businesses and new products should not be viewed as costs. For example, it may be all right if there is an element of fundamental research; the kind that shows results only after ten years or more. However, these days the number of companies that are able to make investments for such undertakings are limited and in most cases companies hook up with organizations such as universities and special corporate bodies that carry out fundamental researches for the purpose of realizing commercialization and productization. Since fundamental research in this case takes place across a considerably long span of time, it is common for evaluation groups to overlook this aspect. At the telecommunications firm, NTT, a representative Japanese company, the research facility is basically positioned in a holding company, and the cost is shared with the operational company. Similarly, even at KDDI, their research facility is established as KDDI's directly controlled subsidiary, and it is believed that expenses are shared among each business department.

An evaluation group needs to determine the extent of what should be evaluated by referring to corporate policies and societal norms. Toward this end, they need to be objective and neutral and if they happen to be from within the company, that will be a plus. With such a setup, even members of a terminated project will be able to reach an understanding and be able to look forward to the next opportunity.

3.2.5   *The standardization (packaging) and withdrawal of successful projects*

Lastly, I would like to offer some thoughts on "how to standardize and package a successful project"; in other words, how to make a successful product or business attain consistent sales. If you cannot do this, you need to think about withdrawing your product or service after bringing it to market.

The newly launched product or business of a successful project will undergo the product life cycle comprised of "the introductory phase → growth phase → mature phase → waning phase," as indicated previously. It will not just simply wait for decline to happen, but instead it will go around the cycle while modifying on the way. If it enters into its growth phase through this process, its price will gradually fall, and when it enters into its mature phase, it will fall into a price competition and become a generic product. In other words, this is the time when it should be standardized (packaged). Furthermore, when it enters into its waning phase, if it is not possible to modify it and return it to its growth or mature phase again, it will become necessary to withdraw it from the market. This is the sequence that should be noted.

However, according to what is known as the Chasm Theory, in the hi-tech product market of these days, in the process of penetration, there exists a large chasm between what are known as the initial markets, which number in the few and are made up of consumers who can be characterized as progressive, and the mainstream markets, which form the majority and are made up of consumers who can be characterized as utilitarian. An advocate of this Chasm Theory,

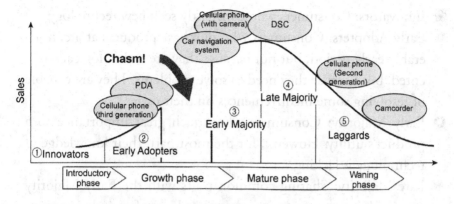

Figure 3-12:   Project Life Cycle and Chasm
Source: Based on Geoffrey Moore's "Chasm Theory".

Geoffrey Moore, categorized consumers of high tech products into five groups as seen in Figure 3-12 and stated that a chasm exists between the early adopter and early majority groups.

As indicated in Figure 3-12, there is a chasm that needs to be crossed to reach the mainstream market. In other words, to reach the mature phase from the growth phase, this chasm needs to be crossed, and standardization can take place only after that. In the mature phase, car navigation systems and camera-equipped cell phones have already been standardized and are dominating markets. With passenger vehicles these days, there are cases where car navigation systems are offered as standard equipment, and most cell phones come equipped with cameras, becoming a threat for digital camera markets in the process (though it can be said that camera-equipped cell phones and digital cameras have been concurrently responsible for creating such a visually oriented society). As for the second-generation digital cellular phone, while it had become standardized in the past, it has already arrived at its waning phase and cell phones using this generation's technology called Personal Digital Cellular (PDC) are gradually disappearing from the market.

❋ Innovators: Consumers who constantly seek new technology.

❊ Early Adopters: Consumers who purchase products at a considerably early period, but not because they are technologically oriented, but because they need to solve problems. They are capable of resolving some inconveniences on their own.

◎ Early Majority: Consumers who attach great importance to a product's utility. However, for the most part, their knowledge of technology is lacking.

✳ Late Majority: Sharing common traits with the Early Majority group, these consumers purchase products after industry standards become fixed.

✸ Laggards: Consumers who purchase high-tech products (in unintentional ways) after they become incorporated and become obscure.

And so by going through such a process of standardization, new products cease to be new products. In other words, they become generic products. In other words, the end result of an R&D project is this standardization. Once a product advances to this state of consistent sales, a single R&D package becomes complete, and by customizing this package, it should become easier to deploy it for other new products as well.

The decision to withdraw after a product or business has passed its growth phase and is in the process of standardizing should be made in the case when it is deemed that it has reached its waning phase after standardization or when it is deemed that a new product or new business was not able to reach the chasm. If you withdraw at the wrong time, it is tantamount to never having truly ascertained the project's unsuccessfulness. In such a situation, you will be substantially increasing your losses, and as indicated in the case example, the error may have an impact on the very survival of your company, leaving you with only two alternatives; seek cooperation from other companies or be resigned to a buy-off.

As can be seen, products and businesses are like living things, requiring you to constantly maintain them in top condition and foster their ability to continue creating. In this sense, new products and new businesses are just like babies, and as such, giving birth to them and raising them are no easy matters. When child rearing brings good results, it is extremely joyful, and with these good results, you will be able to go on giving birth to new lives.

Hiromichi Yasuoka

References

1. Fumio Kodama, Kiminori Genba, *New Business Creation Strategy — Case Analysis According to the Theory of Industrial Creation/Technological Evolution Cycle*, Seisansei Shuppan, 2000, pp. 186–190.
2. Ken Oe, Yasutomi Kitahara, *Strategy for Making Profits — Planning, Assessing, and Examining New Businesses*, Toyo Keizai Shinposha, 2002, pp. 48, 144.
3. Akira Ishikawa, *The Q & A Primer to Information Searching for Developing New Products and New Businesses*, Dobunkan, 1988, pp. 77–78, 85.

Chapter 4

The New Systematization and Assetization of Information

In this chapter, great importance will be attached to new systematizations and assetizations of information for corporations, and the discussions will be based on the recognition that they form the key foundation for R&D and new product and business development. Specifically, this chapter examines proprietors and CIOs (Chief Information Officers) who seek to assure strategic management of developmental information, the analysis of the systematization and assetization of technological and R&D information that serve the executive in charge of developing and managing information, and the systematization and assetization of market development information that play a crucial role in the development of management strategies.

4.1 Systematization and Assetization of Technological and R&D Information

4.1.1 *An approach to the systematization of information*

It is possible to gather and accumulate data relating to research and development from among a voluble amount of technical intelligence and apply them to various administrative actions by effectively systematizing them. To that end, you must build a database related to information technology by grasping the progress and changes of technology up to the present as technological information, while treating accumulated R&D information as basic intelligence.

From the time a present data analysis is made on collected technological information, R&D information will be treated as sources of information for making forecasts for the near future of two to three years ahead, the future of five to ten years ahead, and the long-term future beyond that. The R&D information for the near future will be treated as entries of the Data Base System, while information for longer periods beyond that will be treated as entries of the Knowledge Information System.

However, when seeking R&D information, you should not limit your search to the electronics field and medical product field or the information communication field in particular, but should broaden your scope to include information from all fields. For example, in the case of developing medical products, it is said that in addition to requiring more than ten-odd years to develop one drug product, a cost of tens of billions of yen needs to be spent. In such a process as seen in the development of a drug product, as indicated in Figure 4-1, if you attempt to present a medical product as R&D information, you will not be able to do without not only information related to the securing of present research materials, but also information regarding data that confirm the research subjects of two to three years' time; and furthermore, information regarding the isolation and refinement of active substances of five to ten years' time or information regarding drug designs and clinical trials.

In addition, in order to disperse the R&D risk of medical products, a large, global-scale project has been underway in recent years involving drug-company alliances. Amid such circumstances, the following factors concerning Japan, the United States, and Europe have to be evaluated within your firm or the development team: the level of development progress in each country, the degree of ease in exchanging technical know-how between the countries, the degree of difficulty in carrying out technology cooperation between the countries,

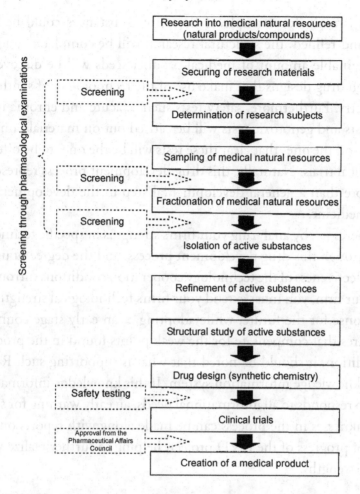

Figure 4-1:   The General Flow of the Drug Development Process

and the extent of the technical level in each country. Through carrying out information management of the development phase of such a drug development process, it becomes possible to clarify screenings based on the indicators of pharmacological tests of research materials that are the focus of future researches of two to three years' time, and to confirm, abstract, and compartmentalize research subjects determined by the discovery of materials having the screened pharmacological actions.

As a result, for example, if the active substances could be isolated and refined, the structural research will be completed, and an unimaginable amount of medical-product seeds will be discovered through drug designs that make use of the technologies of synthetic chemistry. Furthermore, safety tests such as acute and chronic toxicity tests and genotoxic tests will be carried out on materials among these, and the ones that clear these tests will be the ones to be offered to clinical trials. Naturally, this drug development process represents no more than a general developmental step in the development of new medicines.

Therefore, by analyzing your firm's strengths in specific technologies through this drug development process, and the degree of usage and effectiveness of the technology cooperation conditions surrounding your firm, you must extend your firm's technological strengths as a response for the future, while adopting at an early stage countermeasures that compensate for the weak points found in the process. In addition, it should be noted that what is supporting such R&D is the knowledge information system. If this knowledge information system responds to all informational needs, an early warning for signs of weaknesses in the process can be made along with reports on the level of progress of the R&D project, helping to further realize your firm's strengths.

4.1.2 *Systematization and assetization of keywords*

Information is dependent upon various fields, processes, topics, and contents. Thus, predictions of the near future of two to three years time, the future of five to ten years time, and the long-term future of beyond five to ten years can be treated as keywords related to inventions, discoveries, and technological innovations. As indicated in Figure 4-2, the keywords could be described as personal needs in terms of the workplace, office, and occupation, or in terms of municipalities and nations.[1] Furthermore, if you associate the needs with directly or indirectly related categories, you will be able to

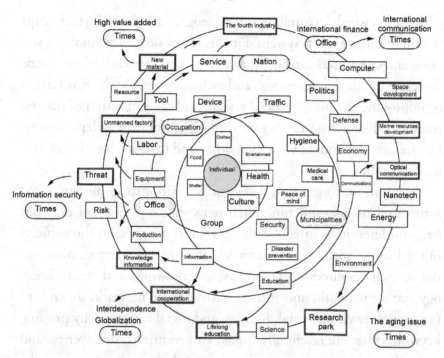

Figure 4-2: Relationships between Needs and Keywords
Source: Adapted from p. 26 of Akira Ishikawa's *The Q&A Primer to Information Searching for Developing New Products and New Businesses*, Dobunkan, 1988.

grasp all keywords not as elements that exist independently, but as elements that have interrelationships with each other.

Therefore, when classifying these needs and narrowing down their scope, it becomes possible to grasp them as inter-network related keywords considered to be concerned with inventions, discoveries, and technological innovations of five to ten years into the future. For example, terms such as nation, municipality, workplace, and individual can be positioned as inter-network related items associated with the keywords "human social system." In addition, terms such as health, hygiene, and medical care can be positioned as inter-network related items associated with the keywords "human organism system." Furthermore, terms such as energy, entropy, and natural resources can be positioned as inter-network related items associated with the keywords "natural resources/geography system," which helps maintain the organism system. Finally, terms such as technology, science, and computers can be positioned as inter-network related items associated with the keywords "technology system," which is related to improving the human social system and the utilization of natural resources. Furthermore, each network does not exist independently, but are interdependent with each other and form an even larger network together.

In addition, to group the keywords positioned in human, environmental, social, and functional networks, one method that can be considered is to integrate the keywords assigned to the subjects of the human social system network, the organism system network, the natural resources/geography system network, and the technology system network, and further narrow these networks down into functional, environmental, human, and social categories by probing keywords that are essentially linked to inventions, discoveries, and technological innovations and by probing the project sphere as well.[1]

If you regard the keywords in accordance with networks, in the case of functional networks firstly, you will be able to subdivide them into sensory functions and work functions. On the other hand, the environmental network can be subdivided into such categories as space, time, object, plant, and animal in chronological order. In addition, the human network could be subdivided into categories ranging from spiritual (introverted) to physical (extroverted). Finally, the social network could be subdivided into such categories as secure and quality living standards, economic efficiency, and convenience.

In carrying out the systematization and assetization of keywords on the basis of the above points, the following two perspectives will prove indispensable.

1) *Identifying master keywords (categories)*

This is about grasping the overall picture of the technology field, especially the R&D field, and identifying categories that allow for collecting, systematizing, and assetizing keywords from a macroscopic perspective.

2) *Adding quantitative expressions*

This approach is about carrying out systematization and assetization by adopting quantitative expressions drawn from a microscopic perspective for the categories drawn from a macroscopic perspective. Specifically, in the process of such an adoption, the approach will help to identify keywords that are directly connected conceptually, structurally, and constitutively, and, on the basis of their interrelatedness, systematize and assetize in accordance with their size, strength, and inclusiveness levels.

4.1.3 *Charting and patterning as means for systematizing*

When expressing the systematization and assetization of keywords, it will prove more effective if you adopt charts or patterns. Among the expressions you can develop, while there is the tree structure[1] diagram showing keywords in a hierarchical layout, there is also the relational structure[2] that interlinks keywords in a tabular format, and additionally, there is the network structure[3] that shows combinations of multiple categories. Furthermore, the matrix structure,[4] which

---

[1] Tree Structure refers to the schematization of the hierarchical relationships of directories and files, designating their most basic component as a "root," from where branches grow, diverge, and spread out.

[2] Relational Structure shows multiple items laterally and a corresponding number of data vertically within a square graph, and displays a collection of mutually related data in a tabular format.

[3] Network Structure attempts to streamline information processing by linking multiple items to each other and having each of them share data in common as well.

[4] The Matrix Structure signifies matrix items with mathematical expressions and displays them within a square framework. This framework is capable of expressing data in terms of the three dimensions of length, width, and height, in addition to expressing them in terms of time and other dimensions.

depicts the fusion of the technologies of different and innovative hi-tech fields, can be used as an expression of new technologies.[5]

For example, such new fusion technologies include fine chemicals,[5] which is a fusion between the chemistry and life science fields, specialty chemicals,[6] which is a fusion between the chemistry and materials fields, and engineering plastics,[7] which is a fusion between the advanced materials field and other fields. In addition, the fusions have also made possible such advanced technologies as biomass,[8] which is a fusion between the fields of natural resources, energy, and biotechnology; and artificial organs (artificial materials), which is a fusion between the fields of materials and life science. Furthermore, the fusions have also made it possible for the development of nanotechnology,[9] which is a fusion between the fields of Information

---

[5] Fine Chemicals refer to a variety of high value-added chemicals found in chemical products, such as medicines, pesticides, synthetic dyes, and perfumes. They require a high degree of processing and are produced in small quantities.

[6] Specialty Chemicals refer to high-performance specialty chemicals such as plastic additives, functional coating materials, water treatment chemicals for manufactured paper, functional textile materials, and chemicals used in home/personal care goods.

[7] Engineering Plastics refer to plastics used in industrial applications such as machine components and structural materials. Primarily used as metal substitutes, they are high functional polymers that have the durability and heat resistance required to withstand their application in industrial products such as automobile parts, machine components, and electronic parts.

[8] Biomass refers to a fixed number of plant materials that can be used as energy and is created by plants through the process of photosynthesis. Biomass is also referred to as phytomass with the prefix "phyto" referring to the fact that its energy is derived from plants.

[9] Nanotechnology is a means for manufacturing at a scale of a one-one billionth meter. One nanometer (nm) is a hyperfine unit that expresses about one-one hundred thousandth of the thickness of a strand of hair, and one-one thousandth of a red blood cell. Nanotechnology is the most researched technology today and once it becomes established, the miniaturization of various machines and electronic equipment will become successful. Furthermore, its establishment will also make the creation of unprecedented high performance advanced materials possible.

and Communication Technology (ICT) and such fields as biotechnology.

Regarding the fusion of technologies that come into being through the integration of various industrial sectors, there are the simple cases that see technology fusions arising from the merger of two industrial sectors, and there are the complex cases that see technology fusions arising from the merger between multiple sectors. With the adoption of the concept of the matrix structure, these relationships can be illustrated as technologies arising from the interrelationships between specific industrial sectors. The direction of such technology fusions of different fields, as it has been consistent with what has been discussed up to this point, is truly about the development from systematizing to assetizing the keywords that will prove essential for discovering R&D themes.

Incidentally, in our approach to information based on the systematization of keywords until now, we have understood such information on the basis of what has been directly apparent; information that revolved around established technologies and materials or products. In other words, with regard to the properties, phenomena, and discovered principles included in each of those technologies, we considered them to be part of what had already been systematized and for this reason did not make use of them as case examples.

Therefore, the technical function map (gene map), which was designed to serve as a foundation for everything, is a tool that truly helps to systematize the properties, phenomena, and principles of established technologies and materials or products and turn them into data that R&D projects can use for reference.

4.1.4 *Compiling keywords into a thesaurus*
Regarding keywords that continue to increase, if you group them by their characteristics, finding what you seek will often be made

easier. This is where the thesaurus,[10] a tool for searching databases, can play an important role. As the number of keywords increase and become more substantial, compiling them into a thesaurus will become all the more indispensable.

In the ISO 2788[11], the thesaurus is defined as "an organized and functional glossary of terms made up of semantic and comprehensive associations that cover specific spheres of knowledge." On the other hand, in the JIS X 0901[12], the thesaurus is defined as "an organized vocabulary index that is arranged in a way to show the anticipatory relationships between concepts.

Such thesauri that are indispensable in the systematization and assetization of keywords are being created in large numbers by various government bodies, institutions, academic societies, associations, groups, universities, and corporations to meet their respective purposes, and even in Japan, there exists such thesauri as the JICST

---

[10] A thesaurus is a glossary of terms used in searching databases and serves as a lexicon to assist in encapsulating with one word those matters that can be expressed in various ways. Thesaurus-based searches suffer from the following drawbacks; inputs of thesaurus terms need to be accurate to be able to produce hits; choosing the correct term from a vast number of words is cumbersome.

[11] The International Organization for Standardization (ISO) is an international authority formed for establishing worldwide standards. Standards are variously established by relevant bodies and are categorized into "company standards," which are standards adopted at the corporate level; "industrial association standards," which are standards adopted at the industrial level; "national standards," which are standards that are assumed to be adopted at the state level; "regional standards," which are standards established at a certain regional level, such as Europe; and "international standards," which are standards established in the expectation that they will be adopted at the international level. ISO is one of the representative international authorities formed for establishing international standards, which are considered to be the most significant standards among the standards mentioned above.

[12] The Japan Industrial Standard (JIS) refers to national standards established for all manufactured products on the basis of Japan's industrial standardization law. In JIS, there are ISO standards that have been adapted for Japan and others that have been originally created for Japan, but in either case, the Japanese Industrial Standards Committee (JISC) deliberates the original proposals of the standards, which are prepared by affiliates of regulating authorities. Upon approval, the cabinet minister in charge officially announces the proposals as JIS standards.

Thesaurus.[13] Field-specific specialist thesauri include the Nikkei Thesaurus (Nihon Keizai Shimbun), the Library Thesaurus (College Library), and the Thesaurus of Medical Terms (Japana Centra Revuo Medicina). In addition, there are many software packages of thesauri available in the market, including The Unabridged Dictionary of Synonyms, Kohjien, The Digital Thesaurus, and The Practical Thesaurus.[2]

Incidentally, as elaborated below, when creating a thesaurus, it is necessary to consider the scope, selection of descriptors, and usage.

1) Scope of the thesaurus

The scope of a thesaurus should not be limited to terms of a specific field and its adjacent areas, but should encompass terms that other thesauri can use. The terms to be included in the thesaurus should be ones that express concepts in their simplest and most unitary forms possible. As for compound terms, they will be disassembled into simpler words to function as index words. The disassembly will be made to the extent that the meanings remain clear for the user. In addition, where complex subjects are concerned, it is important to express them through the combination of individual terms.

2) Selection of descriptors

The selection of descriptors[14] as terms that have been officially approved and formulated for the thesaurus will be made on the grounds of criteria such as structure, usage objective, and usage plan of the thesaurus. The most crucial function of a thesaurus lies in its capability to expose interrelationships that exist between concepts

---

[13] The Japan Science and Technology Corporation (currently Japan Science and Technology Agency) has published the 1978 and 1999 editions of the "JICST Thesaurus of Science and Technology Terms."

[14] A thesaurus shows descriptors (preferred terms) and non-descriptors (reference terms) for the descriptors. For actual searches, descriptors are used.

by clearly distinguishing the basic relationships that exist between terms.

The basic relationships found in the thesaurus are the following three kinds; the synonymous relationship, which is the relationship between descriptors and non-descriptors when a number of words share a similar concept; the hierarchical relationship, which relate words according to how broadly or narrowly they are associated with each other, and the relevancy relationship, which show relationships between words other than their synonymous and hierarchical relationships.

3)   *Thesaurus usage*

The thesaurus must allow a user to clearly confirm descriptor, hierarchical, and relevancy relationships of synonyms. In other words, when carrying out an index search, the thesaurus must allow for the selection of the same terms for identical concepts. This should be so because, for example, by making use of hierarchical relationships, it becomes possible to maintain a consistent index that allows one to conduct a search with a broad term (upper term) and retrieve all literature indexed by its correlated narrower terms (lower terms). In effect, such an arrangement helps to improve retrieval efficiency.

4.1.5   *Evaluating the efficiency of information retrieval systems*

For users of information, to be able to efficiently search for required information anytime is an important factor in evaluating the assetization of information. For decision makers, various information become necessary, fundamental determinants that affect the decision making process in a crucial way. What is important to point out here is that information itself does not take the place of the decision to be made by the decision maker, but is used to help in making the decision.

In evaluating the retrieval effectiveness of an information retrieval system, you should take criteria such as the following five ones into consideration.

1) *Scope and depth*

This is a criterion concerned with whether a database is sufficient in terms of the range of its data or the depth of its contents. In other words, it is concerned about what types of information are included and to what extent its contents are hierarchically structured. These attributes make it possible to efficiently search out required information from within the database via the use of keywords.

In database construction, what are needed are not only the contents that fall under category names of a particular field, but also detailed contents that cover various fields. However, realistically, it is impossible to store all necessary information beforehand. Since there are times when other necessary information become required in the middle of a search, it is necessary to design an information retrieval system with an expandability that can freely incorporate various information, which can be maintained efficiently.

2) *Relevance rate*

This criterion is concerned with the level of relevance rate or precision that should be maintained when searching a database. This is because in an information retrieval system, when searching for only relevant documents and information within this system, if you restrict search conditions, the recall rate drops, while if you relax the search conditions, the relevance rate drops.

In actuality, however, the goal that can help improve retrieval effectiveness is to suppress the number of non-relevant search hits within an allowable range, and make the search hits match as much as possible. Corporations are already constructing and operating information systems and are engaged in accumulating a large volume of information. However, since plenty of paper-based information exists apart from the information stored in databases, the ideal setup can be said to be one that allows for the use of both types of information.

3) *Response time*

This criterion is concerned with the speed of the response of an information retrieval system. An informational retrieval system with a fast response time can be said to be a system with high operability. Since operability means being able to instruct an information retrieval system on how to search for information, with regard to recurring information whose structure are clear to a certain extent, it is also necessary to be able to edit beforehand any information you use into a format suited to those types of information.

Regarding the criterion for response times, the general practice is to assure quick searches for information required to make highly urgent decisions, while for information required for decisions that are not that urgent, the general practice is to see that response times are not designed to be immediate. In addition, it is important to arrange organizational control over response times for such levels of urgency.

4) *Cost effectiveness*

This criterion is concerned with whether the benefit of searching exceeds cost. This is because even if you construct a costly information retrieval system in the company, if the system does not prove to be helpful for users relative to the invested capital, you cannot say that you have assetized information with the introduction of the system.

With regard to benefits, users must be able to quickly grasp the significance of search results derived from an information retrieval system. An information retrieval system, along with particular benefits, must have diverse information retrieval functions that respond to the specific circumstances and issues of the user.

5) *Features*

This criterion is concerned with what type of features various users seek. This is because if there are no features that respond to various usage objectives, it will not be possible to attempt to promote the efficiency of information retrieval operations. With regard to database information features, considerations such as the following need to be made: fitness with the front, middle, and back of a text string; the efficacy of "links," which use symbols to indicate associations beforehand between relevant index words; the efficacy of "rolls," which develop links and add information on semantic relationships between terms to index words; the efficacy of "subtitles," which make specific terms have rolls; and the efficacy of "proximity searches."[15)]

Another feature sought is usability or operability, which involves clarity and ease of use. Users of information retrieval systems include all types, ranging from top management executives, who tend to be inexperienced in the use of such systems, to specialists, who have thorough knowledge of the features of such systems. In this way, since various users will be making use of an information retrieval system, you will need to equip it with features that accommodate both experienced users and novice ones in terms of ease of use.

4.1.6 *Reinforcement through the assetization of information*

To reinforce the systematization of information through assetizing it, you need to offer users information believed to be necessary for the future through applying various approaches and means. In other words, this means being able to allow users to easily and swiftly obtain valuable information that they seek to have the most whenever they need it, wherever they are.

[15)]Adjacent searches are searches for information within a certain distance in databases whose word orderings are the same throughout. Specifically, these searches are carried out when using multiple keywords.

In recent years, thanks to the development of ICT and the spread of the Internet, even without the processing power of a mainframe computer[16] or even if there is no database or knowledge information system installed in your own computer, the circumstances[17] today allow for users to be able to access various data and services inexpensively by making use of open networks. For example, in the case of information systems that have adopted ASP[18] service arrangements, since the use of rental applications makes it unnecessary to install individual applications in a user's computer, it becomes possible to reduce the cost and labor of installing, managing, and upgrading software, which have been a large burden to bear for the information system departments of corporations.

Incidentally, even if you have finished setting up an information system that can offer timely information required by users, the systematization and assetization of information have yet to be completed. In fact, the activity of assetizing information through an information system is one that is a cumulative process carried out steadily on a daily basis without any end in sight. It remains a work in progress forever.

For the user, it is ideal to be able to obtain required information anytime, anywhere, and in a timely fashion. This is a fact. However, it is not always the case that there will be a computer close at hand

---

[16] Mainframe refers to a large-scale, general-purpose computer used for mission-critical task systems in a company. With the mainframe, most components of the computer, including the power supply, CPU, and memory banks, are multiplexed, and performance gains in processing and preventing malfunctions are attempted through parallel processing.

[17] In this present day and age when information networks such as the Internet have become widespread, it has become possible to work or be entertained without being restricted to a particular place, thanks to the fact that access to networks have become ubiquitous, allowing anyone to access them at anytime from anywhere.

[18] An ASP is an Application Service Provider, which is a company that rents out mainly business software applications to customers via the Internet. The user uses a web browser to make use of applications installed in the ASP's server. Additionally, Rental Application refers to the service of renting out business software applications to customers via the Internet.

wherever a user may be. Besides, even if there were one, it is usually unclear whether it would be found in a circumstance that would allow you to access an information system. Therefore, offering such a usage configuration for all users is actually difficult. But even if you were able to obtain such an information usage environment, you will still have to contend with system-related risks, such as whether the information obtained from such an environment was credible; whether the source of information used was reliable; and whether there would have been different results if a different source of information had been used. Furthermore, since there is the possibility that the information that had been required by a user had actually been tampered with or had been deleted due to information security concerns, it may not have been what the user had been seeking. In addition, this same user, upon making comparisons with other information, may seek to verify the details of the obtained information.[8]

Toward this end, by rounding out the features of the information system, it becomes possible to increase the likelihood of realizing a swift resolution to such problems. Furthermore, in the event you realize reinforcement by the assetization of information, along with the introduction of such things as email, TV conferences, and the intranet,[19] you will not be able to ignore the fact that a single user will be receiving information from multiple information providers or that multiple users will be receiving valuable information from a single information provider.

By introducing information systems through creating open networks and through decentralization, it becomes possible to have a communication mode with controllable multifunctional features that respond to needs. This in turn makes it possible to realize information assetization reinforcement.

---

[19] The Intranet refers to a network system built for use within an organization. It makes use of standard Internet technology, including the TCP/IP communication protocol. Since many companies ship products that support standard Internet technologies, the Intranet has the feature of being less costly than a custom-made network.

4.2   Systematization and Assetization of Market Development Information

4.2.1   *Differences between market development information and information/R&D information*

Diverse information can be classified roughly into technological information, R&D information, and market development information. The fundamental differences between these types of information are found in the variance in domains or fields of the treated information.

Technological information and R&D information are those that include detailed content regarding technology and data on their trends. So the concerns of what field's technology gets used by what type of user in what way to produce what kind of results that will help to form what kind of market and develop in what way are of only secondary importance. In contrast, with market development information, strictly speaking, market development becomes the primary concern. Therefore, if certain products prove to be helpful in market development, technological information and R&D information become secondary concerns.

While technological information, R&D information, and market development information all ostensibly have in common primary fields and domains of study, challenges, aspirations to achieve the progress of humanity, aspirations to attain world peace and bring about an individual's happiness, they basically differ in terms of their objectives and goals and show different directionalities. Information systems that allow for exchanging data of such different meanings can be said to have content that is beneficial and different from content up to now and to be accessible only when users show a preference for it. To understand the information discussed, the following eight stages are indispensable. In addition, what should be paid attention here is the acknowledgement of what types of information exchange are the most crucial in each of the eight stages.

1) *Information-gathering stage*

The *information-gathering stage*, which sets the future direction, is a stage that begins with forecast analyses such as market forecasts or technological forecasts.

2) *Goal exploration stage*

The *goal exploration stage*, which is concerned with setting goals, is a stage for carrying out goal-oriented research through marketability research and project research.

3) *Commercialization decision-making stage*

The *commercialization decision-making stage*, which is concerned with setting the policy, is a stage where you can attempt to make appropriate alignments with policies of development requests, sales plans, and development considerations.

4) *Commercialization planning stage*

The *commercialization planning stage*, which is concerned with setting actual measures to be adopted, is a stage where adjustments are made to measures ranging from preliminary design to initial trial manufacturing and production design.

5) *Practical use stage*

The *practical use stage*, which lasts until the launch stage, is a stage where you make adjustments through actual retail prices and additional trial productions.

6) *Introduction stage*

The *introduction stage*, which is a stage for appealing, is a stage for carrying out fine adjustments for appealing through pilot sales and experimental production.

7) *Growth stage/competition stage/decline stage*

The *growth stage*, *competition stage* and *decline stage*, which prepare towards full-fledged production, is a stage for carrying out full-fledged production after coordinating the start of test marketing and the speed of trial runs.

8) *Terminal stage*

The *terminal stage*, which has the termination of production in its sight, is a stage where you can attempt continual coordination and understanding through taking the stages cleared so far into account.

Incidentally, with regard to contents that are essential to market development information, there are three types of information demanded as data that should be provided to those in charge of R&D and product development; customer desire information, customer satisfaction information, and customer attribute information.

Firstly, information should be provided on what functions potential customers seek in a product. With existing products, you should provide information on "customer desires" by grasping what kinds of inconveniences or usability problems potential customers have, and what kinds of functional products they desire to help them circumvent such issues.

Next, with regard to existing customers, you should be providing information on the details of their satisfaction levels. You should provide information on "customer satisfaction" with regard to what customers are dissatisfied with when using existing products. Such points could include information on inconveniences and usability issues, with what functions or features they are satisfied, and with what functions or features they are not satisfied.

And finally, you should provide information on whether the points of dissatisfaction are tied to any regional characteristic or business type. You should, in effect, provide information on "customer attributes" by seeing whether the inconveniences and usability problems customers have with existing products are confined to a particular area or whether they are confined to products offered by particular businesses or whether they apply to all customers in general.

4.2.2 Systematization and assetization of market development information

To attempt an effective systematization of market development information, a market development strategy needs to be described as a corporation's management strategy. Generally, with a corporation's market development strategy, as indicated in Figure 4-3, the corporation itself depicts a growth matrix[20] and devises and deploys

Product/ Service/ Technology

		Current	New
Market	**Current**	(Market penetration) Strategy of attacking the current market with current products	(Product development) The strategy of introducing new products into a current market
	New	(Market development) Strategy of introducing current products into a new market	(Diversification) The strategy of introducing new products into a new market

Figure 4-3: The Concept of the Growth Matrix
Source: Adapted from p. 147 of Genichi Nakamura and Tetsuhiko Kuroda's *Saishin Senryaku Keiei*, Sanno University Press, 1990. This work is a translation of H. Igor Ansoff's *The New Corporate Strategy*.

---

[20] The Growth Matrix is a strategy model proposed by H. Igor Ansoff. It is a tool for analysis that is used when considering a company's growth strategy. Specifically, it is used to broaden growth strategy alternatives and to discuss how to go about allocating management resources.

a management strategy.[10] The growth matrix is a measure to confirm the direction of the corporation's own growth strategy.

The growth matrix is for clearly indicating the type of management strategy to be deployed to attempt the company's growth, and the strategy is determined from the viewpoints of business domain, management environment, and management resources on the basis of the following four perspectives; market penetration, market development, product development, and diversification.

1) *Market penetration*

The market penetration strategy is a strategy for promoting growth in the current market by making use of current products/services/technologies. Some representative examples of this strategy include the strategy of Southwest Airlines, which helped the company gain an advantage by heightening its cost competitiveness through development and productivity improvements of new technologies, and the strategy of Yamato Transport, which helped the company heighten its competitiveness by raising customer satisfaction levels through making it possible to designate delivery times.

2) *Market development*

The market development strategy is a strategy for making an entry into a new market by making use of current products/services/technologies. While the average amount from a single customer transaction remains the same, the strategy involves growing sales by increasing the number of customers, and its representative examples include Starbucks' strategy, which is helping the company advance its multi-store operation by promoting expansion from urban districts to backbone cities and provincial cities, and the strategies of automobile companies, which are helping them advance their globalization strategies.

3) *Product development*

The product development strategy is a strategy for introducing new products/services/technologies into the current market. It involves broadening the assortment of a product, service, or technology lineup to raise the average amount from a single customer transaction by encouraging customers to make additional purchases. Its representative examples include Uniqlo's strategy, which helped the company offer a variety of merchandises using high-performance materials, and Mister Donut's strategy, which helped the company add Yum Cha (Chinese tea and snacks) and noodles into their product lineup.

4) *Diversification*

Diversification is a strategy for introducing new products/services/technologies into a new market. As it is an unprecedented challenge, this field's entry risk is high. Still, it is a field that promises the possibility of gaining a substantial founder's profit, since it is an unexplored area devoid of any competition. Its representative examples include the strategies of many venture corporations, such as ICT and biotech companies.

Corporations need to apply the perspectives of such growth matrices to their market development strategies and clarify what strategy field would contain the strategy that can respond to various factors, and also clarify what type of essential qualities such a strategy should have.

Therefore, the four perspectives pertaining to the growth matrix become essential items that help to put market development information in order and systematize information by responding to various properties of a strategy. Naturally, when you carry out the assetization of market development information, you select strategic attributes from the growth matrix, and, based on these attributes, determine what products/services/technologies are the most desirable.

4.2.3   *Balance between R&D information and market development information*

When you compare market development information with R&D information and technology information, until now, market development information had largely preceded and influenced other types of information. In other words, it had often been the case that the engineering and R&D departments had been coming under the influence of the administrative department or the marketing and sales departments.

In addition, in these times when the management environment is becoming more demanding and the future seems uncertain, it is no longer desirable to have a situation where market development information takes precedence over other types of information when launching a new business to develop new products. In fact, such a situation may even be inviting an outcome that sees your company being left behind in the market competition. Therefore, it is important to attempt to strike a balance between R&D information and market development information in a way that allows you to make use of your company's strengths.

To this end, your company's experts, who possess leading edge information from the technology and R&D departments, just as they possess advanced market development information from the sales department, need to understand the mutual strengths and weaknesses of the different departments and work to compensate for their weaknesses through complementation. For example, if a definitive medical product for restoring hair is developed, a company will clearly be able to dominate this field's market. For this reason, it will be easy to imagine the sales department of a pharmaceutical company requesting the technology and R&D departments to strongly engage in making developments in this field.

However, in the event that you cannot guarantee the development of such a medical product in several months' time or in several years' time, what the sales department should nevertheless be doing is provide the technology and R&D departments with the latest market development information in a timely and continual fashion. Such information would include data on the medical-product developments of rival firms as well as data on the effects and side effects of newly launched "hair-restorers." Naturally, it will be necessary for the technology and R&D departments to convey information laterally to the sales department on such matters as the outlook and progress of new product developments being made through the adoption of new technologies, and on what are the problems and bottleneck issues standing in the way of development.

Up to now, carrying out such a form of information exchange had been impossible unless a conference was held for a limited amount of time to exchange opinions on a face-to-face basis. However, at present, it has become possible to formally or informally exchange information by making use of the information access environment of an in-house information system such as email, TV conferences, and the intranet. Moreover, in information exchange today, it has become possible to quickly obtain many opinions from not only experts within the company, but from outside the company as well, thanks to the information access environment of the open network, which connects the in-house information system to the Internet.

By making use of such an information access environment, what used to be top to down communication will become horizontal in nature, helping to realize a two-way, interactive form of communication where parties can complement each other.

4.2.4 *Assetization of market development information*

It is a top priority to see that market development information, R&D information, and technology information complement each other. However, to deploy the assetization of mainly market development information amid such complementary relationships, you must take into consideration the following three points:

1) *Making development possibilities efficient*

This point pertains to the necessity of having market development information contribute not only to the development of new markets or the expansion of established markets, but also to the promotion of new technologies and R&D. In other words, this means "information that does not involve the promotion of efficiency in the development potential of a product is not market development information."

2) *Reducing the period for possible development*

This point pertains to the necessity of providing market development information that is technical in nature and can help in developing new products in a short period of time. In other words, information that does not help to reduce the period for possible development is not market development information.

3) *Reinforcement of the development system*

This point pertains to the necessity for building and examining the effect and impact of an organizational setup that allows for continually providing market development information to relevant departments within the company and relevant parties outside the company. In other words, "information that does not help to reinforce the product development system is not market development information."

For example, the disposable camera developed by Fujifilm[21] is a new product that was created by a project team comprised by

---

[21] In July 1986, Fujifilm released the disposable camera, "Utsurundesu," but at the outset this was not a product that had taken recycling into account. In April 1990, Fujifilm announced the intention to salvage units that had already finished being used, and at present it is a misnomer to call the product a disposable camera, as most of its components such as the body, lens, and strobe are recycled. In fact, the correct way to refer to this camera is to call it a lens-equipped film.

personnel from the Market Development Department and Technical R&D Department. In this case, the concept for the product was simply derived from the idea advocated by the sales department, which was the expert on market development at first.

This idea was one that believed that the camera, like other products, should be a "disposable good." However, the issue that actually came up in the process of commercializing the disposable camera was the issue of whether it was going to be possible to produce a single-function camera at a sufficiently low price that customers would tolerate. The camera would be premised on the idea that it would be exhaustible. In addition, after the launch of the product, there were changes detected in consumer behavior that accompanied the heightening in awareness of environmental issues. Specifically, consumers began to take interest in how products were going to be recycled and to what extent it was going to be possible to reuse them.

Therefore, drawing from the results of a market survey, it became clear that the crucial factor that would determine the success or failure of this project was whether it was technically feasible to develop below a certain price level a disposable camera that came equipped with a minimum standard of functionality. In addition, during later recycling, rival companies, who had been simply disposing their products up to then, began to exchange recovered cameras among each other and discuss whether it would be possible to engage in a collaborative recycling initiative.

If market development experts have a thorough understanding of your firm's technology, it will be possible to clearly foresee product development potential and the necessary developmental period. In addition, if there is a market development expert advocating the necessity of a product, receiving various proposals from the camp of technical developers as well will make it all the more possible to reduce a product's development potential or the time required for development.

In this way, the assetization of market development information entails the construction of an information system that can help in finding out as early as possible the development potential and feasible developmental period.

4.2.5   *Impact of systematizing management strategy (development) information*

The systematization of management strategy information or development information is having a large impact on market development information, technological information, and R&D information. Figure 4-4 shows the case of systematizing management strategy when a corporation is developing a business. In the systematization of a management strategy, a strategy can be roughly classified as either a "business strategy" or a "functional strategy," depending on whether the strategy directly links to commercialization or not.

With regard to the "business strategy," which is directly linked with your firm's business development, a strategy can be categorized as either (1) existing business strategy, or (2) new business strategy, depending on whether the strategy is focused on either an existing business or a new one. In addition, with regard to "functional strategy," which is not directly linked with your firm's business development, depending on whether a strategy attaches importance to enhancing structure or whether it attaches importance to increasing efficiency, a strategy can be categorized as either (3) structural strategy, or (4) rationalization strategy.

Furthermore, (1) an existing business strategy, depending on the field it emphasizes, can be further broken down as market expansion development strategy or product development strategy. In the case of a (2) new business strategy, depending on the targeted business, it can be further broken down as either peripheral business development or new business development. Furthermore, (3) structural strategies, depending on the type of structure emphasized, can be broken down into the following categories: decentralization strategy,

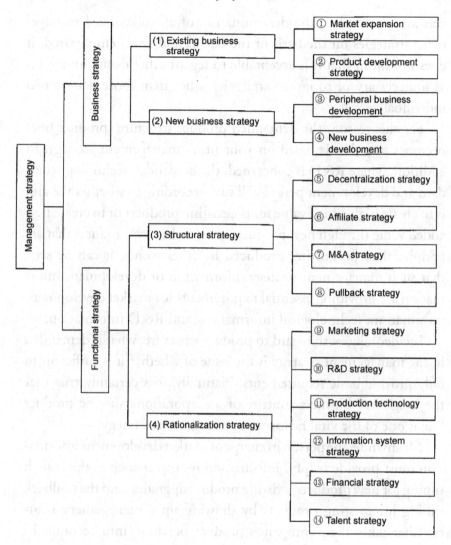

Figure 4-4: An Example of the Systematization of a Management Strategy

affiliation strategy, mergers and acquisition strategy, and pullback strategy. With regard to (4) rationalization strategies, depending on the type of efficiency emphasized, they can be broken down into the following categories: marketing strategy, R&D strategy, production/technical strategy, information system strategy, financial strategy, and organizational talent strategy. However, even though information gets systematized in the determination of all categorized management strategies on the basis of the details and fields emphasized, it does not mean that it is acceptable to regard other details and fields as unnecessary or to ignore strategies other than those determined individually.

For this reason, the demanded product structure (product line) becomes one that is based on your firm's management strategy. In addition, where R&D is concerned, the demanded technology standard and development period will vary according to whether the aim is to create high added value for preexisting products or to create new added value through new products or to make new products that are peripheral to preexisting products. In other words, it can be seen that such management strategy information or development information are providing essential requirements for market development information, technological information, and R&D information.

Incidentally, with regard to product structure, what is demanded in the management strategy is the issue of whether it is sufficient to only provide basic requirements. Naturally, it is certainly true that the long-term business strategy of a corporation's specific product line is one of the vital factors of a management strategy.

Meanwhile, the person in charge of market development information must provide helpful information on topics such as the launch timing for new products, existing product upgrades, and the pullback timing for existing products by drawing up a management strategy that takes their company's product portfolio into account. In addition, the person in charge of technological and R&D information, must categorize and interpret the R&D strategy information contained in the management strategy by product, by function, by amount of technology investment, etc., and provide to the person in charge of the management strategy whenever necessary the feedback information on the validity, feasibility, and implementation timing of the market launch plan for new products and the upgrade or pullback plan for existing products.

In any event, in determining the management strategy, systematized chronological information is necessary. Such information will influence the market development speed and timing, and additionally, the progress of R&D and the timing for introducing new products into the market. For this reason, the more systematized the management strategy information or development information is, the more you will be able to clarify the requirements for market development information, technological information, and R&D information, and thereby raise feedback frequency, which will in turn help you to provide more appropriate requirements. Therefore, the various information systems begin to become more interconnected with each other, helping to reinforce the assetization of information in the process.

4.2.6 *From systematizing to assetizing management strategy (development) information*

To evolve from systematizing management strategy information or development information to assetizing them, you need to first of all clarify the procedures of the systematization, which will form the basis for the assetization. The procedures for systematizing management strategy or development information are as follows: (1) conduct environmental forecasting, (2) perform analysis of opportunities and risks, (3) perform analysis of your company's strengths and weaknesses, (4) perform analysis of the product line, and (5) perform analysis of matters that can be responded to or possibly responded to — i.e., SWOT analysis.

To carry out these procedures, in addition to the limited in-house knowledge information belonging to your company, it is essential to use information or databases found outside of the company. This is because the first step toward evolving from systematizing to assetizing management strategy information or development information happens when gaps in business processes are discovered after taking various procedures into account, and correctives and countermeasures are determined.

Therefore, if there is an error in these correctives or countermeasures, your management strategy information or development information will stay at the systematized level and will not go on to develop into assets.

These correctives and countermeasures will form the basis for determining the management strategy plan. Such management strategy information or development information that have not been analyzed beforehand or that do not have any goal or direction will simply remain as information that satisfies only the person in charge.

To carry out all five of the procedures mentioned above, you must clearly show targets and completion periods by judging your company on the basis of the following points of reference; market share, relative margin, position in the product life cycle, comparisons with other firms' new products, and additionally, plans for plant and equipment investments and key-personnel training. When you are able to clearly show targets and completion periods, it will become possible to carry out a shift from systematizing to assetizing management strategy information or development information.

Incidentally, when making the transition from systematizing to assetizing management strategy information or development information, to promote an effective implementation of the procedures, the following five items are demanded:

1) *Criteria for evaluation*

This pertains to clearly showing competitive (relative) evaluation criteria in the procedures. With this item, the determination of specific correctives and countermeasures becomes possible.

2) *Order of priority*

This pertains to clarifying the order of priority in the competitive (relative) evaluation criteria of the procedures. With this item, it becomes possible to make responses through the allocation of time and management resources.

3) *Targets and durations*

This pertains to clearly showing targets and completion times based on the order of priority of the procedures. With this item, it becomes possible to indicate specific targets and completion times.

4) *Unforeseen situation*

This pertains to preparing alternative targets and completion times upon clarifying contingencies[22)] that make the achievement of the original goals difficult. With this item, you will be required to assume the occurrence of unforeseen situations and make it possible to develop predetermined correctives and countermeasures to minimize any resulting damages and losses.

5) *Pre-adjustments*

This pertains to being fully prepared with a pre-adjusted system that can help in dealing with any difficulties arising in the course of achieving targets. With this item, it will become possible to deal with risks (uncertain factors) that pose as obstacles in running businesses and projects. The idea is to build a pre-adjusted system for the purposes of being prepared to deal with any influential risks that may surface.

4.2.7 *A means for promoting the assetization of management strategy (development) information*

Until now, along with promoting the procedures that help to assetize management strategy information or development information, we have been studying their criteria for evaluation. Logically speaking,

---

[22)] A contingency is something that may or may not occur and implies preparing for the possibility of an unexpected outcome. Its gist, however, is that the outcome is uncertain, regardless of whether it is good or bad.

they are sufficiently understandable. However, if you easily make management-related decisions on the basis of only a superficial set of criteria for evaluation, you will run the risk of attaching excessive importance to specific criteria.

In particular, corporations that have entered into their mature stage and are carrying out a "financial strategy" as part of a stream-lining strategy are highly unlikely to think about escaping from the mature stage by carrying out R&D that strives towards imple-menting new technologies. But corporations that are deploying "new business development" as part of their new business strategy are more likely to lead new technologies and R&D to success, and also realize a continual pace of growth for the company. For this reason, the value of "new business development" will increase.

To this end, it is necessary to review on a fundamental level the issue of regarding a company in terms of its principal field. With respect to technology and R&D, after gaining an accurate grasp of your company's management environment and its conditions, you will have to seriously reconsider questions such as what field should your company demonstrate its technological leadership in, what type of companies should your firm attempt alliances with, and what tech-nological goals should your company aim to achieve after covering such areas as production, raw materials, labor force, and advertising and publicity. Drawing from the answers to these questions, you will then need to develop a set of criteria for evaluation that is not partial to any specific criterion.

The development of digital wristwatches by Casio is the result of a strategy that applied the concept of the analog wristwatch, which uses the conventional long and short hands of a clock, to the digital tech-nology the company itself possessed. This strategy is an exemplary case of bringing about a new technological architecture as a result of a fundamental reappraisal aimed at demonstrating the company's technological leadership.

Casio's core technology had seen a shift from precision-machinery processing to microelectronics, as the company became capable of assembling through automated lines. As a result, it had begun to wield a large influence over markets and industrial structures. For example, by starting to sell Casio wristwatches through distribution channels such as discount stores, stores specializing in watches, supermarkets, and department stores, the company was able to establish its watch's position as a public product among watches.

In addition, improvements in IC technology had paved the way for the emergence of wristwatches with not only simple stopwatch functions, but with value-added features such as games and TVs as well. Furthermore, along with the rapid rate of diffusion of the watches and improvements in their functionality, the price had dropped to levels that had been formerly unforeseeable. Incidentally, in recent times, as a prerequisite for promoting the assetization of management strategy information or development information, the ability to deal with computer system risks has become crucial.[7]

After all, companies will have to bear the losses stemming from defects and inconveniences of information systems that may shut down or malfunction. Furthermore, unlawful computer uses could jeopardize the credibility or reliability of various types of information. To reduce such system risks, companies need to assume the occurrences of malfunctions and accidents and adopt countermeasures that allow for carrying out the dualization of hardware such as machinery and tools, the establishment of a computer center in a physically remote location, and the rigidification of a security system that can facilitate data backup operations.

4.2.8 *Reinforcement of the interrelationships between management strategy information, market development information, technology information, and R&D information*

To reinforce the interrelationships between management strategy information, market development information, technology information, and R&D information, it is necessary to determine a market development strategy and a technology and R&D strategy that revolve around the management strategy.

To reinforce the interrelationships between these sets of information, you must specifically show the activities involved in each of these fields and then attempt to make mutual adjustments. As one measure toward achieving this end, the cross-impact analysis is effective. This approach helps you to foresee what information will be mutually necessary, and what information should be provided to benefit the activities of other fields. With cross-impact analysis, the series of development matters related to the process of developing a product are mutually linked to a number of events such as the probability estimates for the completion dates of the matters.

Consequently, causal relations become clarified and help to predict the impact of those matters. At the stage of making predictions, in the field of market development information "market forecasts" are carried out, and in the fields of technology and R&D, "technology forecasts" and "new product forecasts" are carried out, and in the field of management strategy, "management forecasts" are carried out. However, if these fields fail to satisfy the information requirements of other fields respectively, their directions will be scattered and disconnected. For example, in the management strategy of a certain corporation, when the entry into the biotechnology field is the primary policy in the development of a strategy, by carrying out forecasts through a cross-impact analysis, you will be able to focus the direction of forecasts, whether they may pertain to market forecasts or technology forecasts.

Therefore, from the perspective of a corporation's management strategy, with regard to making a foray into the biotechnology field, by focusing the forecast directions, the applicable technology field will expand. In addition, on the other hand, consideration must also be made for the promising technical fields where research is still underway. They include the development of bioreactors,[23] development of mass cell culture technology, and the development of DNA recombination technology. For example, if definite goals of a plan for the next eight years are made clear to all the members of an organization, you will be able to make focused, medium to long-term market forecasts regarding what type of market is desirable in accordance with the order of priority of those goals.

Furthermore, in terms of technology and R&D, various technological forecasts will be carried out, including forecasts for the possible uses of specific technologies such as the adaptation of regenerative medicines of bioreactors, forecast for the possibility of supplying mass quantities of fine chemicals through mass cell culture technology, and forecasts for the possibility of discovering enzymatic inhibitors concerned with diseases and new microorganisms concerned with specific biologically active substances.

It is through having mutual exchanges of such forecast information between each field that concrete implementation plans of a management strategy can be devised. In addition, non-technological financial information, such as economic outlooks, market forecasts, and industry forecasts, should be treated as important forecast information and their influence at various stages must be taken into consideration, along with the influence of demand forecasts. These stages include the information-gathering stage, the information analysis stage, the target search stage, the goal setting stage, and the implementation stage.

While these sets of information exist in each of the stages mentioned above, by carrying out such mutual exchanges of information and analytical assessments, the smooth and efficient development of new products becomes possible. Furthermore, the information

---

[23] The prefix "bio" in bioreactor refers to "biology," and the word "reactor" in bioreactor refers to "reaction vessel." In effect, a bioreactor is a reaction apparatus that uses the catalytic action of biological organisms to synthesize and decompose materials.

system's role is to support the management strategies of each of the stages.

4.2.9   Centralized/decentralized systems for a variety of information

The change in the system configuration of the corporate information system from a centralized data processing system to a decentralized processing system took place when companies were abandoning the centralized data processing system of the mainframe computer and were promoting business reforms, while adopting a more offensive management style.

The transition from the centralized data processing system of the mainframe was a move to carry out measures for resolving various problems posed by such a system.[7] Such measures included: (1) improvements in processing response and performance during peak business times, (2) responses to the increase in man hours and development times that resulted from the mainframe's incapability to be flexible in the face of additional requirements of individual systems, and (3) reductions in the operational and maintenance costs incurred by an information system. The promotion of business reforms and the change to a more offensive style of management was a response to meet several needs, including (4) the need to introduce a new structure to promote business reforms within the company, and (5) the need to fulfill the requirements of new information systems for management strategy data, market development data, technology data, and R&D data, which became necessary after it became an urgent matter to reform sales strategies as companies began to switch their management strategies from defensive to offensive ones.

As one approach toward meeting those needs, companies began to switch their systems to the client-server type decentralized processing systems. With the decentralized data processing system, the workload lightened relative to the one that had resulted from the centralization of processing in a mainframe computer. Consequently, a flexible client-server type information system was built. In addition, thanks to the ATM-LAN method,[24)] the lines were streamlined and an attempt to construct an integrated information system was made, while carrying out a fundamental reexamination of the mission-critical task system.

With the decentralized data processing system, the restructuring of the R&D information processing system was carried out to help realize seamless business operations. The aim of such a system configuration was to change closed systems, which were confined within disparate departments within an organization, to open systems and realize a system environment that could be accessed by all groups within an organization.

Incidentally, in the case of upgrading the processing system concerned with this R&D information and developing it into an information system that includes various other data such as those pertaining to management strategy, market development, business strategy, human resource strategy, and financial strategy, the general approach is to basically establish and manage a large part of the management strategy information and a part or large part of other information under the centralized control of the Management Planning Department.

As for information such as those that pertain to technology and R&D, human resource strategy, financial strategy, and market development, it is necessary to establish, manage, and control them in a decentralized fashion at various departments in charge, such as the Technology and R&D Department, Human Resources Department,

---

[24)] The Asynchronous Transfer Mode (ATM) is one of the multiplexing schemes that divide a single line into multiple logical lines (channels) for realizing simultaneous communications. This mode carries out transmissions and receptions by dividing the data of all channels into fixed-length data of 53 bytes.

Training Department, Financial Department, Marketing Department, and Sales Department. On the other hand, since all departments will require a small part, or depending on the situation, a large part of each other's information, the sharing of information through the use of mutual networks such as VAN and LAN will become necessary. It is in this way that information management systems are constructed for the development of new products through the use of computer and communications technology.

In the case of building next-generation information systems, AI and automatic translation features and even advanced search features will be introduced into the technology and R&D systems.

Regarding knowledge information systems in particular, it will be highly probable that such a system developed by your own company will be used simultaneously with databases developed by outside firms and intelligent information systems. Consequently, you will be able to access and use the latest information available and apply it for the benefit of your corporation's management strategy.

Tetsuro Saisho

References

1. Akira Ishikawa, *The Q&A Primer to Information Searching for Developing New Products and New Businesses*, Dobunkan, 1998.
2. Scientific and Technical Information Headquarters of the Japan Science and Technology Agency, *JICST Science And Technology Terminology Thesaurus — 1999 Edition*, Japan Science and Technology Agency, 1999.
3. Scientific and Technical Information Headquarters of the Japan Science and Technology Agency, *Digitization Technology of Information — From Introduction to Application (Information Management Supplement XII)*, Japan Science and Technology Agency, 2000.
4. National Center for Science Information Systems, *Full Text Retrieval — Technology And Application*, Maruzen, 1998.
5. Shuji Kondo, *New Product and New Business Search Algorithms through the Technology Matrix (New Edition)*, Japan Management Association, 1985.
6. Yukio Nakamura, *The Foundations of Information Retrieval Theory: Critique and Reappraisal*, Kyoritsu Shuppan, 1998.
7. Tetsuro Saisho, Changes in the Environment Surrounding Corporations and System Risk Management, *Japan Society of Security Management Magazine*, Vol. 19, No. 1, pp. 25–43, 30 September 2005.

8. Tetsuro Saisho, *Installation and Deployment of Information Security Management*, Kanto Gakuin University Publishing Society, 2006.

9. Japan Database Industry Association, *How to Use the Most Up-to-Date Online Information Resources — From the Internet to Databases*, Nichigai Associates, 1998.

10. H. Igor Ansoff, *The New Corporate Strategy*, Wiley, 1988 [Genichi Nakamura, Tetsuhiko Kuroda (translators), *Saishin Senryaku Keiei*, Sanno University Press, 1990].

Chapter 5

How to Advance R&D, New Product Development, and New Business Development: Requirements That Should Be Taken into Consideration Towards These Ends

Regardless of whether we are talking about R&D, new product development, or new business development, as long as the word "development" is being used, these fields have something in common with each other. Furthermore, they all have the quality of being novel and are resourceful pursuits for humanity; pursuits that can be considered to be activities for realizing potential values.

In such a case, the research that forms the essence of R&D is generally categorized as either fundamental research or applied research or even practical-use research. Whereas fundamental research in particular aims to arrive at new theories, discoveries, and inventions, new product development and new business development primarily aim to create new products and businesses for the market.

Therefore, even though the duration, development scope, and development scale and cost may vary by the development project, as far as their implementation is concerned, they all have a good number of considerations that they share in common. In what follows, I would like to investigate various ways to advance development and the considerations that need to be made towards achieving their ends by looking at them from the viewpoints of such topics as information sources, the integration of development, R&D management, and human resources development and management.

5.1   Considerations for Acquiring and Selecting Data from Sources of Information

5.1.1   *Published and unpublished information*

In general, development-related information sources can be roughly classified into the following two categories:

1) Published information (information made available through trade papers, trade magazines, professional journals, books, research papers (industry-specific, field-specific, country-specific, etc.)), reports, DVDs, videotapes, cassette tapes, databases, various TV, cable, and radio broadcasts, and related information obtainable from search sites.

2) Unpublished information (publicly undisclosed information from academic and non-academic organizations and from information professionals and information non-professionals that are exchanged as electronic, paper, telephone information, and person-to-person word of mouth information, using telecommunication networks, fax machines, telexes, various means of communication using man-made satellites, and encryption to collect, accumulate, access, and evaluate).

Among the published information, an examination of just the types and number of science and technology magazines available today reveals that they have increased exponentially over the past four centuries. Even a survey carried out by King Research at the end of the last century reported that the number of scientific and technical information generated in the world was more than 4.5 million per year and moreover has been increasing at a rate of 4%–7% per year.

Meanwhile, the 1988 science and technology white paper points out the problems researchers of leading edge science and technology fields face when acquiring research information. According to the paper, 68% or approximately seven out of ten researchers said that they believe there are problems faced when attempting to acquire research information.

The reasons stated were mainly "difficult to make time," "budget for travel and purchasing reference materials are insufficient," and "available information systems and databases are insufficient." While the top reason for university researchers was "difficult to make time," the top concern for private enterprise researchers was "available information systems and databases are insufficient." Furthermore, nearly 70% of researchers working at national research and development institutions consider their top reason to be "budget for travel and purchasing reference materials are insufficient."

5.1.2   *Difficulties of acquiring data from sources of information*

The difficulty these researchers face when acquiring information pose major problems for development researchers and since researchers of other representative institutions point out different top reasons, it is believed that such problems need to be eliminated by promoting industrial clusters and intelligent clusters formed through industry-academic-government collaborations, which is currently gaining a groundswell of support.

Furthermore, when comparing the setups of available science and technology databases, the number of Japanese document abstracts (for which this writer has previously contributed) related to science and technology in general found in the Japan Information Center of Science and Technology (JICST) (the current Japan Science and Technology Agency, an independent administrative institution) amounted to 5.6 million as of May 1988. Meanwhile, at this point regarding information in English, in the US, the number of database entries related to mainly chemistry is 8 million, and in the UK, database entries related to the fields of physics, electricity, and computers amount to 3 million. In contrast, the number of

English-language files found in JICST related to science and technology in general amount to 500,000, which is only 1/16th of the amount of the entries found in the US. This clearly indicates the discrepancy between Japanese and English document abstracts and shows that the JICST is extremely limited to Japanese information.

In dealing with this problem, the thinking to rely on overseas databases is certainly there, but when taking into consideration the problems of budgetary and time constraints, which were raised as major issues, the option to just neglect the problem is believed to be inadvisable.

5.1.3   *Four basic considerations for selecting information sources*

Next, pertaining to selecting information sources, the following four considerations must not be forgotten.

The first consideration is that preferably the information source is already established and that it is highly reliable. This is essential. However, it is also a fact that even in the case of information published by the government, relatively speaking, their reliability varies greatly.

If you collect same data from different sources, you will often find that they differ accordingly.

For example, if you decide to research the number of Internet users, you will find that the result according to the report carried out by Access Media International varies from the result according to the one carried out by the Ministry of Public Management, Home Affairs, Posts and Telecommunications, even though they are both reporting for the same year. Specifically, the latter reports about 15 million more users (77.3 million) than the former.

According to the *1985 White Paper on Small and Medium-Sized Businesses*, special-interest magazines and trade journals attract the most interest as sources of information for gathering technical information for product development purposes, regardless of company size. The point can be made that the reason for this is they are the most accessible sources of information while also being the most reliable at the same time. Needless to say, among professional journals, there are old ones and new ones, and in the case of specialists of advanced technology in particular, it can be very well understood that interest in new trade papers and professional journals will run high.

Secondly, there is the issue of the cost efficiency of the information source. This is about whether the use of a particular information source is sufficiently effective or has sufficient benefits *vis-à-vis* the cost incurred over its use. While magazines and newsletters that are restrictively purchased by VIPs all over the world are generally very costly, the decision to purchase them is largely due to the fact that top managers and engineers reason that the purchase of these types of publications are necessary for the survival of the company or for the maintenance of its competitive edge.

Furthermore, regarding institutions that strongly promote publications that claim to offer confidential information, the exercise of caution is necessary, since many of them undervalue confidentiality themselves and are solely motivated by the opportunity to make excessive profits.

Thirdly, the unexpectedness of an information source (a.k.a. serendipity in the sense that you might come across a new source through failures and accidents) cannot be removed from the list of necessary requirements.

To create artificial snow, Dr. Ukichiro Nakaya failed over and over again before finally succeeding in creating an artificial snow crystal through the use of a Japanese hare. While this discovery was truly unexpected, an examination of the hair of the hare through a microscope revealed strands of stinging hair growing in many layers. It then became clear that their structure was exactly right for creating crystals of artificial snow. In this example, the very hair of the hare was the directly sought-after information source, but indirectly, the source was an element of the natural environment found outside of the research facility.

Another famous example is the case of Dr. Alexander Fleming, who had sprinkled a bacteria called staphylococcus on a petridish and left it there without sealing it by mistake. Then by chance, some green mould had fallen into the dish. Consequently, although it was completely unexpected, he ended up observing the staphylococcus melting away, and it is said that it was this very observation that had eventually led him to the discovery of penicillin.

A similar case can be seen in the case of Mr. Koichi Tanaka, who had won the Nobel Prize for Chemistry in 2002. Mr. Tanaka was absorbed in his work on the mass spectrometry of the protein. In this case, it was necessary to vaporize and ionize the protein, but while the protein is a substance that is difficult to vaporize on the one hand, to ionize it, a high level of energy is required. However, since applying a high level of energy fails to vaporize the protein and only leads to its decomposition, it had been extremely difficult to ionize something with a particularly high-molecular weight as protein.

He then accidentally went on to mix glycerol and cobalt by mistake and upon attempting to use the mixture as a thermal energy shock absorber, since he did not wish to see it go to waste, he unexpectedly became the first person in the world to completely succeed in such an attempt. This method was named the "soft laser ion method" and it went on to be awarded the Nobel Prize for Chemistry for its achievements.

The fourth important consideration is to clarify the largest obstacles standing in the way when attempting to efficiently obtain necessary information from required sources. According to the findings of the research carried out by Mr. Hiroaki Okamoto, the largest obstacle was the fact that "necessary articles were too dispersed in various kinds of magazines," which was followed by the fact that researchers "could not obtain translations of dissertations written in a language I cannot read," and "insufficient availability of abstract journals." In addition, while researchers of the Science and Technology Agency (the current Ministry of Education, Culture, Sports, Science and Technology) in particular point out that "the available amount of review magazines is insufficient," the top complaint raised by researchers of research institutes was that "there are too many index journals that are hard to use."

The fifth consideration is that a variety of information resources need to be prepared in such a way so as to be able to provide timely and top-quality information.

And finally the sixth consideration is that information sources need to be raised to a level where they can provide, along with first-hand information, estimations and conjectures as the occasion demands. And, they need to be complex enough to be able to avoid becoming defunct, even in the case of an emergency.

5.2   The Relevance between Information Sources and Basic Research

5.2.1   *The significance of the gene (technical features) map*

To link information sources to fundamental research if it is regarding, for example, materials and processing methods, it is extremely important to develop a gene map (a matrix) of the root effects, phenomena, and rules found among their functions.

This gene (technical function) map systematizes such factors as properties, phenomena, and detected rules that are found in each technology, and makes up for any missing data, while removing any duplicates, and indicates an easy study list of items that need to be created as rules and theories by clarifying the direction of the fundamental research (see Figures 5-1 and 5-2).

For example, in the case of Figure 5-1's materials-technology gene map, a matrix is expressed by listing metal materials, inorganic

Functions / Materials	Thermal	Electric	Magnetic
Metallic materials	• Seebeck effect • Thomson effect • Pyroelectric effect • High melting • Thermal expansion • Thermoelectric effect • Melting point depression • High heat conductivity • Peltier effect • Shape memory effect • Invar effect	• Magnetocaloric effect • Surface effect • Meissner effect • Barkhausen effect • Ohm's law • Superconductivity • Free electron transfer • Electrode reaction • Metal absorption of hydrogen • Josephson effect	• Metal magnetization • Electromagnetic induction phenomenon • Back electromotive force phenomenon • Noncrystalline phenomenon • Tunnel effect • Pinning effect • Adhesion effect
Inorganic materials	• High melting • Low thermal conductivity • Low melting • Surface reinforcement	• Conductivity • Piezoelectric effect • Insulating properties • Semiconductor effect • Ferroelectricity • Pyroelectric effect • Ionic conductivity	• Strong magnetization • Hall effect
Organic materials (including living things)	• High melting point • Heat insulating effect	• Ohm's law • Semiconductor effect • Isolation effect • Pi-electron effect • Charge-transfer complex	• Magnetization phenomenon • Electron spin resonance
Composite materials	• Fiber reinforcement • High melting • Heat insulating effect	• Electric charge • Insulating properties	• Magnetization phenomenon

Figure 5-1: Materials Technology Gene Matrix

Source: Adapted from Eikichi Ueki's *Text on How to Collect Technical Information*, Keiei Kaihatsu Senta (Management Development Center), 1987.

Chemical	Biochemical	Mechanical	Optical	Radiation particle-like
• Law of the voltaic battery • Deionization phenomenon • Catalytic effect • Ionization tendency difference • Noncrystalline phenomenon • Electrochemical reaction • Ion nitriding • Kirkendall effect	• Low ionization • Organism stability	• Vibration absorption • Shape-memory superelasticity • Superplasticity phenomenon • Law of geostatics • Noncrystalline phenomenon	• Photovoltaic effect • Snell's law • Zeeman effect • Kerr effect • Cotton effect • Stark effect • Doppler effect	• Thermionic emission • Radiation ray absorption • Atomic collapse • Electrothermal radiation • Nuclear fission • Photoelectric effect • Diffraction phenomenon • Auger effect • Compton effect • Mössbauer effect
• Chemical reaction • Low dissolution charge • Low ionization • Semipermeability • Honda Fujishima effect • Ion diffusion • CVD • Cotton effect	• Artificial crystallization • Medical benefit effect • Poor solubility • Organism stability	• Machinability • Durable solidity • Antifriction • Self-lubricating	• Kerr effect • Photochromic phenomenon • Snell's law • Chemical reaction • Photovoltaic effect • Photoconductivity phenomenon • Spectral phenomenon, interference • Diffraction phenomenon • Electrochromic	• Radiation ray absorption • Radiation ray electromotive force • Flicker effect • Kramer effect • Schottky effect
• Chemical inertness • Chemical reaction • Absorption phenomenon • Surface activation • Surface tension • Semipermeability	• Hydrophilic property • Poor solubility • Enzyme • Medical benefit effect • Chemical reaction • Semipermeability	• Machinability • Fiber reinforcement • Molecular force binding • Movability • Vibration absorption • Surface reinforcement • Self-lubricating • Fault tolerance	• Translucency • Liquid crystal phenomenon • Photochemical reaction • Selective reaction • Snell's law • Spectral phenomenon • Diffraction phenomenon • Raman effect	• Photochemical reaction • Radiation ray electromotive force • Radiation absorption
• Chemical inertness • Surface tension	• Organism inertness	• Fiber reinforcement • High solidity • Composite reinforcement • Self-reproducibility	• Snell's law	• Radiation ray absorption

Figure 5-1:   *(Continued)*

Function / Processing method	Thermal energy type	Electromagnetic energy type
Cutting	• Plasma oscillation phenomenon • Arc discharge phenomenon • Combustion behavior • Joule effect • Explosion phenomenon • Fusion phenomenon • Hot shortness phenomenon • Nernst effect	• Discharge phenomenon • Electrolysis phenomenon • Charged particle beam Ion beam • Electrophoresis phenomenon • Attachment phenomenon
Change of shape/Fusion/Solidification response	• Thermoplasticity • Fusible alloy phenomenon • Combustion phenomenon • Explosion phenomenon • Heat transfer phenomenon • Thermosetting property • Solidification • Amorphization • Thermal stress phenomenon • Frictional heat generation • Thermal diffusion • Arc discharge phenomenon • Magnetocaloric effect	• Discharge phenomenon • Joule heating effect Superconductivity • High frequency guidance phenomenon • Plasma oscillation phenomenon • Electro-deposition phenomenon • Magnetothermal effect • Ettingshausen effect • Magnetocaloric effect • Meissner effect
Junction	• Positive adsorption phenomenon • Absorption phenomenon • Capillary phenomenon • Arc discharge phenomenon • Combustion fusion phenomenon • Plasma oscillation phenomenon • High temperature condensation effect • Vapor deposition phenomenon • Heat transfer phenomenon • Thermal diffusion phenomenon • Interface wetting phenomenon • Peltier effect	• Joule heating effect • High frequency induction heating effect • Discharge phenomenon • Electro-deposition phenomenon • Electric heating value effect • Righi-Leduc effect • Charged particle beam

Figure 5-2:   Processing Technology Gene Matrix
Source: Adapted from the same source cited in Figure 5-1.

Light energy type	Chemical energy type	Mechanical energy type	Radiation energy type
• Stimulated emission phenomenon • Solid-state laser radiation phenomenon • CO2 laser radiation phenomenon • Liquid laser radiation phenomenon • Photoresist phenomenon • Photoetching phenomenon • Photoelectromagnetic effect • Photochemical reaction	• Combustion behavior • Solvent action • Chemical milling • Ion etching • Plasma etching • Spark etching • Maskant recycling • Absorption phenomenon	• Acoustic wave amplification phenomenon • Plasticity • Distortion hardenability • Internal friction phenomenon • Low-temperature brittleness phenomenon • Friction phenomenon • Diffusion phenomenon • Nitryl effect • Nitro roller dislocation • Notch effect	• Radiation phenomenon • Permeation action
• Stimulated emission phenomenon • Thermal radiation phenomenon	• Explosion phenomenon • Implosion phenomenon • Combustion behavior	• Superplasticity effect • Shape memory effect • Lubricating effect • Cooling effect • Bridgman effect • Distortion speed effect • Consistency effect • Creep phenomenon • Rolling friction • Age hardening • Elastic after-effect	• Hot electron effect • Kramer effect
• Laser stimulated emission phenomenon	• Diffusion phenomenon • Conjugated double bond • Substitution reaction • Condensation dispersion response • Aspell Kanner effect	• Internal friction phenomenon • Supersonic vibration phenomenon • Pressure adhesion effect • Age hardening • Shock wave phenomenon • Diffusion phenomenon	• Radiation polymerization reaction

Figure 5-2:   (*Continued*)

materials, organic materials, and compound materials on the vertical axis and the many properties peculiar to them, such as namely thermal characteristics, electrical characteristics, chemical properties, mechanical characteristics, and photocharacterizations on the horizontal axis. In so doing, the matrix enumerates in each element the various effects, properties, detected representative rules and hypotheses that correspond to each material and individual characteristic. These can also be enumerated in chronological order or by the depth of relationships *vis-à-vis* the content of the research project. Therefore, these tables do not simply function as a set of keywords for the purpose of obtaining an output through their input, but in fact, function to filter every material through different perspectives, creating a highly valuable map that in effect becomes a wellspring of expected (and unexpected) outputs.

5.2.2   *Case examples*

In the gene map of Figure 5-1, electron tunneling is an effect that exists where metallic and magnetic properties intersect. The fact that this became the harbinger of the transistor age is an all too famous story. This phenomenon is the apparently improbable appearance of electrons on the base side of a compositional surface in a manner that suggests that they have passed through a tunnel. Dr. Reona Esaki had discovered the phenomenon and had announced it to the domestic Physical Society, but the reaction of the scientists was extremely indifferent, as it was seen to apparently violate the theories of classical physics at the time. However, it is known that the discovery began to attract attention once Dr. Esaki received acclaim from Dr. William Shockley, a pioneer in transistor research, after Dr. Esaki announced the discovery at an international convention in Brussels upon publishing an article on the discovery in an American journal in 1958.

In addition, while this is not indicated in the gene maps shown in Figures 5-1 and 5-2, I would like to show how such a map could point towards the development of such a drug as Aricept. Generically known as donepezil, Aricept is a drug developed for the treatment of Alzheimer's disease. It was developed by a technician at Eisai and had received a special commendation in the 1997 UK Prix Galien Awards (the Prix Galien is considered the equivalent of the Nobel Prize for medical research). In a materials-technology gene map, let us enter the category of neurotransmitter in the vertical axis and the category of enzyme properties in the horizontal axis. At the intersection of these two points, you should find the Choline hypothesis, an idea that was falling into obscurity at the time. Nevertheless, this hypothesis drew the attention of the Eisai technician and eventually paved the way towards its development into a drug whose sales went on to exceed 100 billion yen in Japan alone (as of 2002).

In this way, when linking information sources to fundamental researches, it can be understood that it is extremely important to first of all carry out an exhaustive investigation of rules, hypotheses, and effects that can offer the direction for the discovery and development of fundamental research themes, and secondly, to arrange and display the information sources that make such an investigation possible, and thirdly, to have a person fulfilling the role of an intermediary between these two sides.

5.3   Relevance between Sources of Information and Applied Research

When attempting to deepen the relevance between information sources and applied research in the context of the preceding paragraph, since the key to reinforcing relevance and realizing successful applied research, productization research, and commercialization research is believed to lie in a broad sense in investigating the matching or synchronization of seeds with needs, and in a narrower sense, in the thesaurization of keywords and in the carrying out of technical relation analysis, I would like to touch upon these topics.

5.3.1 *Matching needs with seeds (synchronization)*

When matching and synchronizing needs with seeds, you should begin by enumerating the keywords that correspond to market diversification and dramatic market changes, and then follow up by writing a brief on the changes in technological seeds and their multi-faceted circumstances. And then, as a third step, you should match them according to their relevance to ascertain themes and directions of new products and new businesses. In other words, this is an approach that attempts to figure out what is the best way to express relevancies between inputs and outputs, assuming that you consider an information source as a cause (input) and the result, new product, or new business derived from an applied research as an effect (output). In the end, this approach entails the creation of a checklist of needs and seeds (a matching table) (refer to Figures 5-3 and 5-4).

In addition to this approach, by coming up with the following functional and psychological expressions, it became possible to capture over 120 new product themes and actually create unique proprietary products: "add or subtract," "try to change the shape," "change the product (the material)," "think the opposite," "apply fundamental principles or phenomenon," "think again by returning to the starting point," "attempt unification," "consider instantization," "apply analogies," "use waste matter," "consider in terms of healing and nature," and "capture the changes in the minds of users."[5,7]

5.3.2 *Thesaurization of keywords*

The thesaurization of keywords refers to the adoption of a tool that helps to control terms when converting keywords used by people searching indexes from their vernacular form into more specialized system terms or documentation terms or information terms. As

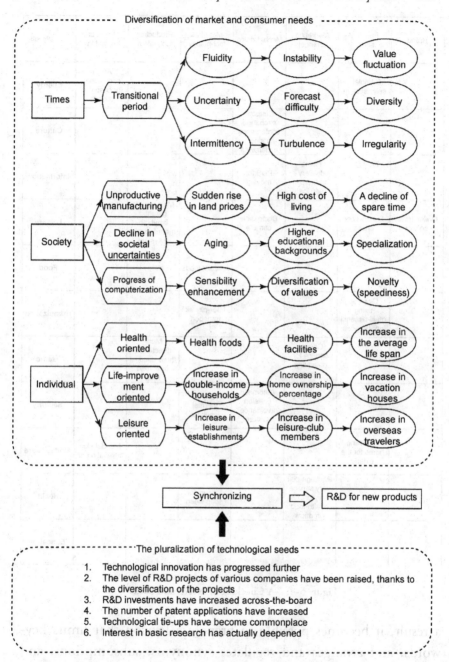

Figure 5-3: Synchronizing Needs with Seeds[1]

Creative Marketing for New Product and New Business Development

Brand	Funding ability	Marketing channel	Mechatronics	Materials technology	Production technology	Product technology	Seeds/Needs
	Complete solar system					An air conditioner for changing moods	**Energy**
			Cultural-exchange conferences using multimedia				**Culture**
		Home delivery information service	PDS for moving				**Information**
Online travel service	Luxury liner cruise		Disposable camera		Multi-variety gigantic labyrinth manufacturing system		**Leisure**
				Artificial foods			**Food**
	City map using multi-dimensional spaces			Inter-city air transport			**Urbanization**
		Courier service for delivering hope			Multi-directional, three-dimensional road map		**Traffic**
			Automatic collision avoidance system	Super thermal insulator			**Security**
	A fulfilling home for the elderly					Artificial skin, artificial organ	**Medical care**
		Package-delivery service for health-food products		Pillows for deep sleep			**Health**
							Education

Figure 5-4:   A Checklist of Needs and Seeds[1]

a result, it becomes possible to prepare a lexicon that limits key-words, and arranges and regulates synonyms, subsumptions, and related terms when attempting to search specific terms in information sources.

The history of the thesaurus began when Dupont introduced one in the 1950s. Since then, a large number of them have been created to respond to various needs of organizations, such as governmental institutions, various academic societies, the International Organization for Standardization, United Nations Educational, Scientific and Cultural Organization (UNESCO), and newspapers. The thesauri created in Japanese include the "JICST Thesaurus" for use in exploring science and technology in general, and the specialized "News Thesaurus" (Chunichi Shinbunsha) and the "Textile Thesaurus" (Textile Machinery Society of Japan) for use in exploring specific fields.

To create a thesaurus, you need to follow the following steps:

1) Confirm whether it is possible to use other thesauri covering specific areas and adjacent areas related to information sources.
2) Determine the selection of descriptors (as terms or symbols that have been officially approved and formulated throughout the thesaurus) in accordance with the thesaurus' structure, usage objectives (whether the thesaurus is designed for manual use or mechanical retrieval), and planned scope.
3) Evaluate the effectiveness of descriptor candidates with the following key considerations:

   • (Expected) frequency of appearing in documents
   • The high probability that the candidate will be posed as a question during search
   • Relevance with descriptors that have already been approved
   • Validity as a term that can be used generally
   • Degree of usability and comprehension when alluding to or clarifying specific ideas.

5.3.3 *Technical relation analysis*

Thirdly, I will explain technical relation analysis. One aim of this type of analysis is to attempt the linking of information sources with appropriate themes and keywords of applied researches by incorporating tabulation and patternization into the systematization of keywords mentioned above.

It is possible to depict charts and patterns through various structures and processes such as tree structures, network structures, and their hybrid structures, and technical relation analysis is also a method that applies these structures.

In technical relation analysis charts, it is common to show various cutting-edge innovatory technology fields on the left-hand side, and to show the results of mixing different technologies on the right-hand side.

For example, when citing the fields of fine chemicals and specialty chemicals as cutting-edge innovatory fields in the area of chemistry and combining them with the field of new materials, you get the hybrid technology of engineering plastics; when linking natural resources to energy, you get the development of the fuel cell; and when you link life science to biotechnology, you give rise to the possibility of fields such as artificial organs, artificial skins, and artificial blood.

These combinations of different technologies can be completed with just two types in the simplest cases, but in most cases, such as in the case of artificial organs, the combination is the result of various attributes, including at least mechanical, material, bioengineering, and medical. Additionally, if you attempt to express their relational analysis little more closely, it will become necessary to portray their interrelationships through multidimensional charts and diagrams.

Furthermore, if you aim to successfully realize the development of a certain undeveloped or insufficiently developed artificial organ, a new product development management map that includes elements such as the management strategy, product strategy, product development, and experimental design will become essential, and without the cooperation of an entire organization that strongly shares values in common with you, you will not be able to realize anything successfully.

Regarding this point, I would like to touch upon several topics, including market analysis, R&D budgetary control and human resources development/management. It is often the case that the research environment and the personal-property motivation of researchers exert a definitive influence over the development and realization of new products and new businesses. I will elaborate with concrete examples.

5.4 Effective R&D and Personnel Training Management

5.4.1 *Effective criteria for evaluating R&D projects*

As a means to lead R&D management to success, effective criteria for evaluating an R&D project and the timeliness of its evaluation are indispensable. Thus, I present to you the following points adapted from a research study carried out by the Massachusetts Institute of Technology (MIT):

1) *Sales figure or sales revenue*

Increase in transactions, additional amount of production that does not accompany additional investment, market share, percentage of R&D products, ratio of new product sales to old product sales, growth rate of new customers, etc.

2) *Costs for materials, personnel expenses, and overhead costs*

Amount saved in patent fee payments, amount saved in costs for materials, reduction in personnel expenses, improvement in the utilization of surplus equipment, decline in indirect costs, increase in the productivity of unit processes, etc.

3)   *Profit*

Differences in the profits of new and old R&D products, R&D expenses per profit unit, changes in the rate of return, etc.

4)   *R&D stage of completion*

Differences in the completion stages of new and old R&D projects, differences between actual completion stages and forecasted completion stages, differences in per-unit cost completion stages, relationships between completion stages and anticipated results, etc.

5)   *Customer satisfaction and receptivity*

Growth rate of sales volume, types and amounts of returned products, rate of defective products, number of customer complaints and their seriousness, etc.

6)   *Level of contribution toward technological development*

Number of new ideas, advanced materials, extent of introducing new processes, level of preparation and development of the specification sheet, extent of technology mix and collaboration, responsiveness to technical requirements, etc.

7)   *Level of success of technological solutions*

Success rate of R&D issues, application patents, number of new industrial designs, details of unresolved technologies and the impact they have on failures.

8)   *Cost/effect (effectiveness)*

Profit per unit cost, effectiveness of up-to-date information, difference in the cost-benefit ratios of new and old projects, and the variance in the differences.

9)   *Environmental management and CSR*

Recycling rate, environmental sustainability, level of societal contribution on a cost per unit basis, risk aversion ratio, etc.

According to a survey conducted by A.H. Rubenstein,[1] the top five evaluation criteria used by 37 US research institutes are as follows:

- Time and cost required in technology solutions
- Sales figure or sales revenue
- Amount saved in materials costs, personnel expenses, or overhead costs
- Output of R&D information
- The level of success of a technology solution.

5.4.2 *Effective evaluation organizations for projects*

Next, ideally, the formation of the following five organizations or organizations with the following five functions are considered to be necessary for evaluating projects:

- Organizations that inquire closely into the very details of an R&D project and evaluate whether such details are truly in alignment with the aims of medium to long-term management plans, strategic plans, and R&D plans.
- An organization that considers the operations management method for R&D projects and evaluates whether human, material, and information resources are being fully utilized.[4]
- An organization that carries out cost-utility analysis for R&D projects and evaluates whether sufficient benefits are being obtained or whether sufficient effectiveness is being achieved or is in the process of being achieved *vis-à-vis* investment efforts (including cost-effectiveness analysis of project risks).
- An organization that evaluates the extent of an R&D project's contribution toward environmental protection.

- An organization that evaluates the extent of an R&D project's contribution toward achieving a company's Corporate Social Responsibility (CSR) targets.

For example, the central laboratory of company T is made up of a special mobile unit, which is set up as a temporary organization to deal with new projects, and mobile room units to which general researchers belong. The laboratory does not have permanent setups and general researchers formed into A, B, C groups in accordance with themes, but instead it acts as a permanent organization that forms future kernels in accordance with research studies of long-term projects and themes, while also performing activities as a special mobile organization in some cases. In effect, the laboratory is a complex organization prepared to assume contingent roles.[1]

In this way, the company is believed to be increasing its chances of being able to deal with unexpected situations (such as new discoveries, acts of God, and man-made calamities) in an agile manner.

Next, I would like to point out that the relation between new product development and marketing research is particularly indispensable during the planning and trial manufacturing stages. Figure 5-5 shows what types of product concepts are appropriate for elucidating the demand structure of labor-economizing equipment, and what types of marketing research need to be carried out for planning new product development strategies.

5.4.3   Personnel training management

Lastly, I would like to touch on the matter of developing and training human resources.

Mr. Masamichi Ishii, in his book *The Conditions of Originality* (NTT Publishing, 2005),[2] analyzes successful cases of original product development such as the lens-equipped film "Utsurndesu," the entertainment robot "AIBO," and Quartz wristwatches, and states that the four abilities the developers of these products shared in

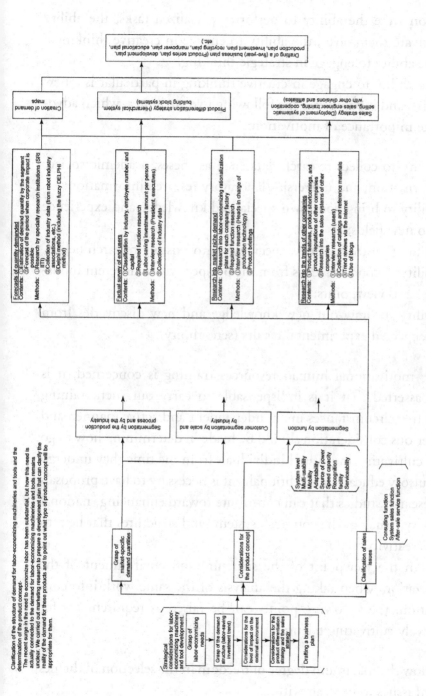

Figure 5-5:   For Drafting a New Product Development Strategy[3]

Source: Adapted from R&D Guidebook Editorial Committee's *R&D Guidebook (Seventh Impression)*, Union of Japanese Scientists and Engineers, 1984, p. 298.

common were the ability to perform specialized tasks, the ability to motivate themselves, the ability to engage in creative thinking,[6] and the ability to engage in strategic thinking.

The ability to engage in creative thinking in particular is a new approach and it comprises the following five attributes, which advocate the importance of motivation:

1) Ability to collect research data such as theses, academic society information, and university/laboratory research information;
2) Ability to bring your own specialized knowledge and experience into new fields;
3) Ability to introduce new specialties into existing research fields;
4) Ability to conceive ideas from the perspectives of different industries and viewpoints;
5) Ability to draw out new knowledge and new discoveries from unexpected experimental results (serendipity).

Where motivational human resources training is concerned, it is being asserted that it is indispensable to carry out such training under free circumstances in an independent and active manner, and that serious consideration should be made in determining how to go about cultivating motivated individuals from the time they undergo compulsory education. Additionally, it is necessary to have proposals and research studies that can contribute toward enhancing "national creativity," such as the country's systems and structures that help to boost creativity.

From the viewpoint of the structure and environment of the organization, when taking the analysis of the same work into consideration, the following points can be raised as requirements for effectively cultivating talent:

1) Allow the maximum degree of freedom in the selection of themes and issues to be dealt with.

2) This should be allowed even when continual support from the top or your superiors proves difficult.

3) Provide as many measures as possible that will promote separation and independence from day-to-day business affairs and from the supervision of headquarters.

4) For the purposes of carrying out research, give the opportunity to freely participate at domestic or overseas universities, laboratories, and academic societies as occasion demands.

I would like to end, however, by emphasizing that the foundation of successful R&D projects, new product developments and new business developments goes beyond the scope of individual capability. The foundation, in fact, lies in the securing and sustainment of boundless passion and motivation and in the environment and structure of an organization that makes maintaining and increasing such zeal possible.[8,9,10]

Akira Ishikawa

References

1. Akira Ishikawa, *The Q&A Primer to Information Searching for Developing New Products and New Businesses*, Dobunkan, 1988, pp. 54–55, 66–67, 82–83, 85–87, 106–109.
2. Masamichi Ishii, *The Conditions of Originality — How Epoch-Making Products were Born*, NTT Publishing, 2005, pp. 142, 150–151.
3. R&D Guidebook Editorial Committee, *R&D Guidebook*, Union of Japanese Scientists and Engineers, 1984, p. 298.
4. Masatsugu Kawai, *The Manual for Developing Hit Products with CD-ROM Attached*, ASUKA Publishing, 2001.
5. Nikkei Business Daily, *Ultra-Tech — Japan's Underlying Strength*, Nihon Keizai Shimbun, 2003.
6. Takahiro Kawashima, *How to Create a Genius*, Kodansha International, 2004.
7. Makoto Takahashi (editor), *Encyclopedia of Creativity*, Mode Gakuen Publishing Bureau (Incorporated Educational Institution), 1993.
8. Akira Ishikawa, *Theory of Strategic Budgetary Control*, Dobunkan, 1993, pp. 333–376.
9. Akira Ishikawa, Makiko Okuyama, Toshitaka Kobayashi (editors), *The Cybernetic Renaissance*, Kogyo Chosakai Publishing, 1999.
10. Akira Ishikawa (editor), *Global Information Network*, The Nikkon Kogyo Shimbun, 1992.

Part 2

PRECEDENTS OF NEW PRODUCT/NEW BUSINESS DEVELOPMENT

The Role of Information Search in the Development of "Karada Meguri Cha^{TM}" (Body Circulation Tea Based on Traditional Chinese Medicine)

It was March 2004 when the Health Product Group of the Innovation Health Product Group started in Coca-Cola Japan as a department under the direct control of the President with a mandate to develop products that can absolutely dominate the market. Since this time, the product named "Karada Meguri Cha^{TM}" was developed over a span of around two years and two months and was finally released in May 22, 2006. This product was a full-fledged health-tea beverage that was marketed as Japan Coca-Cola's major new product of 2006 and hired the celebrity Ryoko Hirosue to feature in its advertising campaign. Sales progressed smoothly and after two months since its launch, it had outstripped expectations by 35%, and the product even experienced a shortage at one time. I would like to present the development of this product as a case study in the hope that you will come to understand what type of a new product development process is one that can make a difference.

6.1 The Beverage Business Today

6.1.1 *The beverage selling space is very crowded*

Initially, I would like to slightly touch upon the environment surrounding the Ready to Drink (RTD) business (RTD beverages are contained in PET bottles, cans, and paper packs and are made for immediate consumption). A distinctive characteristic of the RTD business can be said to be its tough competitive environment. New products keep being released all the time one after another at the beverage counters of convenience stores and supermarkets. The showcase is indeed congested with a resplendent variety, offering not only completely new products, but also an assortment of flavors of existing brands, seasonal products, and products that have undergone package renewals. In the soft drinks industry, there are 1,000 brands launched every year in one form or another, and it is said that only three from among these make it to the next year. The marketers of the soft drinks industry, continue to engage in a trial and error process every day to determine how to go about successfully winning against the competition posed by the products of their own company and those of other companies under such a tough environment, and ultimately acquire the shelf space of stores.

6.1.2   *The philosophy of new product development*

So what should be done to attain a full victory against the competition? One answer is to create an innovative product. Many products in recent times have been incremental innovations that made progressive performance improvements over the products found in existing markets. In other words, companies have been basically responding to market needs by tweaking their products to make them a little newer, then safely mass producing them and swiftly and stably supplying them to top automatic vending machine networks established nationwide and to major supermarkets and convenience stores, with whom they enjoy strong relationships. However, it is a fact that a cloud began to hang over this model. The reason is that it has no longer become possible to sufficiently respond to consumer needs with incremental innovations. The times are such that markets are overflowing with similar products that have reached their saturation points and consumers needs have become diversified as consumers have become more discerning in the selection of their products. This reason is also true for the makers of other industries as well, including consumer electronics makers, toiletry makers, cosmetics makers, and automobile makers.

The requirement for development necessary during these times when existing technologies, sales networks, production networks, distribution networks have started to vie in these ways is disruptive innovation; innovation that destroys concepts of existing products to create new markets. A look back into the past reveals that markets have gone through fundamental changes when paradigm shifts occurred, which were caused by the introduction of a disruptive innovation that gave rise to "an invention with a new concept." Examples of such innovations include the following; the paper-cup juice→ the bottled Coca Cola, the cloth diaper→ the disposable diaper, the portable stereo→ the hard-disk model portable stereo, the detergent and the softening agent→ the detergent with a softening agent in it, and the gasoline car→ the hybrid car. In the manufacturing of these products, it may prove difficult to realize differentiation even if there were differences to a small or large extent. Toward realizing differentiation, effort has to be made in realizing disruptive innovation. To bring about such disruptive innovation, it is essential to not find out what are the products that can satisfy existing consumer needs, but what are the unmet needs (latent needs) of consumers and create new concepts or reframe existing ones (through combining existing concepts to create new needs). In the field of marketing research, various approaches for such creation and reframing are being proposed.

However, the excavation of latent needs at present relies on the ability of the individual developer to look ahead and detect future needs, except the needs that emerge from the introduction of new technologies. Therefore, it is vital to engage in forming a setup that will help the developer probe for and forecast future needs with a high degree of precision. Innovative product development begins by having developers, researchers, and outside experts discuss the latent consumer needs among each other to probe for those needs and then carry out productization at an early stage. The Health Product Group of Coca-Cola Japan is carrying out health-focused product developments on the basis of such thinking.

6.2   Investigating the Marketplace

6.2.1   *Left-brain analysis and right-brain analysis*

I would like to begin this discussion by elaborating on the topic of "searching for new concepts that can help to meet the unmet needs of consumers." The basic process begins by observing the market with a perspective that makes a well-balanced use of the left and right brain modes of thinking and by consequently ascertaining whether there are any gaps in the market. The human brain is divided into the left brain and right brain, which respectively work in different ways. The left brain has the function of performing analytically and is proficient in grasping the present situation by organizing perceptions logically.

On the other hand, the right brain has the function of instantly associating inputs from the eyes and ears with images through spatial patterning. So the left brain is in charge of chiefly looking at data analytically and making calculations based on them, and the right brain is in charge of associating images with experiences, such as looking around at stores and talking to people. Therefore, the cognitive model being discussed here basically states that unmet needs are the gaps that exist between the results of the right brain's analytical thinking process and the left brain's image-oriented thinking process. This line of thinking is not only adopted in the field of consumer marketing, but also widely adopted in the discipline of fundamental medicine, such as in the area of searching for new genes.

6.2.2 *Situational understanding and hypothesis construction*

In the development of "Karada Meguri Cha™" (Body Circulation Tea), the people in charge firstly carried out some data analysis to grasp current phenomena that were occurring in the world. In this analysis, to determine what the competition was up to, what consumers were thinking about, and how company resources should be used, they examined left-brain observations of various events from several angles. The sources of their observations were such items as: 1) existing market data, 2) market trends in chronological order, 3) consumer awareness data, and 4) beverage-purchase surveys. When looking back at the phenomena that occurred over the past several years, it becomes clear that a health-oriented boom had arrived. In fact this is clear at a glance whether you are looking at the growth of the supplements market, the index of fitness club openings, the extension of the market for designated health foods, the new product trends of electrical equipment manufacturers, and the moves made by the medical care industry. Upon looking at the beverage market, it became clear that markets that had been appealing health and nature as selling points had seen rapid growth. In the case of the non-sugar tea market in particular, it was a time when major makers were introducing green tea brands on a large scale, such as "Ooi Ocha," "Yemon," "Namacha," and "Hajime" as the overall non-sugar tea market leaned toward green tea beverages. In addition, tea beverages that had acquired special health designations such as "Ban So Rei Cha," "Sasso," and "Healthya Rokucha" were overwhelming the market. "Healthya Rokucha" was typical of the type of beverage that was specially designed to serve as diet aids.

An investigation into the common denominators shared by these phenomena occurring in the beverage market revealed such denominators to be comments such as "good for the body" and "it's natural and therefore not bad for the body." To explain the factors behind such phenomena, we probed consumer awareness and the living conditions of the consumers. According to the Survey of Consumer

Sentiments, among all people, regardless of their age and gender, uncertainty toward their own state of health registered extremely high. Such an attitude was reflected by statements such as "I feel my body is filthy," "I could fall sick any time and that wouldn't surprise me," and "I don't think I can live long." A large reason behind the demonstration of such anxiety of the Japanese people, whose life expectancy is among the highest in the world, has to do with the sudden changes in social structures, such as the deterioration in dietary habits and in the work environment. This is the result of factors such as working late into the night to compensate for a labor shortage caused by a protracted economic depression, skipping dinner and eating box lunches purchased from convenience stores every day, experiencing a chronic lack of sleep, compensating for a lack of vitamins by taking supplements, and resolving any feelings of illness by just taking pills.

It can be conjectured that products appealing such points as "Good for the body" and "It's natural and therefore not bad for the body" were highlighted due to the context mentioned above. Now, let us consider the difference between "Good for the body" and "It's natural and therefore not bad for the body" from the perspective of the research findings on beverage purchases. "Beverages good for the body" according to these research findings are, in addition to the so-called "natural drinks" such as vegetable juices and *aojiru* (a soup made by squeezing green leaf vegetables such as kale and/or komatsuna), the "health-designated beverages" that have acquired the seal of official approval from the Ministry of Health, Labour and Welfare. On the other hand, products considered to be "natural and therefore not bad for the body" are for the most part non-sugar teas and 100% juices. In terms of market scale, the ratio between "Beverages good for the body" and "Beverages considered to be natural and therefore not bad for the body" is approximately 1:5, clearly showing that the market scale of the latter category is overwhelmingly larger. When examining the wording of the two expressions, it becomes also clear that "good for the body" sounds more effective for health maintenance than "bad for the body" and therefore should be a more favorable phrase. However, this is to the contrary in the market. So what is the reason behind the contrast between one expression that is favorable, but in a limited, "niche" way and the other expression that is passive in tone but enjoys a large market nevertheless?

6.2.3   *Interviewing experts*

In order to explore the reasons behind the difference between "Beverages good for the body" and "Beverages that are natural and therefore are not bad for your body," we interviewed experts on what we knew about the present situation related to this matter.

In the beginning, we carried out an interview with the members of the various sales teams that were in charge of convenience stores. They have on-site knowledge of market trends and are well-informed on what buyers at convenience stores are thinking. Their opinion is that "while the probability for a sale increases when there is an absolute functional value, it also decreases when there is no emotional value at all." If a product has both functional and emotional values that are strong in their own ways, and current primary customers of convenience stores, who are largely characterized to be capricious, see it as something new, then the product will enjoy a substantial chance of being sold. While the market seeks products with the wording "good for the body" more than they seek products with the wording "not bad for the body," what turned out to be important was understanding what the extra benefit was as a new product. In addition, sales personnel who were in charge of supermarkets remarked that housewives, who are the primary customers of supermarkets, are extremely sensitive to price. However, they went on to claim that this is true insofar as commodities were concerned and that housewives are in fact highly sensitive to health concerns, believing that it is their mission to protect their overall family's health. If a TV program on health broadcasts that *aojiru* is good for improving blood circulation, the next day, high-priced *aojiru* will become sold out at supermarkets. Their conclusion was that if a product has value that housewives truly seek, then there will be no need to be concerned with the price, and even if it is something that tastes bad, it will still be able to dominate the market.

In other words, the difference between "beverages good for the body" and "beverages that are natural and are therefore not bad for the body" was made up by such factors as "deliciousness," which is a basic attribute of beverages, and the "ease of obtaining the product" as in being able to purchase it every day, and "price." Certainly, the health value of the *aojiru*, which is "a beverage that is good for the body," appears to be very high. However, it suffers from the hurdles of being unpleasant to drink, troublesome to buy, and being expensive. In addition, it is chiefly focused on its health-benefit function and ingredient-name appeal and is devoid of any emotional value.

On the other hand, the green tea, which is a "beverage that is natural and therefore not bad for your body," may not clearly convey how it may be beneficial to your health. Nevertheless, it evokes an emotional image associated with being natural, going well with food, being pleasant to drink, and being available anywhere at a reasonable price. The top three reasons generally stated for buying a beverage is "I can chug it down," "it goes well with food," and "it's delicious," and the basic question for product development then becomes what extra benefits can be added on top of these reasons. The reason why the *aojiru* is actually being sought after only in a niche market when it should be sought after on a much larger scale lies in the fact that it lacks in the "emotional value" of a soft drink, in addition to being "expensive" and "unpleasant to drink."

6.2.4   *Redefining the value of health*

We decided to carry out a workshop based on the analysis made to date. The workshop is a sandbag, so to speak. It is a process that involves having planners criticize your hypothesis that has been drawn from researched data and your rationale that has been inflated by your own words and images. Through arguing and defending against their criticisms, you will discover points of weaknesses in your logic so as to be able to brush up and improve your hypothesis. I feel that for such a brush-up session, you should assemble a group that is diverse as possible to be able to carry out a debate from various angles. For our workshop, we assembled a group made up of a total of eleven individuals who were from the Health Product Group, the Strategy Planning, which brought objectivity to the table with their databases, and from an ad agency whose planners had both creative expertise and up to date information resources concerned with domestic and international matters related to the industry. Extracts of opinions expressed in the course of the workshop are shown below:

- Recent health checkups seem to be fanning uncertainty. For example, I can understand up to things like total cholesterol levels, HDL, and LDL, but it gets irritating when they start talking about arteriosclerosis levels and resistance values of the capillary. Is having a high capillary resistance value something that's so unhealthy as to instantly link directly to death? They talk about the arteriosclerosis index, but is it a criterion that applies to all people? If you lead a contemporary urban lifestyle that is irregular and then get threatened by the fragmentary items of a health checkup, it is only natural to be seized by a sense of unease regarding your health.

- The Japanese people had originally been able to stay healthy by consuming seasonal, local products and by keeping it in mind to prepare well-balanced diets. In other words, the Japanese people had an innate understanding that a natural state of health = "ishoku dougen" (the idea that food and medicine come from the same source). This knowledge had been passed down the generations. However, together with the advent of the nuclear family, and the fact that people's days have become busier, people have become contented with low-priced food imports and processed foods that are easy to prepare. Consequently, such societal trends have put an end to the dietary habits of ancient Japan.

- Seized by such worries, housewives tend to flock around "products based on themes of natural health" such as *aojiru* and black vinegar, and men tend to gather around health-designated beverages for aiding weight loss, but it remains a question whether these products are responding to the consumer's concerns over health at a fundamental level.

Perhaps it may be possible to fulfill the extra-benefit part of a new product if you can clarify what a product is supposed to deliver, and if you can upgrade its value by meeting price and taste preferences and by creating a compulsion to drink it through appealing on an emotional value.

While looking at the information derived from analyzing the data and the findings derived from the interviews, we debated various points from subjective and objective angles that related to "natural and good for your body," which is the type of product sought after by consumers. The goal of this debate was to redefine the expression "natural and good for your body" as a health value and attach it to a product that had this redefined value. The conclusion arrived through the workshop was that "what is natural and good for your body" is precisely what the Japanese wisdom of "ishoku dougen" has been saying all along since ancient times; that both medicine and your daily diet are equally important in helping you to build a healthy body, the kind that helps you to prevent illness. In other words, the panel of debaters had liked the idea of a product claiming that even if you lead a busy life every day, if you consume a product that is based on the "ishoku dougen" concept, you can aim to build a body that will help you to prevent illness. In effect, they had concluded that this idea was novel and that it was in sync with the current of the times and therefore stood a good chance.

What is a good workshop?

I believe a good workshop is first and foremost a medium that helps to bring out in the open the knowledge and experiences of participants to the maximum extent possible and then advise which direction to take. So what should you do to lead the workshop toward showing this direction?

The success or failure of a workshop hinges on prior preparation. To lead the workshop toward a certain outcome with an output, the facilitator must work toward creating an effective flow. By creating gimmicks that can offer unexpected stimulation to participants, it becomes possible to generate ideas that go beyond the established framework of discussion. In previous workshops, we did such things as put on short plays and engage in thinking sessions while lying down on the floor. As for the participants, they need to prepare for the workshop with regard to the theme. When gaps between knowledge and participation levels exist, the quality of the workshop will decline, so participants need to take note of this fact.

Regarding how to carry out a workshop, first of all, it is necessary to encourage all participants to actively speak on various situations (regarding targets/times/scenes, etc.). Since this is an initial stage to promote the generation of ideas, participants should avoid becoming attached to their own ideas. Additionally, everyone should attempt to refrain form rejecting anyone else's opinion and for the time being simply accept all opinions expressed. Then on top of all these opinions expressed, a participant should add their own ideas and diffuse them with what has already been expressed.

There is one more important thing to remember when making remarks at a workshop. That thing is to keep an open mind.

To promote active exchanges of opinion, it is also important to create a conducive atmosphere. Appearing high-handed or passive will never work towards your advantage. It is necessary to constantly keep in mind that the workshop is not a place for winning over others with your opinions. Next, you will enter into the stage of producing an output by tying up all the diffused ideas, but what needs to be pointed out here is that you should not force out a conclusion. Naturally, it will be necessary to narrow down the ideas through grouping them, but each idea thought up by the participants are valuable and should prove to play a large role during concept development. Once the workshop arrives at a stage where options for future directions are proposed, I believe the workshop can be said to be a success. I believe that the significance of implementing a workshop lies not in finding solutions to everything, but in making options for future directions available to the person in charge so that they may make their selections and consequently generate concepts with higher precision in the process.

Since people at the "Karada Meguri Cha^{TM}" workshop were all accomplished and were all brimming with ideas, I personally found the experience to be very stimulating. After the workshop finished, however, I was so fatigued that I didn't even feel like standing up. Still, two years later, with the product's market entry having been made, I now find my time at the workshop to have been a deeply moving experience.

Atsushi Saito
Director of the Innovation Group of the Health Product Group of the Coca-Cola Japan Company

6.2.5   Compilation of keywords

Based on the output of the workshop, the expression "natural and good for your body" was defined as "building a body that helps you to prevent illness." At this point, we brainstormed and extracted keywords associated with what consumers actually do to build strong bodies resistant to illness. These keywords included moderate exercise, regular lifestyle, simple diet, macrobiotics, yoga, and Pilates. Roughly categorized, they can be divided into the dietary-habit improvement group and the exercise group. At this point we began to focus our attention on ideas and exercise methods that had Eastern roots, such as yoga and macrobiotics. A certain segment of consumers had begun to realize that a good approach towards realizing optimal health was not the Western way, which involves taking medicines and supplements to reinforce your body, but the Eastern way, which involves carrying out exercises and practicing daily dietary habits. These consumers had even begun to implement this preference. Even though the data did not show this, a look around cities certainly revealed that there are various types of yoga classes proliferating, and women's magazines had been covering them as special features on a constant basis. Personally, my only impression of yoga was that it was associated with India, and I doubted that consumers were attending yoga classes because they were fond of the country. I inferred that they had related to yoga's way of thinking, had adapted it to suit Japanese tastes, and incorporated it into their daily living patterns.

As we sorted through these phenomena while taking beverages into account, the motif that surfaced was Chinese medicine. The difference between Chinese medicine and Western medicine lies in the difference between symptomatic treatment and prevention. In other words, in contrast to Western medicine, which identifies trouble spots and performs treatment on them, Eastern medicine probes for root causes of illnesses and removes them, while also aiming to remedy illnesses through elevating the body's ability to heal itself. To embody the principle of the product, which is "to build a body that does not fall ill," we arrived at the assumption that it would do well to adopt the concept of Chinese medicine (Eastern thinking). Based on this assumption, we decided to create a product concept that incorporated the motif of Chinese medicine, which is representative of the Eastern way of thinking.

6.3 Oriental Way of Thinking

6.3.1 *China, a country that manages health through tea*

We established Chinese medicine as a motif for fulfilling the product development theme, "natural and good for your body." To establish the "concrete benefits this product should offer," we began by gaining an understanding of traditional Chinese medicine (Kampo). During my graduate school days, I had majored in Oriental medicine and therefore have a general understanding of the subject. However, I had no expertise in creating a product of this kind from the ground up, so for all practical purposes, my knowledge was useless. In this case, instead of researching the field on my own, it was quicker to ask someone who knew the subject well, so I went on to contact a trading company that had ties to my company and were dealing in ingredients of Chinese medicine. They introduced me to an expert and after explaining the circumstances so far under confidential terms to this person, I was referred to a practitioner of Chinese medicine who belonged to this person's network. Consequently, I flew to Beijing.

This practitioner was someone who used to be the attending physician of a certain chairman and is currently active in the Chinese and US academic worlds. I had him lecture me on many aspects, such as Chinese medicine's basis in Inyogogyo Ron [Chinese cosmological theory of the cosmic dual forces (yin and yang) and the five elements (metal, wood, water, fire and earth)], the actual circumstances of Chinese medicine within China, the internationalization of Chinese medicine, the thinking behind the different usages of Western and Chinese medicines, and the thinking behind effects and benefits. I also had him advise me on touring factories where materials were produced. The following is a summary of what I had ultimately learned from him:

- Chinese medicine is the fruit of clinical experiments carried out over the span of 3,000 years, and its marketed products have a proven track record. In addition, many Chinese medical remedies blend multiple materials in ratios validated through experience to amplify effect (this is known as the harmony effect).
- Since Chinese medicine mainly attempts to cure illnesses by promoting self-healing, it could take a long time for any effect to show. However, depending on the case, there are times when Western medicine and Chinese medicine are alternately prescribed.
- The thinking behind prescribing Chinese medicine can be roughly categorized into the following two approaches: add something to cure symptoms and eject something to cure symptoms.
- National American medical institutions are helping to realize the internationalization of Chinese medicine. In effect, they are studying the efficacy of Chinese medicine, which is a medical science grounded in experience, through the evidence-based process of Western medicine. Through this process, they are aiming to realize the internationalization of Chinese medicine.
- Even the Chinese feel that Chinese medicines taste bad. Therefore, what is considered to be health tea is in fact Chinese prescription medicine that has been mixed mildly to help people continue enjoying it on a daily basis. In this way, it is deeply rooted in the practice of daily health maintenance.

The most interesting facts here were that even Chinese people were feeling that Chinese medicine tasted bad and preferred not to take it if possible, and that people were managing their everyday health by drinking tea that had been created for such a purpose. It occurred to me then that China is a country where health is managed through tea consumption. As a concept, I felt this to be interesting. In addition, the idea of treating symptoms by firstly eliminating toxins was novel.

In Western medicine, the general approach to curing a symptom is to alleviate it by adding medicinal properties that target its focus. However, in the case of Chinese medicine, it is the reverse in that this form of medicine places emphasis on firstly subtracting rather than adding. Apparently, this way of thinking is unique to Chinese medicine. We made this factor a key element in our product's line of thought.

6.3.2   *Consumer awareness of traditional Chinese medicine*

I returned to Japan and began to organize the collected information when I was struck by a realization. This was that despite the fact that Chinese medicines had already entered into various fields in Japan and also had won acceptance at the consumer level to a certain degree, even the medicines being sold by major Japanese companies handling Chinese medicines could not be considered to have attained mass penetration by the standards of the drug industry. To find out why this was so, I went on to perform a factor analysis. I began by proceeding to the Chinatown found in my neighborhood to browse through stores selling Chinese medicines. The impressions I received at those places included "old-fashioned," "Chinese image despite being located in Japan," "expensive prices," "no credibility," "smelly," and "grotesque."

On the basis of these observations, I then carried out a web-based survey that saw responses from 1,500 general consumers. Their responses confirmed what I had felt and they included ones such as "I believe Chinese medicine is good for your body," "I would like to use from now on," "I can't believe its effects," "too pricey," "it takes too long for any effect to show," and "tastes awful." Of special note here is that the number of consumers who responded "I believe Chinese medicine is good for your body" and "I would like to use from now on" were more than expected. In other words, the results of the analysis suggested that Chinese medicine was not reaching mass levels because of negative impressions that were offsetting its potential. This finding did not change by age, gender, or area.

6.3.3 *Changing the way of thinking from a Western one to an Oriental one*

Since I had reached an understanding of Chinese medicine's business potential and consumer potential, I established the idea of eliminating toxins as the product value. This, after all, was based on Chinese medicine's principle of preventive medicine. The concept of eliminating toxins is not found in Western medicine and it is unique to Chinese medicine in that it is focused on firstly removing bad elements, instead of adding elements while the bad elements remain stored inside the body. This concept resembles what is known in English as detoxification or detox, and back in 2004, it started to become a buzzword found in women's magazines. I digress here, but I should mention that during the development of the product, Shiseido released a Chinese medicine-based cosmetics product called "SHINOADORE" and Kao released a Chinese medicine-based cosmetics product called "ORIENA" and a hair-care product called "ASIENCE," which incorporated oriental concepts. Additionally, with ideas and products that were focused on Oriental health and beauty concepts beginning to become popular, such as yoga, Pilates, and macrobiotics, I was able to confirm that the concept for our product was not heading in a completely wrong direction. The only regret I had was that others had released their products before we released ours.

6.4 Sorting Out Development Requirements

6.4.1 *Who should be offered detoxification by Chinese medicine?*

The keywords began to gradually shape into "natural and good for your body/toxin elimination through Chinese medicine, which incorporates the concept of preventive medicine." At this point, we inspected whether the consumer need of toxin elimination existed in the first place. While we went on to carry out another web-based survey, we put our thoughts in order on detoxification to establish the questions that were to go into the survey. An Internet search of women's magazines turned up a very high volume of articles, indicating that the topic had already become a boom among women.

Detoxification is a way of keeping healthy through eliminating toxins found within the body. One method appears to be through releasing sweat by undertaking activities such as yoga, Pilates, and half-body bathing, while another appears to be through the consumption of approximately two liters of oolong tea or mineral water per day to excrete the body's waste materials through the process of diuresis. Yet another method apparently is through the consumption of foods prepared with ingredients that promote the excretion of the body's waste materials. Such ingredients include coriander, red pepper, and onion. As for the toxins mentioned here, we found two views that define them; one was the concrete view that toxins are heavy metals such as mercury and cadmium and the other was the more conceptual view that toxins are associated with thick or viscous blood that could be converted to become more fluid through exercise and the consumption of healthy food. The more fluid the blood was, the more it would then be able to help in eliminating stored fat and waste materials. Although I did not find any academic verifications to support these views since the information sources used were the Internet and women's magazines, I was able to somehow or other relate to the views on a conceptual level.

To determine market size and the targets at this point, we carried out a web-based survey again to find out answers to the following questions: Who are the people interested in detoxification? How many of them are out there? What sorts of awareness do they have? What tastes do they have? What types of lives do they lead? Consequently, on the basis of the answers to these questions, we carried out factor analyses and multiple regression analyses through the use of health-related keywords and categorized the overall market into health clusters shaped by consumer perspectives. Firstly, regarding the recognition rate for the word "detox," on average it was around 10%, so it was not that high, and understanding of the method of detoxification was diverse, varying by the individual. So it appeared that the word itself did not offer any royal road to reaching consumers. However, a certain consumer cluster showed strong interest in detoxification, and moreover, they had already incorporated the practice into their lives. This cluster was comprised of women in their late twenties through late thirties residing in urban districts who had a strong interest in beauty-oriented health, and women in their forties through fifties with a relatively high household annual income residing in the Tokyo metropolitan area and the Kansai region who had a strong interest in health. These two groups were estimated to comprise approximately 30% of PET bottled sugar-free tea users, and to comprise approximately 15% of all user types.

We then decided to listen to their stories to profile them in detail. The method adopted was the focus group interview (FGI), and the interviewees totaled 36 individuals who comprised four advanced health-interest groups, which were made up of women residing in the Tokyo Metropolitan and Kansai areas, and two groups of men and women who were general RTD sugar-free tea users. A summary of the findings of the FGI sessions as they pertain to development follows:

- Strong needs were confirmed to exist among the members of the advanced health-interest group. However, in light of the fierce vying for share at convenience stores, it was deemed necessary to capture the women's sugar-free tea group, which comprised the mass market.
- The men's sugar-free tea users are slow to react to new products themselves (approval among men could spread once women show their approval). They should not be actively pursued.

- A product and communication development that realizes an attractive drink to enjoy on a daily basis for these two groups is necessary.
- The key to promoting "daily consumption" lies in providing a moderate peculiarity that provides a sense of an extra effect in addition to thirst-quenching deliciousness and palatability.

Research that creates needs

I believe there are many marketers and researchers who have come to believe that individual consumers who have obtained what they desired no longer have any further needs or that the very notion of picking up ideas from consumer voices is starting to become unreasonable. While it is the fate of marketers of all ages to utter the words, "I can't perceive the needs," the consumers of the present age are satisfied as fetuses in a mother's womb and have become apathetic insofar as discovering new needs for themselves is concerned. Asking consumers who have obtained everything they desire will not produce any answers. Does this then signify the limits of marketing research?

To break through this blockage, we can find hints in extremely basic techniques. One of them is motivational research. This research came into the limelight along with the father of the Focus Group Interview technique, Mr. Ernst Dichter, in the 1950s and was criticized for being merely a tool to measure individual experiences within a laboratory environment and therefore was inadequate for measuring a market as a whole. For this reason, this field fell out of prominence. Another technique is the observational research. As the name suggests, this approach does not involve any direct contact with consumers, but involves making observations from a distance to grasp facts and make interpretations. As a technique, this one also cannot be said to be a new one in any way. After 40 to 50 years, these techniques are making a comeback. What the two traditional approaches mentioned above can be said to have in common is that they do not perceive consumer behavior through fragmentarily monitoring moments of purchase and consumption, but instead they strictly perceive consumer behavior as a succession of actions and apprehend them in terms of subconscious motivational drives. However, the revival of these two approaches is gaining momentum precisely because of a new feature that has been added into them. This feature is the task of contextualizing all behaviors.

As to the question of how to contextualize the behaviors, to find the answer, a trial and error process continues to this day. Specifically, experts are asking questions such as the following: What concrete features are required to make contextualization possible? Could it be such things as storytelling, a photo collage, or some other form of nonverbal communication that can convey an image through pictures and sounds? Could it be role-playing that reproduces the behaviors in question? However, one certain matter is the point that the work of the researcher will no longer be what it used to be and that they will be expected to be competent in creative and expressive abilities that could help them contextualize the circumstances of individual consumers.

To put it in an extremely straightforward manner, the revival mentioned above parts company with the questionnaire. In other words, the revival is promoting a shift from the "measurement of what is observable and the estimations made from the combinations of such measurements" to "the understanding of essential commonalities shared among human beings and the building of hypotheses for the motivations that drive those commonalties." Rather than chasing after superficial phenomena in fields that individual consumers can easily acknowledge and recognize and that marketers find easy to understand, having consumers themselves daringly step into fields that are difficult to comprehend, having researchers themselves contextualize the circumstances, and having the consumers resolve questions in the form of making realizations will prove to be a shortcut toward achieving product developments and marketing strategies. This gives rise to the "needs-creating researcher." So will this momentum begin to question the validity of the distorted new-product development trend that leans toward newness and thereby put a stop to the ephemeralization of new products? Will it put the brakes on the ritualization of the focus group and depth interviews? The consequence of the shift will most likely be evident in the products that stand to win the most sympathy from now on.

Shigekazu Sugiyama
Business Knowledge Director of Coca Cola Japan Company

6.4.2   *Innovation committee*

In the development of products at Coca Cola Japan, there is an approval process that involves a committee called the Innovation Committee, which is responsible for authorizing product releases. A presentation is made to a group of managers that includes the President and unless approval is granted from them, a developer will not be able to start official development geared towards a market launch. The committee is focused on finding out whether what is being proposed can offer completely new values to the consumer or not. We incorporated some insights into the assumptions made until this point, and presented the general concept along with supporting research data and consumer inputs. Alternately, we also presented ideas on target consumers, product concept, expected volumes, the entry category, and the development schedule. While there were a number of follow-up sessions that followed, in the end we received a clear go signal. This happened in January 2005.

6.5   Towards Commercialization Development of the Formula, Name, and Packaging

6.5.1   *Rethinking formula development*

After safely receiving approval from the Innovation Committee, we made an official request to the R&D department for the development of a formula. The formula concept was "detox tea rooted in Chinese medicine." However, since we regrettably had no Chinese-medicine experts inside the company and since we expected developing from the ground up on our own would take a considerable amount of time, we decided to loan the idea to an outside entity. Toward this end, we established the following two routes: a trading company specializing in herbal medicines introduced to us by the Raw Materials Procurement Department; and the Chinese-medicine practitioner in China whom we relied on during the time I was gathering information on Chinese medicine.

Specifically, the request was for the procurement of raw ingredients that exhibited novelty, that were delicious, that had the function of eliminating toxins, that could be supplied stably, and were suitable for releasing within Japan (and China). We took advantage of the trading company's network and had them prepare more than 100 varieties of materials and dispatched a team of individuals from the R&D department and the Health Product Group to the trading company's factory located in the Kansai area. Among those prepared by the trading company were interesting materials that were referred to me by the people I came to know in Chinatown when I was browsing through Chinese medicine drugstores found there. These materials included *fukucha* (said to be the mysterious tea of the Silk Road), *yukicha* (70% fat-breakdown rate), *koukeiten* (an analeptic used by cosmonauts during the Soviet era), *kuteicha* (the diet tea of popular choice among Shanghai celebrities), *happoucha* (a tea for health and beauty care that became the talk among flight attendants of a Hong Kong airline company), *natsume* (a natural vitamin compound), *hipokou* (a favorite cough medicine among the Chinese), *saji* (a juice much loved by Genghis Khan that is believed to have anti-aging properties), *shinjyufun* (a legendary Chinese health and beauty ingredient), and *banrankou* (an anti-viral drug that attracted attention due to SARS).

Upon arriving at the factory, we found the 100 plus varieties already prepared for us, giving off distinctive aromas. Since we had to finish tasting all of them in one day, we breezed through the formalities and began tasting right away. We started with *kuteicha*, which is endorsed by Shanghai celebrities and which we deemed to be the most promising. The first impression was that it was bitter. Actually, I had never tasted anything that was as bitter as this. It was simply intolerable. Upon inquiring the person in charge of R&D, I was informed that the bitterness was the kind that no amount of blending technology could ever hope to mask. This tea was therefore immediately rejected. Next, we tried the also promising *yukicha*, which is considered to have a 70% fat-breakdown rate. The taste was hard to describe. I had never tasted anything like this before, and if I were pressed to give an analogy, I would have to say it tasted like the water in a goldfish bowl. Slimming down didn't seem to be worth it, if you had to tolerate something so foul. All of the collected materials tasted strange or had flavors that I had never tasted before.

Having consecutively used gustatory senses that I didn't normally use, I began to feel dizzy. As expected, Chinese medicine turned out to be unappetizing. It also seemed like we were tasting similar ingredients endlessly. Then we shifted perspective and came up with the idea of mixing several ingredients to produce a better flavor instead of relying on one ingredient. Upon consulting with the person in charge of the ingredients about this, we received the response that the trading company dealing in these ingredients had no expertise or experience in developing formulas and that if none of the prepared materials were adopted, then there was nothing they could do. The proposals from the practitioner of Chinese medicine in China were okay in terms of taste and effect, but there were issues involving the stability of supply, the safety of the materials, and the price, so even his proposals could not be accepted for practical use. We had taken two months to prepare for this search for ingredients, but it had ended in complete failure. I began to wonder whether the problem we were tackling even had an answer to be found in the first place.

6.5.2 *Collaboration with Nihondo*

To find some hints for developing a formula, we decided to search for a Chinese-medicine professional. The candidate that immediately came to mind was the company Nihondo, who would later become our marketing partner. Nihondo is a Chinese-medicine consultancy and pharmacy based in Shinagawa and operates 41stores nationwide (as of August 2006). This company was gaining popularity, thanks to its fashionable, welcoming interior design, simple and modern product packaging, easy-to-understand product explanations arranged in ways that suit Japanese tastes, and gentle style of attending to customers, which is oriented toward women.

When I carried out a search for information on Chinese medicine, I came to know about a seminar titled "Whitening with Chinese Medicine," which was being held by Nihondo for the general public, so I attended it myself. The lecture was extremely easy to understand and conveyed the difficult subject of Chinese Medicine in a modern, accessible way through presenting Nihondo's expertise and their unique worldview. Within a seating capacity of 80, 79 seats were occupied by women in their twenties through thirties, clearly indicating an overwhelming support for the company by women. This is most likely due to the fact that they provide solutions to various concerns the modern woman has, including fair skin, diet, stress, and atopic dermatitis in ways that incorporate Chinese medical theories. While I was not clear about the details of the company, I judged that the firm seemed to be capable and went on to promptly contact Mr. Yohei Suzuki, the lecturer. After explaining my objectives, I received his willing consent to cooperate relatively smoothly and went on to immediately coordinate with the legal department and the procurement department to draw up a contract and begin development together with Nihondo.

There were two matters that turned out to be difficult at this point. One was the fact that this was the first time for Nihondo to be involved in a project related to RTD beverages and the other was the problem of coming up with a balance between function and taste that would please both the core users of the advanced health interest group and the women's non-sugar RTD tea users, who formed the satellite group of users. The users of the advanced health interest group were quite discerning and were not convinced by effect alone. To hook them, there had to be a slightly unpleasing or unfamiliar taste. On the other hand, the women's non-sugar RTD tea users were not convinced even if there was an effect. To be viable for them, the product had to offer good taste and be easily drinkable. Therefore, the direction of development became focused on tastes and functions that could please both parties. With regard to toxin elimination, the previous FGI sessions had made the following consumer signals clear (effects that would convince them that toxins were being eliminated); the diuretic effect, the disappearance of constipation, the disappearance (or reduction) of shoulder stiffness, and improvement of skin condition. Consequently, we included these points as key elements in the development of the formula as well.

The following is a compilation of the thoughts on the development of the formula:

- While we do not intend to produce an image-oriented product, it must belong in the soft drinks category.
- Include consumer signals extracted from FGI sessions.
- The taste needs to convince both the core users who make up the advanced health interest group and the satellite users who make up the female sugar-free RTD tea user group.

- Since a little bitterness and sweetness stimulates the sympathetic nervous system and tends to increase the urge to drink again, the flavor hook needs to be at a level that is not too unsavory.
- The ingredients to be used should be usable in the making of soft drinks and should also be those that can be stably supplied.
- Pay sufficient attention to allergies.
- The product should be drinkable by the elderly, children, pregnant women, and people suffering from and recovering from illnesses.

6.5.3   *A formula that restores the circulation of qi (vigor), blood, and water*

The development of the base formula began in March 2005 and extended for a period of two months. Ultimately, the idea bore fruit to use Nihondo's Kenkocha (health tea) as a point of reference. The ingredients included matrimony vine, lotus, chameleon plant, eucommia ulmoides, low and striped bamboo, orange peel, bracket fungus, and Panax ginseng, and they were blended according to certain proportions. The R&D department expressed some disappointment, since the blended ingredients were all ones that could be obtained easily. Nihondo, however, insisted that they were confident about the product.

So we decided to prepare tea bags based on this formula and have the development team test them for two weeks. Regarding the flavor, there were many negative impressions voiced by men. However, in terms of effect, they reported that their visits to the restroom had increased, that they felt their bodies becoming lighter every time they had the drink, and that they felt their skin becoming somewhat tighter. Many female testers reported that they experienced relief from constipation, stiffness in the shoulders, and sensitivity to cold. When we reported these results to Mr. Suzuki, he commented that the human body is thought to be comprised of three elements — *qi,* blood, and water. *Qi* is vigor/power, blood is a liquid for conveying nutrients throughout the body, and water is a liquid for preventing the body from becoming dry. A state of physical imbalance indicates that there is a deficiency or glut in the supply of *qi* (vigor), blood, and water or in the supply of some of them and that the three elements are not circulating smoothly.

In the case of most Japanese people, the cause of the imbalance is a water glut. This is due to the distinctive high temperature-high humidity climate of Japan. At any rate, the important point here is to facilitate the release of surplus water accumulated in the body. Toward this end, if you prescribe an herbal medicine that can heighten the level of *qi* (vigor) and can facilitate the discharge of "water," then the circulation of "blood" will naturally improve and the three elements will begin to circulate smoothly as well. It is said that many of the problems troubling people today, such as pimples, dry skin, constipation, and stiffness in the shoulders can be handled without resorting to any medical treatment simply by restoring the three elements to their original state. This is indeed detox the Chinese medicine way. Having received concepts and ideas on Chinese medicine, we then moved on to the tasks of naming and packaging, while entrusting the tasks of improving the flavor, procuring the ingredients, and coordinating for mass production to the R&D department.

6.5.4 *Naming*

The key point in naming is to assure that the name clarifies what the product can do for the consumer and that consumers can readily understand it. In addition, it is necessary to be careful concerning the Pharmaceutical Affairs Law, the National Health Promotion Law, and the Trademark Law. In pharmaceutical regulations, there are two general rules that need to be heeded. One is that the words of body parts such as skin, liver, and blood cannot be used in any communication aimed at consumers. The other is that there should be no message that appears to be making a claim about the product's effect or performance. This means that sellers cannot appear to be making statements such as "this product is good for producing such and such an effect." In addition, expressions regarding Chinese medicine that are evocative of medical products are prohibited as well.

We carried out the naming process while taking heed of these factors. We purchased an entire store's worth of magazines and newspapers and spread them out on desks to help trigger ideas as we brainstormed in earnest as a team. Words that described the product concept such as "Kampo (Chinese medicine)," "detox," "toxin elimination," and words that related to the effects of detoxification, such as "beautiful skin," "improvement of internal functions," "fine tuning of mind and body," "Chinese medicine concept" were all unusable since they conflicted with the Pharmaceutical Affairs Law, so the naming work proved to be extremely tough going. We had the team members come up with several proposals for the name and then debated about them repeatedly. The initial members involved in the naming were just the individuals of the development team of the Health Product Group.

However, in the case of difficult themes, instead of relying on individuals found within the same circumstances, assembling a diverse group of people and having their equally diverse ideas stemming from a variety of expertise and experiences clash against each other and synthesize into new ideas would in most cases yield better outputs. We therefore requested the participation of copywriters, graphic designers, and strategy planners of an advertising agency with whom we had an established relationship. These individuals were experts of various fields. Ultimately, in addition to these members, the Marketing Director of Coca Cola Japan, the Director of Sales Department and the Director of the Creative Department joined the team, so we ended up carrying out the naming process with a very remarkable group of people.

As a result of carrying out desk research, workshops and discussions while taking into account the product concept, target consumers, and the context of the times through multiple filters, we were able to develop more than one hundred candidates for the name. Thereafter, after undergoing a necessary process and ultimately realizing a product concept that did not conflict with the Pharmaceutical Affairs Law, we gave birth to the name "Karada Meguri Cha[TM]", a name that clearly conveyed what the product could do for the consumer.

6.5.5   *Packaging*

For consumer goods, since packaging is one of the components of the Four Ps of marketing (Product, Price, Package, Promotion) and since in the beverage market in particular, where products are consumed quickly, the packaging of a product is compared with the packaging of other myriad products displayed on a shelf before buyers make snap decisions, packaging design is an extremely vital factor. The development of the package for "Karada Meguri Cha[TM]" concentrated on the reexamination of the shape of the bottle and on assuring novelty in its design.

6.5.6   *Observing fads by becoming a consumer*

In the course of developing the package, we carried out a first-person research to understand the tastes of the targeted advanced health-interest group by following their everyday activities. In the web-based consumer survey previously carried out, we identified health clusters and profiled the targets according to their age, taste in drinks, taste in foods, where they shop, and where they reside. With this data, we visited and browsed around places that the women of the group actually chose to visit, such as basement food sections of department stores, high-class supermarkets, exclusive department stores that had recently opened in Ginza at the time, and Northern European designer furniture shops that had opened in Roppongi.

Food shops located in the basement of department stores and high-class supermarkets attempt to offer added value for consumers by focusing on fresh and healthy foods, including local produce. Additionally, by making use of natural materials in the packaging itself and by incorporating naturalistic designs, these places were investing time and effort in offering a sense of quality and were changing not only the content but also the external appearance of their items. By adding a sense of freshness, health, and quality to the conventional value of deliciousness, they were, in effect, attempting to offer added value.

As a similar value-added strategy, there were the exclusive department stores and Northern European designer furniture stores. Clearly setting themselves apart from the usual all-around strategies, they were pursuing thorough quality, providing items that could not be found anywhere else, and pursuing functional beauty over general designs. In this way, they were boldly ignoring the mass market and were concentrating on targeting the high price range segment. What these two parties can be said to have in common is that they are both aligning themselves with the luxury orientation, work-pleasure balance orientation, and health orientation of progressive consumers of this age.

6.5.7 Collaboration with Sony Digital Design

As a result of having pursued the preferences of these targets, we decided to express discerning qualities in the design, instead of resorting to the usual PET bottle form factor and design. For the PET bottle, we decided to adopt a 410 ml screw-type bottle with an atypical form factor. This bottle was specially designed by thoroughly investigating the drinking habits of female RTD beverage consumers and taking into account such factors as their insights into beverages, average volume consumed, the form factor that takes the size of their hands into account for an easy grip, the storage capacity of their bags, and design. We raised the following elements as prerequisites for the development of the bottle; modern Chinese medicine (which is the product concept), modern health, sense of high quality, good sense, visibility at stores, soothing quality of a tea drink, and deliciousness.

As for the motifs, we modeled them after simple and functional designs that we found in places such as yoga studios, luxury spas and massage studios in addition to the basement shops of department stores and Northern European furniture stores that we visited in the course of our first-person research. Additionally, since this product was going to be clearly something different from the traditional tea product, we wished to implement a different grammar of design that avoided the usual motifs for tea products, such as "a vivid green color" and "design patterns showing water drops dripping down a tea leaf." Upon consulting a packaging design management company, they boldly referred us to Sony Digital Design, a company that was out of the field for this project.

This was to be their first development project for a beverage, and for Coca-Cola Japan, it was to be the first time to do business with the company. While we did have some reservations about request-ing a company whose expertise was in developing designs for such products as computers, TV sets, and cellular phones, we adopted the approach of "out-of-box thinking" and decided to take a bold gam-ble on Sony Digital Design. After briefing them, they took several months for the delivery of the first design proposal. Thereafter, we engaged in discussions with them many times before finally narrow-ing down the number of proposals to approximately twenty. As a result of carrying out quantitative package-screening research for the final three design proposals and further revising the findings of this research, we finally settled on the current package design that uses a white color base and is moderately inlaid with the images of Chinese medical ingredients contained in the product. The white color was bold for a tea product. This package design won an approval rating from general consumers that significantly exceeded in-house norms (reference values) and approval ratings for competing products in all the criterion categories we had aimed to satisfy, which were healthiness, shelf visibility, deliciousness, refinement, sense of high quality, and impression of the product being a Chinese remedy.

What is a good package?

People have asked me this question and my plain response is whatever that can generate huge sales. While it goes without saying that to survive a 3/1000th struggle for existence, the content (taste) is essential for assuring that consumers make repeat purchases. However, if they do not try out the product, or in other words, if they do not reach out and buy it at least once, then the product will never be able to reach a stage where repeats can become possible. In this sense, one interpretation of a good package is a package that can acquire trials.

In addition, I also consider a good package to be one that can be described simply. This is because a product will be made distinctive and easily recallable (or committed to memory) with a good package design. With such a design, you will be able to convey the product in descriptive terms such as, "it's this kind of color and shaped like that," when requesting someone else to shop for the product. For example, in the case of Karada Meguri ChaTM, it can be described as "that tea drink in a slim white bottle with the picture of leaves fluttering about in various ways," and in the case of a Fanta drink, it can be described as "that drink in a bumpy PET bottle with the swirls."

We would be very fortunate if people in general were to commit product names to memory at a single glance, but in a world overflowing with goods, the reality is not that simple. Since many people rely on their senses to commit things to memory, the originality of elements like the images and shapes of colors are extremely vital, and a package design that allows such features to be conveyed in a plain and simple way is what can be said to be "a good design." Incidentally, the package of Karada Meguri Cha^{TM} was designed with not only trial acquisitions in mind but also naturally with other considerations to assure repeat purchases as a favored item. Consequently, several points came up.

First of all, we deemed it important to have a design that would help the product stand out relative to other tea products displayed on shelves, while giving a well-balanced impression of being healthy for the modern consumer and being delicious in a natural way. Consequently, for the color design, we decided on using white (a color associated with "purity" from the chromatic standpoint) to help the product stand out from other products on shelves mostly filled with products prominently embellished with the green color of green tea. With regard to the graphics of the ingredients, we took into consideration a spacing scheme that would prevent any overshadowing of the white color. Additionally, to reflect a Northern European taste, we stuck to a natural tone for the logo and other places. Even though we intended to appeal at stores with a look that was different from the look of others, we wished the product to have a distinctive bearing that would allow for a firm feel when holding it in the hand and didn't become a hindrance when it was placed inside a bag or on top of a desk. In fact, we intended for people to feel comfortable with the design. Currently, we are hearing numerous high praises from mainly women for the package design. We are also hearing that they have become repeat customers.

The fact that the compliments are coming mainly from women is good news because they are known to be sensitive to design features. As the manager in charge of packaging, I couldn't be more grateful.

Hirooki Kobayashi
Senior Manager of the Design Management Section of the Brand Marketing Department of Coca Cola Japan Company

6.5.8   *Final bundle research*

A market-viable beverage formula was completed at the same time the naming and packaging developments were finished. Now all the constituents needed to create the product were present. We then had these constituents assembled at the factory line to form a prototype that came close to a marketable model and carried out a simulation research known as the final bundle survey to gauge the level of general consumer receptivity for the product. While I cannot write about the design of the survey in detail since it is the final in-house hurdle to be cleared prior to market release, to put it plainly, it is a survey that allows us to quantitatively see to what extent a product may be bought and what level of impact a product may have upon its release. The scores yielded by the survey are statistically compared against Coca Cola Japan's previous data and are thoroughly analyzed according to attributes and beverage categories. Depending on the type of results obtained, product launches can be postponed or even revoked, making the survey a terrifying ordeal for the product developer. The results of the survey were submitted from the Business Knowledge department in December 2005. As it turned out, compared to all the results of bundle surveys carried out in 2005, our scores ranked in the top class.

Of particular interest were the forecasted change in market share (Source of volume: SOV) and the level of impact to other products of the company upon the release of the Karada Meguri Cha^{TM}. Based on these survey results, we moved on from the product development stage to the selling stage where we began preparing communication and sales strategies geared towards the market launch.

6.6   Information Transmission of "Karada Meguri Cha^{TM}"

6.6.1   *Basic strategy*

In the case of a mass-market product, to let consumers know about its existence quickly, it is necessary to carry out proactive communication. Due to the progress of the Internet and mobile phones, the consumer's contact with media has been changing. For this reason, the communication for Karada Meguri Cha^{TM} was focused on a cross-marketing plan that incorporated both conventional and modern approaches. The representative cases of the conventional consumer-oriented communication approach include TV, train station, magazine and web ads, product exposure at stores, and PR. In addition to these approaches, we considered modern communication approaches such as Internet discussion boards, blogs run by individuals, and experience-based promotions such as sampling to be vital, so we proactively deployed them. Sampling in particular is an important opportunity for people to come into contact with the product and since it offers a three-dimensional form of product information, which is essential to a drinking experience, it becomes possible to motivate the sampler to willingly transmit information. These approaches form the basis of buzz marketing (word-of-mouth marketing) and facilitate the drastic spread of information and impressions across the Internet and into the consumer's everyday world.

The cross-marketing plan for Karada Meguri Cha^{TM} aimed to optimize its effect by arranging complex combinations of media that served as points of contact with consumers. At this point, I would like to discuss the fusion between mass marketing and buzz marketing.

6.6.2 *Fusion between mass marketing and buzz marketing*

The challenge of communication is to make the consumer interested in a product, and have them feel that it is necessary to have it, and consequently, have them take action to purchase it. Toward this end, how you link a communication campaign, which makes use of a variety of media, to buying behaviors will prove to be crucial. The most important thing about the purchase motive of Karada Meguri Cha™ is to create a structure that promotes the following lines of thought: consumers see how the product's benefit of "improving circulation" is necessary; consumers become generally aware of the necessity of detoxification and that they have harmful elements stored in their bodies. As a result of promoting these lines of thought, they will sympathize with the product concept and reach for the product to solve the problems posed by the concept.

Karada Meguri Cha™ was developed with the aim of mainly targeting the advanced health interest group and the women's sugar-free tea user group. However, the key difference between these two groups lies in whether the necessity of having a good circulation is understood or not by just listening to the word "meguri" (circulation). To respond to the difference in the level of such understanding between these two clusters, we varied our communication campaigns in terms of message, media, and approach according to whether we were communicating to the advanced health-interest group or to the women's non-sugar tea user group.

Firstly, for the advanced health-interest group, we aimed to promote understanding for the product by having them share among each other the challenges of "meguri" or maintaining a good circulatory system by having them try out the product prior to its launch. Toward this end, we carried out sampling sessions and released product information prior to the launch of the product at places where these women enjoyed visiting, such as yoga studios, ganbanyoku (hot-stone spas), germanium hot baths, and foot massage parlors. In addition, we promoted understanding of the word "meguri" itself by running articles that plainly explained health approaches to improving circulation in magazines favored by the targets. For the sugar-free tea users, we attached great importance to topicality and ran the sensational campaign copy "Ryoko Hirosue begins Plan Purify" in television commercials, in newspapers, at train stations, in store POP (point of purchase) ads and aimed to garner more attention. In addition, for the mass consumers including men, we conveyed the product to newspaper and magazine reporters as a business interest story, which involved the collaboration of the three companies, Coca Cola Japan, Nihondo, and Sony Digital Design.

Next, we carried out on-site samplings immediately after the launch of the product. With the aim to convey the product features, the sampling involved having people experience the product at a symbolic site where circulation tended to become bad. The site chosen for this purpose was inside an airplane in mid-flight on a long-distance route, where anyone can easily understand how circulation can deteriorate, since you have to remain seated for a large duration of the flight. The deterioration in circulation arising from such a situation is highly recognized as the economy-class syndrome. Since Coca Cola Japan had been enjoying a business relationship with Japan Airlines for a long time, the company permitted in-flight samplings in all domestic flights for a period of one week. In addition, we provided information on products and carried out samplings for 2,500 flight attendants of Japan Airlines at Haneda airport who were going to serve drinks. Consequently, we were able to deepen their understanding of our product before they served it.

Additionally, in addition to fitness clubs, ganbanyoku (hot-stone spas), foot massage parlors, and hair salons, which are representative places where people go to improve their circulatory system, we carried out samplings practically everywhere we could, including advertising agencies, think tanks, research institutes, trading companies, magazine firms, media companies, and news agencies, which were all places that we had regular dealings with and that we believed to be

workplaces that were not conducive to promoting a healthy circulatory system. Furthermore, each team member's friends and acquaintances were also given the opportunity to sample our product.

The synergy effect of these simultaneous and omnidirectional
advertising and PR sampling campaigns was great, and several hundreds of articles and photographs of the product attained exposure in
all kinds of magazines and newspapers. In addition, on the morning
of May 24, information on Karada Meguri Cha™ was released all at
once through informational TV programs, nationwide newspapers,
and sports papers. At noon of the same day, the information was
exposed as news on the top page of Yahoo! with the sensational catch
copy, "Ryoko Hirosue lends a helping hand." This news then went on
to register as the No. 1 article to be accessed in Yahoo!'s entertainment
section for the same day. At the same time of the Yahoo! exposure,
access to the official website of Karada Meguri Cha™ saw a rapid rise
that it became impossible for even myself to access the site and I was
the administrator of the site. To stoke the fires of this momentum, a
large volume of television commercials, magazine ads, magazine articles, large-scale poster ads at major train stations, street ads, and store
POP (point of purchase) ads were deployed all at once and written
comments on Karada Meguri Cha™ began to increase rapidly at
various blogs, Internet discussion boards, and various websites oriented towards women. In effect, the buzz (word of mouth) on the
product was breaking out from many places.

Even at the time of this writing in July 2006, the buzz continues to spread in various contexts such as product fields, convenience
stores, commercials, celebrity culture, health and Chinese medicine-
related fields, and is believed to be having a considerable influence
in improving product recognition levels. In addition to these various promotional activities, the various market development measures
that were jointly developed with the sales department are contributing to the smooth change in sales, distribution, and market share at
present.

6.7   Conclusion

I believe the most important aspects of searching for information in the course of developing a new product are the spirit of inquiry and footwork.

Approximately 11 years have passed since I began my career at P&G and went on to undertake product development at Coca Cola Japan. Over the course of this time, I have come into contact with all sorts of planners including those belonging to competing firms and I can safely say that a good planner is someone who invests a good amount of time in making advance preparations. Compared to the cost incurred for withdrawing a product from the market because it failed to sell as expected due to a lack of preparation before its release, the cost incurred for investing a lavish amount of time and money for the development of a product prior to its release is overwhelmingly cheaper. This is particularly true in the case of the consumer goods industry where the cost for television commercials is great, requiring several billions of yen to be invested.

Therefore, when developing a new product, I believe you should invest your time, resources, and passion during the planning stage. Also, when developing a new product, I believe you can never go overboard in searching for or verifying information. In addition, since many executives in the marketing industry have graduated from the same types of schools, received the same types of education, and have landed similar kinds of jobs, the possibility that their strategies will necessarily overlap is high. Therefore, I believe that the leaders of the market are the people and companies who understand that they can obtain the fast-mover advantage by being half a step ahead of consumers to be able to quickly formulate distinctive strategies. In effect, the key to their leadership lies in their uniqueness and agility.

Hideto Maeda

Acknowledgments

The success of Karada Meguri Cha^{TM} came about as a result of not only the product development strategy, but also a combination of other strategies, including a detailed communication strategy, PR strategy, market development strategy, and store development strategy. However, since the theme of this book leans towards information search, accounts of those other strategies have been omitted. During the development of the product, I had countless debates with good partners without whom the project would not have succeeded. Below, I would like to introduce the passionate staff members who were involved in a host of activities ranging from concept development to branding. To them, I owe my gratitude.

Coca-Cola Japan Company, Limited
    Innovation
        Atsushi Saito
        Keiichi Shimizu
        Akiko Usui
    Brand Marketing
        Koji Shinohara
        Hirooki Kobayashi
        Shu Imanishi
        Nagi Furukawa
        Akie Horiai
    Business Knowledge
        Shigekazu Sugiyama
        Masayuki Sato
        Hiroaki Suemasa
    Retail Marketing
        Kingo Yamakoshi
        Shigeyoshi Fukuda
        Naoki Takagi
    Scientific Regulatory Affairs
        Keiko Hinamoto

Legal
  Masaru Adachi
  Ayako Handa
Strategic Procurement
  Takehiro Kojima
Corporate Branding & Communication
  Kanako Kumazaki
  Maki Morino

Coca-Cola Tokyo Research & Development Co., Ltd
  Keiichi Ono
  Hiroshi Asahi

Dentsu Inc.
  Kunihiko Kitahara
  Akira Kagami
  Hirotaka Komiya
  Kaoru Ozawa
  Tetsuya Tsukamoto
  Hiroko Kunimasa
  Kota Touhata

Nihondo Co., Ltd.
  Yohei Suzuki
  Takeaki Nishikubo
  Masae Kawabata

Sony Digital Design K.K.
  Toru Ichikawa
  Kouki Yamaguchi
  Takeshi Ichimura
  Chiayao Lin
  Chiya Watanabe

Development of the "Oshiete! Kaden" ("Tell Me! Consumer Electronics") Website — Recommending Merchandises Through the Deployment of a Web Recommendation Engine

With the emergence of the Internet, the ways of searching for information for the purpose of developing new businesses has changed dramatically. To launch the product recommendation website, "Oshiete! Kaden," within a span of several months, it was essential to engage in the gathering of timely information, the sharing of information, and the management of information. I will give a brief description of the Web recommendation engine, "Bull's eye," and "Oshiete! Kaden" and then move on to present concrete case studies to comment on information search methods implemented in all the stages, ranging from the stage of conceiving the idea for a business development to the stage of website development and initial operation.

7.1 Web Recommendation Engine

7.1.1 *What is a recommendation?*

An Internet business that specializes in customizing the selection and display of information according to what may appear to be interesting to an individual customer is generally designated as a recommendation service. If your website were to know what items or services its visiting customers were looking for or what their preferences were, you will certainly be able to realize an ultimate form of one-to-one marketing.

For the customer, if a website only displays information that interests them, there will be the merit of being able to save time, as it will become unnecessary for them to select their required information from vast amounts of data. For the business offering the website, on the other hand, there will be the merit of being able to expect an increase in sales by being able to acquire new customers at low cost, prevent the loss of existing customers, and improve purchasing frequency and amount. Additionally, the business can also expect to acquire customer satisfaction through the delivery of appropriate information. Web recommendation is indeed a key technology that assumes the role of true Customer Relationship Management (CRM).

7.1.2 *The history of recommendation*

From the latter half of the 1990s to the beginning of the 2000s, the recommendation engine began to heat up. Net Perceptions Japan, a Japanese subsidiary of the US Net Perceptions,[21] released in December 1999 a software that could refer to the personal purchase history of customers to automatically select the products they are likely to buy next and propose those products to them. The software went on to be adopted by Amazon[2] and later by Nissen Online[20] as well.

In August 1998, Thomas Foley, a US software engineer, and Junko Nishimura, an entrepreneur, established the company, Silver Egg Technology,[16] and in the autumn of 2000, this company released "Aigent," a service based on "deep knowledge" technology. Specifically, Aigent uses artificial intelligence technology to analyze on-site buying and browsing patterns of individual customers and display the most suitable products for them.

Soon after, the recommendation market cooled down temporarily, but this was not because of any problem with the technology.

Rather, it was mainly due to the fact that the cost effectiveness of introducing the relatively expensive recommendation engine was not clear and the fact that the network infrastructure and Web technology were still in their formative stages, making it difficult for the engine to sufficiently function.

With the arrival of Web 2.0, the cost of servers declined drastically while their performance rose dramatically and affiliate networks and the drop shipping system began to appear on the scene. Consequently, the environment for the recommendation engine began to see a remarkable change. Amid the rise of various portal sites and comparison sites such as "Kakaku.com"[10] (Price.com), anticipation for the recommendation engine to provide a competitive means of differentiation has become substantial. It is expected that there will be a rise in the number of companies, such as "Kenko.com,"[14] that will install their own recommendation engine, and companies, such as "Yamada Denki Web.Com,"[27] that will install external systems such as Bull's eye through ASP.

7.1.3   *Types of recommendation engines*

There are several ways to classify recommendation engines. Here, I will basically explain the kinds of data used for the purpose of making recommendations. Following are some examples of such data:

1) Attribute data acquired from customers
2) Data of preferences acquired from customers
3) Customer purchase history data
4) Customer web browsing data (Web log data)
5) Product specification data
6) Product sales data (POS data, etc.).

One way of implementing the first type of data above is to acquire data on the gender and age of customers at the time of their registration or enrollment and recommending products based on predetermined age and gender-specific rules when those customers visit the site again. For example, if the customer is a man who is forty years old, then the recommendation could be a golf club. The most basic method of this kind is known as "questionnaire-based filtering." The second method is one form of the questionnaire-based filtering technique, as it requires visitors to declare their preferences before the website offers product recommendations related to those preferences. The preferences are indicated through multiple answer questionnaires, often times revealing personal interests and hobbies. While the recommendation algorithms for these methods are simple, prior registration is necessary so recommendations cannot be made for first-time visitors. Additionally, there is the problem that these methods are too standardized, making them capable of offering recommendations of commonplace items only.

The third method of implementing customer purchase history data is called "rule-based filtering," since it involves making product recommendations by following a predetermined rule that follows the following line of thought; people purchasing product A are highly likely to purchase product B. This is the so-called basket analysis, which is based on the "if-then" line of thinking that is evident in such cases as recommending diapers to people who buy beer. What sets this method apart from the questionnaire-based filtering method is that visitor attributes and preferences are not linked to recommended products, but instead rules are set once product to product relevancies are established based on multivariate analysis and data mining approaches.

The method known as collaborative filtering, which is famous for being the method adopted by Amazon,[2] employs data of purchase histories of customers in the way method No. 3 does, but the analytical algorithm is different. In making product recommendations, this method does not observe the rule of assuming that people who buy product A will also buy product B. Instead, this method makes product recommendations on the basis of assuming that people who buy similar items are similar themselves and therefore the items bought by similar people will be bought in similar ways by other similar people. In other words, this method is based on making assumptions that are rooted in affinity-based reasoning.

7.1.4   *The web recommendation engine "Bull's Eye"*

Bull's eye (Figure 7-1) was developed by Albert Inc.[3] and the data it employs are the No. 2 and No. 5 ones mentioned in Section 7.1.3. However, what is distinctive about this engine is that it does not acquire customer preference data in advance, but instead acquires such data in real time when it makes recommendations. Therefore, it can also recommend products to people who visit a website for the first time. Since rule-based and collaborative filtering techniques select products on the basis of making statistical, probabilistic inferences, the recommended products may not always be the products actually sought out by customers. However, Bull's eye is capable of recommending items that customers definitely want since it directly inquires them about the level of importance they attach to sought-out features and characteristics.

At the heart of this approach is the fact that consumer selections are determined through overall evaluations. Individual differences between evaluations are the individual differences in the level of importance attached to product attributes and in the individual evaluations for standards. The system is fundamentally based on the concept that consumers will choose to purchase from a multiple number of choices those items they evaluate the most highly. In effect, the system possesses detailed data of specifications of all potentially

Figure 7-1:   Recommendation Engine "Bull's Eye"

recommendable products, and based on the narrowing down of choices by customers and their declarations of how important certain product attributes are to them, it becomes possible for the system to faithfully make recommendations of products that are closest to the ones that customers seek. Furthermore, there is the merit that the system will be able to offer precise recommendations of even completely new products, since it does not employ data pertaining to personal purchase records.

7.2   Product Recommendation Website "Oshiete! Kaden"

7.2.1   *What is "Oshiete! Kaden"?*

In this present age that has seen the advent of the networked society, consumer behavior patterns are changing from AIDMA, to AISAS® (Figure 7-2). AIDMA was proposed by Roland Hall and is an acronym for Attention→Interest→Desire→Memory→Action (purchase). It is also considered to be a process of reacting to communication. AISAS®, on the other hand, is an acronym for Attention→Interest→Search→Action→Share, indicating that a change is taking place in the process after the stage when a consumer gains interest. (AISAS® is a registered trademark of Dentsu Inc.) In these present times, for the purpose of attracting attention, Internet banner and text ads have become as viable as radio, TV, newspaper, and magazine ads and selling through the Internet is becoming

Attention	Attention
Interest	Interest
Desire ⟶	Search
Memory	Action
Action	Share

Figure 7-2:   From AIDMA to AISAS®

more commonplace. Amid such an environment, consumers are increasingly making use of search engines, such as Google[12] and Yahoo[24], and of comparison sites, such as Kakaku.com[10], to research about products that interest them immediately prior to making purchases. In other words, for a consumer searching with interest, the Internet has made it possible for them to make speedy purchases.

Furthermore, after purchase, an unprecedented pattern has been added. Namely, this involves making use of online bulletin boards, blogs, and Social Networking Services (SNS) to share information on what had been purchased or consumed. Thanks to this new pattern, it has become possible for consumers at the search stage to receive opinions expressed by people who had already made purchases. In fact, it has become possible for many people to make decisions on the basis of what has been written on comparison and community sites.

However, with regard to consumer electronics products, whose product specs are becoming more complex and whose variations continue to increase, the amount of information available is too vast, and for individuals of the follower group, who do not understand the specs necessary for conducting effective searches to narrow down their choices, the task of choosing the right product is certainly confusing for the most part.

In addition to helping customers make product selections, "Oshiete! Kaden" is a website that offers solutions for all sorts of concerns and troubles that may arise from the time after a purchase is made to the time of making replacements (Figure 7-3). As for providing product-selection support, the website offers the following three recommendation features, while also offering search features, various information services, and support for repair and throwaway replacements.

Figure 7-3: The Front Page of "Oshiete! Kaden"

7.2.2 *Three recommendation features*

1) *Recommendation by Bull's eye*

The recommendation engine, "Bull's eye," is a system that can make real-time recommendations of products and services that perfectly meet various user needs. Many product recommendations can be found not only on the Internet, but also in the analog world of newspapers, magazines, and word-of-mouth. However, not many of them have structures that make it possible to offer recommendations of products from a neutral standpoint and in a quantitative manner so as to be able to offer products that truly meet personal needs.

Regarding the products customers want, Bull's eye inquires them about what they deem to be necessary features and characteristics and what level of importance they attach to them. In other words, Bull's eye acquires the previously discussed individual evaluations that weigh the importance of product attributes and standards. The weighing is realized through the use of a slider interface that allows a visitor to indicate their answers to simple questions on an impulsive level (Figure 7-4). In so doing, it becomes possible for the system to search for products that are considered to be optimal for the visitor. Consequently, the system displays these products in the order of how well they match the features requested by the visitor (Figure 7-5). Additionally, with regard to difficult questions and specifications, the system is designed to provide easy-to-understand

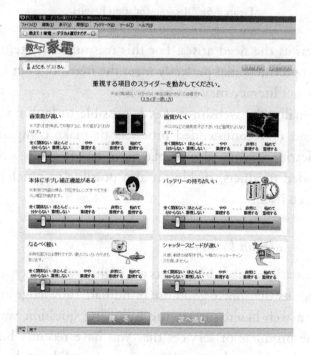

Figure 7-4:   Inputting Assessments of Importance with a Slider Interface

Figure 7-5:   Recommendation Results

explanations as the need arises. For this reason, the system will be able to find products that perfectly meet the needs of even followers whose product literacy may not be high.

Additionally, the website makes it possible to look up detailed specifications of recommended products or make comparisons of the specifications, while also displaying a list of stores selling the recommended products, making it also possible to purchase them from the web itself.

2)   *Recommendation by experts*

Recommendations made by experts are highly valuable types of recommendations that make good use of human knowledge and experience. In a web-based survey, the following question was asked: Among the products or services that you have recently bought or are planning to buy, what products or services did you have or are having much trouble in choosing, if any? Include up to three items in your response. The top three responses were as follows: No. 1 was the PC, No. 2 was the digital camera, and No. 3 was the DVD recorder. Upon asking about how they went about resolving their concerns and making final decisions, the No. 1 response was "consulting with a shop assistant," and the No. 2 response was, "consulting with friends or acquaintances." In other words, it came to light that many consumers were resolving their issues or their indecision by consulting with shop assistants or friends or acquaintances rather than by making use of company websites and search engines.

In response to these findings, Oshiete! Kaden created the system, "Ask the shop assistant," which made it possible to directly pose questions to experts through the web (Figure 7-6). These experts included actual staff members of consumer electronics mass retailers and repair and installation agents. In effect, the website made it

Figure 7-6:   Screenshot of a Page Where Questions to Shop Assistants are Asked

possible to resolve concerns over matters of consumer electronics by transcending temporal and spatial constraints. The questions asked to the shop assistants through this system were not only regarding product recommendations, but also regarding usage and support for times when products malfunctioned, and the assistants are providing sound and honest answers.

Furthermore, the questions and answers are displayed at the top of the web page to allow anyone to read them freely and the page is set up to update in a timely fashion to show new posts of questions and answers (Figure 7-7).

3) *Recommendations by general users*

Thanks to the growing rate of Internet access around the world, the practice of consumers transmitting information through blogs and social networking services has become commonplace. Media known as Consumer Generated Media (CGM) are media from which

Figure 7-7:   Screenshot of a Page Showing Responses from Shop Assistants

individuals or consumers transmit information and they can only be realized on the Internet. While there have been several other forms of media to date such as the telephone and the fax machine, until the emergence of the Internet, it has never been possible for an individual to transmit information at a global level. This information can be easily read by anyone and can also be stored, searched, and analyzed. Such information are also a source for making recommendations, and the company, "ALBERT,"[3] has developed the social networking service titled "Oshiete Na" ("Oh tell me, won't you?"),[9] which connects consumers with each other according to their mutual interests in products and introduces a structure that allows people who are interested in certain products to hear the opinions of others who already own them (Figure 7-8). Additionally, they have also introduced contents such as photo galleries and product reviews that make it possible for users to easily and enjoyably share useful information (Figures 7-9 to 7-11).

Figure 7-8:   Front Page of Oshiete Na[9] SNS

Figure 7-9:   Product Detail Page

Figure 7-10:   Comments on Products

Figure 7-11:   Writings Posted on a Bulletin Board

7.2.3   *Search by specification and keywords*

Oshiete! Kaden has spec-search features for users with a relatively high level of product literacy. It allows users to read through a list of product choices and narrow them down through specifying their preferred specs, such as preferred maker, model number, characteristics, and features (Figure 7-12). In addition, since it is also possible to search the "ask the shop assistant" pages, the photo galleries, and product specification pages by keywords, a user can effectively obtain various information regarding specific products and features (Figure 7-13).

7.2.4   *Offering useful information*

Oshiete! Kaden transmits valuable information that cannot be obtained anywhere else. Specifically, the website periodically runs columns by well-known experts titled, "Consumer Electronic Products That Can Enrich Your Life" and "Consumer Electronic Products That Offer Value" (Figures 7-14 and 7-15). In addition, the site also

Figure 7-12:   Specifications Search

Figure 7-13:   Keyword Search Results

Figure 7-14:   The Consumer Electronics Blog for Richer Living

Figure 7-15:   The Beneficial Consumer Electronics Blog

updates trivia from shop assistants and seller rankings in a timely fashion to support making product selections in a topical way.

7.3   The Role of Information Search in the Business Development of "Oshiete! Kaden"

7.3.1   *The back story that led to business development*

For businesses, it is no exaggeration to say that a highly accurate forecast of consumption behaviors is the ultimate sales promotional strategy. For the general consumer, selecting just the information that truly suits them from vast amounts of information made available through the power of the Internet — a medium that enables anyone to easily and instantly access information found all over the world — is a Herculean task. Meanwhile, for businesses, due to the diversification of user needs, it has become extremely difficult to accurately grasp what consumers desire to have and how much they are willing to pay for them.

For this reason, companies have introduced the method know as Customer Relationship Management (CRM) and are attempting to implement a full-fledged one-to-one marketing approach. CRM is said to be one of the business strategies available for maintaining favorable relationships with customers, while also being one of the necessary approaches available for businesses to communicate with customers to promote their repeat purchases of products and services. Additionally, it is also considered to be a marketing technique for finding out about customer attributes, tastes, and consumption trends for the purpose of recommending products and services that meet their individual needs.

The act of offering the most suitable products through gaining detailed knowledge about individual customers probably was practiced since the Kyoho period of the Edo era, when the retailing industry of Japan became established in its prototypical form. What is the difference then between CRM and the strategy of the neighborhood grocery, which has been in existence since the Edo era?

The greatest difference is that one has the powers of IT and the database on tap, while the other does not. A grocer who is good at their trade would communicate with their customers and find out information on such matters as what they have bought the previous day, what they have cooked, what their family make-up is like, and whether their grandmother is currently visiting from the countryside. Based on such information, they would make recommendations for particular vegetables for the day. These days, consumer electronics stores located in towns have considerably dwindled in number. They know such matters as when it is about time to replace a TV set at which household, or even when it is time to replace the batteries of a wall clock.

However, regrettably, their knowledge of such matters is limited to their own surrounding areas, making it impossible for them to grasp the situation of several thousands or even tens of thousands of customers for the purpose of servicing them. During the Edo era when IT was nonexistent, detailed records of transactions were kept in an old-fashioned account book called "daifukucho," which was for all matters and purposes the database of the times. Storeowners used to enter into this account book all types of information, including information on customers, products, deposits and withdrawals, and it was indispensable for realizing an efficient business operation. What IT, data mining, and database marketing have made possible is not the capability of grasping a massive number of customers in aggregates as clusters, but instead it has, in effect, realized a modern version of the "daifukucho" system, which allows us to grasp customers as individuals. In fact, this is the essence of CRM.

To understand customer consumption patterns, you can refer to such data as sales data derived from point of sales systems (POS), personal histories of web-access patterns, and data on what materials were requested prior to making purchases. Consequently, many companies often carry out data mining approaches that analyze these sets of data and draw out certain principles that help them to predict consumption patterns in advance. The fact that the pattern of "people buying beer and diapers at the same time" was extracted as a rule is a famous case in point. However, it is extremely difficult to predict future consumption behaviors by examining just buying patterns, which are information of outcomes. We must instead begin by examining the determinants of consumption behaviors. In a cause and effect chain of events, if a consumption behavior is the effect, then the cause of this effect can be described as one of the following three factors:

1) Psychological,
2) Demographical, and
3) Informational.

The psychological factor refers to the values and lifestyle peculiar to an individual and has a strong relationship with consumption behaviors. Furthermore, values and lifestyle are influenced by personality and ability, which are in turn influenced by temperament. Consumption behaviors, in addition to these psychological factors, are determined by demographical factors such as gender, age, occupation, and domicile, and furthermore, by external factors such as contact media, friends, acquaintances, storefront information, and advice from shop assistants.

To predict future consumption behavior in a more detailed manner, it is advisable to carry out data mining for not only the data of outcomes such as the data pertaining to completed purchases, but also for the data pertaining to causes.

However, from the viewpoint of protecting personal data, acquiring data on psychological and demographical factors becomes very difficult, requiring some new thinking. With recommendation engines that only use data of outcomes such as data derived from

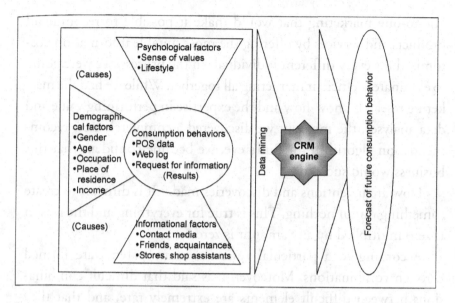

Figure 7-16:   Consumption Behavior Forecasting Model

collaborative filtering, algorithms that predict consumption patterns are also frequently used (Figure 7-16).

Amid such a context, the "Teiin-san.com" (Shop assistant.com) was truly a project that started with the idea of building a site that can offer personable services, just like local, neighborhood consumer electronics stores. (At the time of initial development, "Oshiete! Kaden" was called "Teiinsan.com".)

When a customer visits a website, if the site knows well about the visitor and understands the preferences of the person without inquiring about them, and is able to offer relevant information and products, just as a shop assistant might of a store they often visit, then there is nothing more efficient for the company or for the consumer for that matter.

We resolved to launch this project with a strong and passionate determination to pursue a large dream of revolutionizing marketing in Japan. Toward this end, we aimed to realize an ultimate form of one-to-one marketing that would make it possible to recommend products and services by offering the most suitable information customized for every different individual. In the process, we were going to eliminate inefficient marketing all together. While we had the marketing research know-how and the expertise in performing value and data analyses, the moment we discovered a completely new recommendation algorithm for Bull's eye, we became confident that this business would succeed.

How are inventions and discoveries made? It is difficult to create something out of nothing. This is true for everything and the reason is zero multiplied by any amount is zero.

According to a particular research, many patents are formed through combinations. Moreover, it is said that difficult combinations between difficult elements are extremely rare, and that they instead tend to be difficult combinations between simple elements, and simple combinations between difficult elements. The pencil equipped with an eraser is a simple combination between simple elements, so it can be considered to be an idea, but it will not stand as an invention or be worthy of a patent. The recommendation algorithm discussed here is something that occurred to me when I was having a chat in a veranda with a certain person. This person had served as a consultant for a certain EC site and was talking about how he had failed in an attempt to select products from a choice of tens of thousands of other products by implementing a certain method. When he told me why he had failed, I remembered the cluster analysis method, which is a multivariate analytical technique, and became convinced that it was possible to develop an optimal recommendation engine through combining the two methods. I then went on to immediately create a product database in Excel, and made full use of sorting and filtering features to develop the prototype of the recommendation engine. Even though it was an engine that I had created, I was unable to foresee how it would turn out, and when I eventually ended up with a product that made me say, "Oh yes, this is it!," I was moved.

So regarding the start of Bull's eye, I can say that it all began with the small talk I had at the veranda. There are times when breakthrough inventions and discoveries result from person-to-person communication, and even if we are living in the age of the Internet, the sharing of information through personal, face to face exchanges is very important.

7.3.2   *Business development and information search*

The speed of business development is evolving dramatically due to the emergence of the Internet. Even when looking at the time it takes for a company to make a public offering of stocks, up to now a period of 10 to 20 years was considered to be quick and it was said that it would usually take three generations. However, since the 1990s, venture corporations achieving a listing within a span of only several years has been on the rise. With the progress of IT, the performance of servers and PCs improved rapidly and the cost declined substantially in parallel. The development of Internet-based businesses is moving away from the model of borrowing large sums of money from the bank and purchasing land to build a factory to install a production capacity to a model where a small capital investment is made to prepare an IT infrastructure that a talented engineer takes advantage of to promote the business at an extremely fast pace.

Amid such circumstances, information search media and tools revolving around the Internet are evolving to a great extent. Groupware such as "Cybozu" are used for purposes of facilitating management, various application filings, and making settlements (Figure 7-17). In addition to these features, groupware such as Cybozu have many products equipped with features such as schedule management and project management. In addition, email is ordinarily used as a means to transmit information. Compared to the telephone and making a visit, the email has extremely substantial

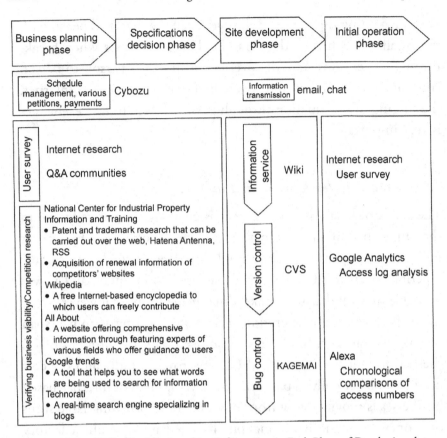

Figure 7-17:　Media Used for Searching Information in Each Phase of Developing the Business of "Oshiete! Kaden"

merits, such as being able to have the receiver receive your message at a convenient time for them, being able to share information among many people at once, being able to attach documents, and being able to leave behind a record. However, the tone of an email message can sound blunt and devoid of any feeling and therefore become a source of hurt feelings. For this reason, it is important to try to communicate at a genuine level.

In addition, when you do not wish to hold a conference in particular, but instead wish to carry out a discussion within a relatively short span of time, chat software such as Skype[17] and Yahoo! Chat[26] are often used. While they are useful for exchanging highly confidential personnel and financial information, there are instances when the intent is not communicated well as in the case of email. So for complex issues, I recommend that you change the venue and hold face-to-face discussions.

Business development steps can be largely classified into the following three categories; the business plan and spec determination phase (Plan), the development phase (Do), and the initial operation phase (See). I have summarized below a number of new information search media and tools for information sharing according to each phase.

7.3.3 *The phase of determining the business plan and specifications*

When starting a new business development, you must first of all verify the validity of the business. Even if you are confident that it will succeed, there are a large number of matters you will need to investigate. For instance, you will need to know if user needs really exist, what its strengths and weaknesses are, what its competitive situation is like, and whether it is a business that can develop in the middle to long-term period.

1) *Patent search*

Toward developing the recommendation engine, Bull's eye, it was first of all necessary to study existing technologies and the developments made by competitors, so we used search engines to collect all kinds of data on corporate websites, press releases, and announcement materials of academic societies and went on to analyze them.

In addition, with regard to information on patents, we were able to very easily search for them over the Internet. At the website of the National Center for Industrial Property Information and Training[15], if you conduct searches by entering keywords or the names of inventors, you will be able to browse all types of materials, such as patent advertisements and related PR materials. When developing a new core technology, it is necessary to carefully carry out patent searches and if you discover any patents that may conflict, you need to consult with a patent attorney and deal with the matter immediately. In addition, you should file a patent application at an early stage for any new technology developed by your own company. (The application for the patent of Bull's eye has already been filed.)

2) *Internet research*

In business development, financing is necessary. To receive financing, you need to create a business plan first of all and then give a presentation to an underwriter. Specifically, you need to clarify business goals, the details of the business, sales and earnings targets, the particulars of the service to be offered and the differentiation from and superiority to existing services and further perform a market analysis that covers market trends and the competitive situation. On that account, sufficient prior research is necessary.

For the user survey required in developing the business of Oshiete! Kaden, we mainly carried out our research over the Internet. Up to then, face-to-face interviews, mail surveys, and telephone surveys were actively used. However, since the emergence of the Internet, the shift toward Internet research has rapidly advanced, thanks to the fact that it is cheaper and less time-consuming. It is no exaggeration to say that there are no businesses now that ignore the Internet for the purpose of carrying out market research. For Internet businesses in particular, surveys are carried out for Internet users, so the targets naturally coincide, and for this reason, it can be said that it is the most efficient solution.

In carrying out a marketing research program, the most crucial element is framing a hypothesis and verifying it. In addition, it is absolutely necessary to tie the results of a research to an action.

Without a hypothesis, you will not be able to design the survey nor the questions. The questionnaire should be thought of as something that cannot yield anything beyond what is asked, and that 80% of its success is determined by the design of the questions themselves. It just goes to show how important and highly difficult it is to have the expertise to be able to construct a good hypothesis and reflect it in the questions. In addition, if the results turn out to be unexpected, there are times when researchers simply ignore them, but as long as the survey is being commissioned to help make decisions, you must investigate the cause of even such results and rebuild your hypothesis and tie them to some kind of action.

For this business development, we came up with the following hypotheses:

1) In the course of selecting products and services, consumers become troubled and hesitant.
2) To resolve their concerns, many of them seek advice from shop assistants.
3) Only people with in-depth knowledge of products make use of price comparison websites.

In addition, we examined the following issues:

1) When consumers purchase products or services, which ones make them troubled or hesitant?
2) What kinds of information do consumers require? What criteria do they use when deciding to make a purchase?
3) Specifically, what types of questions do they ask shop assistants?

To find answers to these questions, we carried out Internet surveys several times. The survey sample was comprised of the members of Scope Net,[18] which is operated by Interscope.[4]

In the survey, we asked, "Among the products or services you have bought or are planning to buy, if there were or are any that you experienced difficulty in deciding to purchase, then please tell us what they were or are. Reply up to three items." We analyzed the responses through text-mining analysis and found that that the overall top three products were the PC, digital camera, and the DVD recorder, or in other words, they were the so-called brown products of consumer electronics (Figure 7-18). Since the progress of the technology of PCs and digital cameras is quick, and since new features continue to be added one after another, it is extremely difficult to decide which products to choose among the many found at stores, making such products typically difficult for consumers to choose. When examining by gender-specific preferences, in the case of women, such items as insurance, trips, country inns, hotels, and cellular phones ranked higher than DVD recorders.

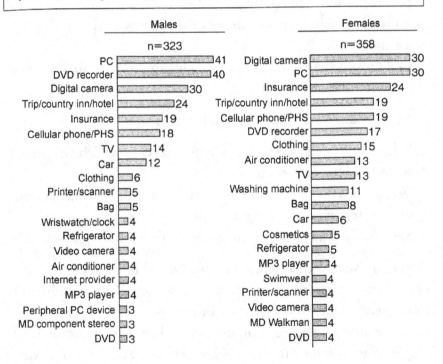

Figure 7-18:   Products Consumers Hesitate to Buy When They are About to Buy Them

In addition, we found out that 89% of the subjects had made inquiries at the time of purchasing a PC, television set, or an audio product, while 50% of them hesitated at the time of purchase. Based upon the foregoing, we realized that when consumers purchase brown-goods consumer electronics such as the PC or the digital camera, half of them were having trouble deciding and that specifically they were having trouble deciding in the following order of items: PC, digital camera, DVD recorder, cellular phone, and television.

Next, we inquired what they did to resolve their issues whenever they were troubled or at a loss. The results overwhelmingly showed that many people consulted shop assistants (Figure 7-19). This was followed by making inquiries to friends and acquaintances,

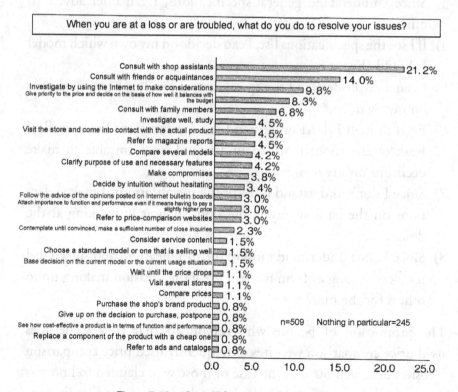

Figure 7-19:   Steps Taken to Resolve Concerns

researching over the Internet, and carrying out searches. While there were many people who used the Internet to resolve their questions and concerns regarding their decision to make a purchase, overwhelmingly many people consulted actual shop assistants to achieve this end.

Next, we inspected the assumption that "only people with indepth knowledge of products use price comparison websites." We asked beforehand product-specific questions that required them to choose from the following answers, which would indicate their level of product literacy, and then inquired on how often they used price comparison websites.

1) I know as much as shop assistants.
2) For an amateur, I know things that experts would know.
3) Since I understand general specifications, I can offer advice to others.
4) If I see the specifications list, I can decide on my own which model I should choose.
5) I generally understand the specifications list, but I cannot decide on my own.
6) Even though I don't understand the specifications list so well, if I ask others about it, I can understand, so I am able to make decisions on my own.
7) Since I don't understand most of the specifications, I make selections on the basis of my impression, such as by looking at the design.
8) Since I don't understand most of the specifications and since I feel it's okay as long as I can use it, I leave the decision making up to others for the most part.

The proportion of people who responded that they sometimes used price comparison websites or frequently used price comparison websites exceeded 80% in the case of those who claimed to know as much as shop assistants. But the lower the level of product literacy,

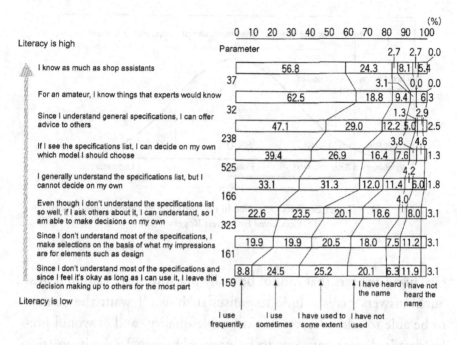

Figure 7-20: Relationship between Literacy Levels and Use of Comparison Websites

the more the usage frequency dropped, and in the case of the group with the lowest product literacy level, we found out that their frequency of usage was extremely low, with little less than 70% of them answering that they had used such sites a little or had never used them or didn't know about them at all (Figure 7-20).

The innovators and early adopters — as mentioned in the diffusion theory put forward by Everett Rogers (Figure 7-21) — make decisions based on their understanding of specifications, so these groups are not resistant to the idea of narrowing down their product choices through looking up specifications. However, the majority of the members of the follower bracket base their decisions not on specifications but on benefits. So for example, if they were to be asked, "what pixel count would you like your digital camera to have" or "how much clock speed do you prefer for your CPU," they will not be able to reply properly. In fact, they will only be able to

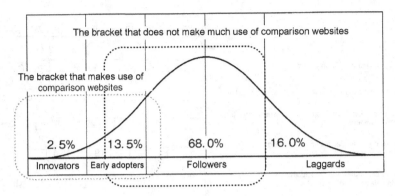

Figure 7-21:   Target Brackets Described in the Diffusion of Innovations Theory
Conceived by Everett Rogers

give fuzzy answers that cannot be easily put into specification terms. Such answers may include responses such as, "I want the camera to be able to take pictures of reasonable quality" and "I would prefer that it doesn't turn out to be unwieldy when I take it on trips with me."

In this sense, if shop assistants are able to respond via the Web and recommend the most suitable products by giving fuzzy answers in kind, the site promises to be valuable for the follower bracket as well.

In Figures 7-22 and 7-23, you will find the results of my investigation into how buying decisions are made and into what questions are asked to shop assistants. We were able to successfully develop the business of Oshiete! Kaden[7] by accurately capturing user needs and meeting them via the Internet through investigating the behavior and mindsets of consumers at the time they were making a purchase.

3)   *Other tools for acquiring information*

Media that can prove useful for the purpose of verifying the viability of a business and for grasping user needs include community

How did you decide or are in the process of deciding to buy a product? Please be as detailed as possible in your answer. (PC)

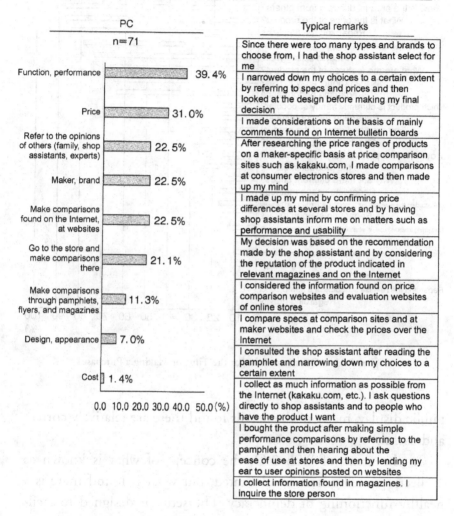

Figure 7-22: Determinants for Purchasing a Product (PC)

sites such as Hatena[22] (Good Gracious!), Oshiete! goo[8] (Tell me! goo), and Yahoo! Chie Bukuro[25] (Yahoo! Wisdom Bag). These Q&A communities are structured in a way that lets people post questions on the Internet and receive replies from someone within a matter of several minutes. Since these questions and answers are on

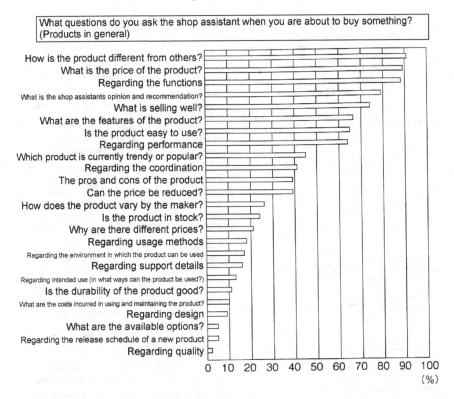

Figure 7-23:   Questions Asked at the Time of Making a Purchase

public display, many of the details found there are relatively correct and useful.

In the arena of Web 2.O, the concept of what is known as "collective intelligence" is advocated, but what is found there is a healthy functioning of democracy. The setup is designed to facilitate the power of revision through allowing the participation of many people in the act of revising and polishing answers put forward by others. So even incorrect answers will eventually become valuable.

A representative example of collective intelligence is the Wikipedia,[5] which is an online encyclopedia that provides a forum for users to freely contribute entries. As of October 2006, there are

280,000 articles contained in the Japanese edition and the encyclopedia is aiming to become the largest one in Japan.

Key policies

You don't need to read any Wikipedia policies before you contribute. However, the following policies are particularly important to the project, as they have been shaped through experience, and the sooner you understand and use them, the better:

Avoid bias — Articles should be written from a neutral point of view, representing views fairly, proportionately and without bias.

Respect copyrights — Wikipedia is a free encyclopedia licensed under the terms of the GNU Free Documentation License. Submitting work which infringes copyrights threatens our objective to build a truly free encyclopedia that anyone can redistribute, and could lead to legal problems. (See Wikipedia: Copyright for details.)

Wikipedia is an encyclopedia. Its goals go no further. (See What Wikipedia is Not for details.)

Respect other contributors — Wikipedia contributors come from many different countries and cultures, and have widely different views. Treating others with respect is key to collaborating effectively in building an encyclopedia. (See Wikipedia: Etiquette, Wikipedia: Civility, Wikipedia: Dispute Resolution for details.)

Cited from the Japanese edition of Wikipedia.[5]

While you can look up definitions of terms through search engines, very often, there are too many search results to choose from. Since Wikipedia is founded on the above-mentioned policies, it serves as a very valuable, exhaustive tool that meets various information gathering needs of business development.

There is another media — a consumer-oriented one — that offers more detailed information, even though it is not as exhaustive as Wikipedia. This media is the website called "All About,"[6] and it features many experts of various fields as guides who offer information that help consumers in their daily living. Specifically, it offers only reliable information carefully selected by the experts in the form of articles, link collections, and e-mail newsletters. Since the site offers information that is relevant to daily living, it is largely useful to use as a reference for finding out how to choose household electrical appliances.

"Google trends"[13] is a system that allows us to check how many words or expressions are searched through search engines. Using a time-series graph, Google trends can confirm the rise and fall of the frequencies of specific words or expressions searched. Since links to related news items are displayed, when the graph indicates a peak, it is easy to grasp what types of events have occurred. In addition, since you can find out from which country or region a user had entered a particular keyword, you can understand search-word trends. Additionally, the sites appearing below are also resourceful:

- Search Engine Ole http://www.seoseo.net/
- SEO TOOLS β(SEO tools) http://www.seotools.jp/

"Technorati"[19] is a search engine that specializes in blogs, and can be used to carry out real-time searches of words and phrases found in blogs in the order of the newness of the words and phrases (Figure 7-24). The difference with regular search engines is that the time required for an article to be reflected in the search results after it is posted is extremely short, requiring less than several minutes. Nowadays, it is not unusual to see news images in this media ahead of any other media. In addition, the fact that search results are displayed in the order of their newness is one of this media's distinctive characteristics that set it apart from conventional search engines. For the purpose of acquiring evaluations, word of mouth information, and the latest information on various topics, it is a very valuable media.

Figure 7-24:   Blog Search Engine

The following search engines for blogs also have similar features:

- NAMAAN blog search engine   http://www.namaan.net/
- livedoor blog search   http://sf.livedoor.com/
- goo blog   http://blog.goo.ne.jp/
- Yahoo! Blog search   http://blog-search.yahoo.co.jp/
- Ask.jp Blog search   http://ask.jp/blghome.asp
- Search Engine MARS FLAG   http://www.marsflag.com/

7.4   The Role of Information Management in the Development Phase of the "Oshiete! Kaden" Website

7.4.1   *Information sharing*

While information sharing during development is carried out through face-to-face communication and email, when collectively managing documents such as those with specifications, you can realize further efficiency if you make use of a system that allows anyone to rewrite documents from anywhere in a network using a web browser application. A typical system of this kind is the "wiki." Wikipedia is well-known for being a website that makes use of the wiki for both browsing and editing purposes, and if you look up the term "wiki" on the Japanese edition of Wikipedia, the following entry appears.

A wiki or a WikiWiki is a system that makes it possible via web browsers to rewrite hypertext documents stored in web servers. The software used in this system and the collection of documents created using this system are at times referred to as a wiki.

WikiWiki means fast in Hawaiian and alludes to the swiftness of creating and renewing a wiki page. With a wiki, anyone can rewrite a document from anywhere within a network, so it is suited for the collaborative creation of documents. Due to such a feature, it has been remarked that the wiki is a collaborative tool. At present, many wikis have appeared as a result of improving upon the first version or as a result of drawing upon from it.

Additionally, there are systems known as local wikis. These systems have been configured to work without web servers and are being used for the purpose of convenient storing of personal notes. With such systems, it is common to use a dedicated application instead of a web browser. While there is the merit that constructing an engine is unnecessary, there is also the demerit that the mark-up syntax varies by the application.

The characteristics common to all wikis are as follows:

- The ability for anyone to be able to rewrite and store documents from anywhere within a network at any time.
- Only a web browser is required for rewriting documents.
- The document mark up language unique to the wiki is comparatively easier than HTML and is therefore easy to learn.
- Linking between documents within the same wiki is easy, making the creation of a complex collection of interrelated documents also easy.
- Usually no prior permission is required to make changes and the wiki is open to anyone who can access the server where the wiki resides. There are many wikis that do not require users to register and create personal accounts.

Cited from the Japanese edition of Wikipedia.[5]

Regarding the use of the wiki, there are several services such as the Livedoor Wiki[28] that are available for free. However, from the aspect of information management, making use of an external server is problematic, so it is advisable to use tools such as PukiWiki[23] that are free of charge to build your own system within the corporate server (Figure 7-25).

7.4.2 *Version control*

In system development, version control has become common sense. Mainly, it is a procedure that is used in the development of programs to manage source codes and other data, and is generally used in commercial software development projects and open-source community projects that involve many people. In the event several engineers revise a source code at the same time, there is no problem if the revisions are for different sections of the code, but if the same section was changed at the same time, the decision of choosing which revision to adopt

Figure 7-25: Information Sharing

cannot be made by the server. The version control tool can prove useful for such situations, since it merges revisions while confirming who added what changes.

Concurrent Versions System (CVS) is the version control system used by Oshiete! Kaden. It records and manages changes made in files, and is mainly used in the sharing of text files (saving and extracting), including source-code files that accompany software development. It can also manage branched off versions of text files. While the software is not limited to text files and can carry out version control for files such as image files and Office documents, in the case of text files, it allows the inspection of differences between versions. In addition, it can also extract a source code entered at a certain point in time. In the development of the Ohsiete! Kaden website, most files were managed with CVS.

7.4.3   *Bug control*

The bug control system is for systematically managing and amending bugs (discrepancies, malfunctions, obstacles) that occur in the course of carrying out a project, and is mainly used in software development projects.

In the development of software, how a system efficiently discovers and amends errors and defects found in a program (in its coding) is vital. To build a perfect program by amending bugs without letting them leak, it is necessary to share among all project members numerous data regarding a bug, in addition to the data on its particulars, and have the members manage them as well. Such data include the date and time of a bug's discovery, name of the person reporting the bug, classification of the bug, its treatment method, its reproduction method, its level of priority, its level of severity, the name of the person in charge of its revision, and the level of progress. In bug control, there are times when mailing lists and bulletin boards are used, while at other times even direct discussions and meetings are carried out. But in the case of developing the Oshiete! Kaden website, we made use of a dedicated bug control tool called "KAGEMAI."[11] KAGEMAI is a purely Japanese bug management system and is easy to use. Because multiple projects progress in parallel, the bug reporter writes the details of a bug after having chosen a project. The administrator receives the report and then assigns a person in charge to manage the progress. You will find more detailed information on other bug control tools at http://www.swtest.jp/tools.html# management.

7.4.4   *Regarding security when utilizing tools*

Regarding the above-mentioned tools, it is necessary to take caution when using them.

What you should be most careful about is the use of external services. An external service is a tool that is located inside an external server. In the case of Oshiete! Kaden, the corresponding services are email and messaging, and depending on the mode of operation, even the wiki and CVS are realized through external services. Regarding the sections where external services are used, it is necessary to take care not to enter any information that will prove to be problematic if it is leaked, such as personal or confidential information. During the development of the Oshiete! Kaden website, we took security into consideration and configured systems such as the wiki, CVS, and bug control programs within our in-house server and in that way managed to reduce security risks. In addition, anytime we used email facilities provided by external services, we reduced the damage brought about by any possible leaks through making use of encryption technology. Furthermore, regarding messaging, I cannot say that the security was always tight, since we used an external service as previously mentioned. Still, we went with Skype, since its messaging features incorporate a high level of encryption. For information on Skype's privacy policy, which includes information on encryption, refer to http://www.skype.com/help/faq/privacy.html.

7.5   The Role of Information Management in the Early-Phase Operations of "Oshiete! Kaden"

7.5.1   *User survey*

When launching a website, it is necessary to confirm how the site will be evaluated by actual users. Among the methods that can be adopted to evaluate a website, there are expert surveys, which are taken by experts, and user surveys, which are taken by general consumers. With expert surveys, experts evaluate predetermined topics. The topics vary by the research company and also by the site and the evaluator. While such surveys are considerably excellent in the sense of being exhaustive in the evaluations they offer, they do not cover the likes and dislikes of design aspects, so the results of these surveys are not always in alignment with the results of general consumer evaluations.

User surveys are carried out for general consumers and are either carried out at physical venues where the test subjects are assembled or are carried out over the Internet. Surveys carried out at physical venues are suited for evaluating websites prior to their launch and for confirming their usability — specifically by having inspectors seated next to people to monitor them while they actually access and browse a website. In the case of Internet surveys, they can be used for only evaluations of websites that have already been launched. However, since there are no regional and temporal constraints, subject samplings can be made easily, making them suited for carrying out quantitative evaluations.

7.5.2   *Access log analysis*

An access log is the data of records of fixed processing functions carried out by a web server, and an access log analysis helps to grasp the usage situation of a website by performing an analysis on how users have accessed the site (Figure 7-26).

An access log comprises data such as IP addresses and domain names of users, access times, the names of accessed links and files, browser types and operating systems. If you analyze this vast amount of data with an access-analysis software, you can collect all sorts of necessary information such as where visitors come from, around how many have visited, around how many pages they have viewed, how long they have stayed, and what operations they have carried out at the site. By making use of these data sets in marketing, you can reassess the structure of the website and search-keyword settings and thereby increase the number of visitors.

Figure 7-26:   Access Log Analysis

A great many businesses are offering access log analyses services, but Google Analytics is offered free of charge, so this service can certainly be used without reserve.

7.5.3   *Competitive research*

Competitive research can be confirmed by referring to the findings of expert surveys of competing websites or through carrying out user surveys, but the easiest way to achieve this end is to research page views. They are the most basic feature of the access log analysis and you can compare them with those of the websites of other companies to help you readily understand the effectiveness of not only your own firm's promotional and advertising campaigns, but the competition's as well. Alexa[1] is also offered free of charge, so it is enjoyable to check the page views of not just the websites of the competition, but of also much talked about websites in general.

Yoshisuke Yamakawa

Acknowledgments

In the course of developing and writing on "Oshiete! Kaden",[7] I was fortunate to have received considerable support and advice from the following people. I would like to express my sincere appreciation for them here:

ALBERT Inc.
    Takashi Uemura
    Megumi Sato
    Kei Tsuji
    Hidefumi Tamura
    Hiroaki Tamura
    Shogo Ota

Interscope Inc.[4]
    Chiharu Hiraoka
    Reiko Shirakawa

Kagawa Nutrition University
    Mayomi Haga

References

1. Alexa, http://www.alexa.com/
2. Amazon, http://www.amazon.co.jp
3. Albert, http://www.albert2005.co.jp/
4. Interscope, http://www.yahoo-vi.co.jp/
5. Wikipedia, http://ja.wikipedia.org/wiki/
6. All About, http://allabout.co.jp/
7. Oshiete! Kaden, http://mitsukaru.jp/
8. Oshiete! goo, http://oshiete.goo.ne.jp/
9. Oshiete Na, http://www.oshiete-na.com/

10. Kakaku.com, http://kakaku.com/
11. Kagemai, http://www.daifukuya.com/kagemai
12. Google, http://www.google.co.jp/
13. Google trends, http://www.google.com/trends
14. Kenko.com, http://www.kenko.com
15. National Center for Industrial Property Information and Training, http://www.inpit.go.jp/
16. Silver Egg Technology, http://www.silveregg.co.jp/
17. Skype, http://www.skype.com/intl/ja
18. Scope Net, http://www.yahoo-vi.co.jp/panel/scopenet_data.html
19. Technorati, http://www.technorati.jp/
20. Nissen Online, http://www.nissen.co.jp
21. Net Perceptions, http://www.netperceptions.com
22. Hatena, http://www.hatena.ne.jp
23. PukiWiki, http://pukiwiki.sourceforge.jp/
24. Yahoo!, http://yahoo.co.jp/
25. Yahoo! Chie Bukuro, http://chiebukuro.yahoo.co.jp/
26. Yahoo! Chat, http://chat.yahoo.co.jp
27. Yamada Denki Web.Com, http://www.yamada-denkiweb.com/
28. Livedoor Wiki, http://wiki.livedoor.com/

Chapter 8

Robot Development Case Examples — The Intelligential and Functional Approaches

In this chapter, I will survey the current situation of robots and then introduce concrete case studies of robot development from a functional perspective and an intelligential one as well. While there is no need to emphasize the importance of industrial robots, which are exemplary of the type of robot technology that pursues functional excellence, it should be noted that the market for robots such as AIBO that appeal to human emotions is expected to grow large as well in the future. In the final part of this chapter, I will discuss the development of Honda's ASIMO and contemplate how a globally leading-edge robot came to be created.

8.1 The Current Situation of Robots

8.1.1 *What is a robot?*

Upon hearing the word "robot", we Japanese are apt to be reminded of robot characters that appear in comics and animation films of the Astro Boy variety. The robots appearing in comics and animations can be like Astro Boy on the one hand and have superior abilities that let them do things humans can only dream of doing, or they can be like Doraemon on the other hand and have abilities that are equal to or even less than those of humans. However, what they all share in common, I believe, is that they are all humankind's best friend and partner. Compared with Westerners, it is generally said that the Japanese have a more tolerant view regarding the impact of robot technology on society and one reason for this can be attributed to the fact that Japan has been having a love affair with the robots of the comic and animation lore. Perhaps it is due to this reason that Japanese robot technology is considered to be top-class in the world.

However, it is clear that robots being currently developed are not reaching the technologically advanced levels of a robot like Astro Boy. Astro Boy can walk and run through various environments using his two feet and can even fly across the sky. In addition, he is conscious like humans and seems to feel all the emotions such as joy, anger, sadness and humor. With the current state of our technology, we certainly are not able to create sentient robots and we can only have them walk in restricted surroundings.

However, it is rash to become pessimistic about robot technology for just these reasons. If we look at the manufacturing industry, we can see that industrial robots are continuing to work days and nights at factories around the world to engage in such tasks as assembling cars. The manufacturing industry will not stay viable without these industrial robots today.

In this way, robots can be seen to be very diverse and therefore it is difficult to clearly define the word "robot" to begin with. In the "Terminology for Industrial-Use Robots" contained in the Japanese Industrial Standard JIS B 0134, there are entries for the word with modifiers such as "industrial robot" and "intelligent robot," but there is no entry for the word "robot" itself.[1]

One reason why it is difficult to define this word is the fact that the word is not really a technical term, but instead is a term that has anthropomorphic connotations. For example, we do not call the crane used in an arcade game called UFO Catcher (a claw vending machine) a robot. However, a machine that automatically grasps parts in a factory is called an "industrial" robot. Why is it that we do not refer to the crane in the game as a robot?

Incidentally, the word "robot" was coined by the Czech writer Karel Capek and was used for the first time in his stage play titled *R.U.R.* The word "robot" is said to come from the Czech word *robota*, which means labor or drudgery. Judging from this derivation, it seems appropriate to define a robot as a machine that frees humans from labor and drudgery. However, nobody calls an automobile — a machine that helps people with the labor of transportation — a robot. (However, the movement to take advantage of the fruits of robot research for automobile development has become conspicuous in recent years.[2])

8.1.2 *The history of the robot*

The premiere of Karel Capek's play, *R.U.R.*, took place in 1920, but the first industrial robot, which was called the playback robot, was created in 1960. This means that it had taken 40 years from the time the word robot was coined to the time an actual robot was put into practical use, and also that only 50 years has passed since an industrial robot had been put to practical use (see Figure 8-1).

In addition, it was in 1942 that Isaac Asimov had described the famous Three Laws of Robotics in the short story titled *Runaround*, which means that these laws actually precedes the practical use of industrial robots by nearly 20 years.

This playback robot was introduced into Japan in 1967, after which industrial robots began to spread remarkably throughout the nation. The output of domestic robot production overtook the output of American and European robot production in the 1970s, and by the latter half of the 1980s, more than half of robot installations around the world were made in Japan.

Year	Event
1920	Karel Capek's stage drama, *R.U.R. (Rossum's Universal Robots)*
1942	Isaac Asimov's Three Laws of Robotics
1960	The first industrial robot (the Playback Robot)
1967	The industrial robot is introduced into Japan
1967–	Development of the WABOT at Waseda University
1972	Successful mass installations in an automotive factory (GM in the US)
1980–1990	Project for developing "Robotics for Extremely Dangerous Work Environments" initiated by the former Ministry of International Trade and Industry
1982	Establishment of the Robotics Society of Japan
1991–2000	"The Micro-Machine Project" initiated by the former Ministry of International Trade and Industry
1996	Honda's ASIMO
1998–2002	"The Humanoid Robotics Project" initiated by the Ministry of Economy, Trade and Industry
1999	Sony's AIBO
1999–2000	The Ministry of Economy, Trade and Industry initiates the project for the "development of robotics that supports the Prevention of Nuclear Energy-Related Disasters"
2002–2004	The project for "forming the foundation of robotic development through software preparations" is initiated

Figure 8-1:   Robot-Related Milestones

Source: Ministry of Economy, Trade and Industry's Society for the Study of Robotic Policies, *The Society for the Study of Robotic Policies' Report*, May 2006.

The backdrop to this achievement was the large amounts of investment put into research and development for robot-related national projects and the active R&D carried out through an industry-university collaboration, which was made possible through the investment. The representative robot-related national projects of Japan that have been completed as of 2007 are "Robotics for Extremely Dangerous Work Environments," which began in 1980, "Robot Systems for Collaborating and Coexisting with Humans," which began in 1998, "Robot Development for Supporting the Prevention of Nuclear Energy-Related Disasters," which began in 1999, "Software Preparation for Forming the Foundation of Robot Development," which began in 2002, "The Initiative for Reinforcing

Development of Robotics for Extremely Dangerous Work Environments	1983-1990	Development of robots to be used in hazardous environments in the nuclear energy, oceanology, and disaster prevention fields.
Micro-Machine Project	1991-2000	R&D for micro-machine systems that bring about the miniaturization of production equipment and also carry out inspections, repairs, and diagnosis in narrow places such as inside pipes of power plant facilities and inside the human body.
The Humanoid Robot Project	1998-2002	R&D for robots that can be manipulated through remote control via the use of communication networks to assist human beings where they work and live by carrying out complex tasks and moving through divergent terrains.
Robotics Development for Supporting the Prevention of Nuclear Energy-Related Disasters	1999-2000	Development of robots that are resistant to high levels of radiation, robots that support work supervision, miniature robots for light work, work robots for opening and closing valves, and robots for heavy-weight transportation.
Software Preparations for Forming the Foundation of Robotic Development	2002-2004	The development of middleware that make the construction of diverse robots possible by combining various robotic elements through communication networks. This development aimed to realize the limited production of diversified products.
The Initiative for Reinforcing the Foundation of Strategic Technologies (including the field of Robot Components)	2003-2005	Support for the development of robotic components carried out by small and medium sized companies. This project aimed to help improve the technological development of such companies.
The Next-Generation Robotic Applications Project	2004-2005	Development, experimentation, and demonstration of the prototypes of robots expected to carry out tasks such as cleaning and policing in the near future. The project was featured at the World Exposition in Aichi.
The Human-Assistive Robot Applications Project	2005-2007	Development of nursing robots that support patients and caregivers. From the start, this project was carried out through partnerships between users (facilities, hospitals, etc.) and robot makers.
Common Foundation Development Project	2005-2007	R&D for the modularization of robots that took into account the fruits of the RT Middleware Development Project (The project for making software preparations for forming the foundation of robotic development).

Figure 8-2:   Robot-Related Large-Scale Projects
Source: Ministry of Economy, Trade and Industry's Society for the Study of Robotic Policies, *The Society for the Study of Robotic Policies' Report*, May 2006.

the Foundation of Strategic Technologies (including the Robot Parts field)," which began in 2003, and "The Next-Generation Robotic Applications Project," which began in 2004. In addition, projects that are ongoing as of 2007 are "Human-Assistive Robot Applications Project," which began in 2005, and the "Common Foundation Development Project," which also began in 2005 (see Figure 8-2).

8.1.3   *Robot development in Japan and future challenges that should be heeded*

When regarding the robot from a market-oriented perspective, it can be seen that industrial robots account for a large portion of the robot market in Japan.

According to the statistics provided by the Japan Robot Association, the shipment of industrial robots in 2005 amounted to 689 billion yen. Most of these industrial robots are in operation at factories of manufacturing industries. While nearly 40 years have passed since industrial robots were introduced into Japan, its market is in no way an old one that has become saturated. As long as unprecedented new products continue to be developed in the manufacturing industry, the development of new robots will be carried out for the production of those products. With the rapid spread of thin-screen TVs in recent years, the market for clean-room robots, which are used in the transportation of glass substrates for liquid crystal televisions, has seen sudden expansion.[3] Along with industrial progress, new needs for robots promise to arise from now on as well.

Meanwhile, the market size for robots other than those for industrial use is believed to be of a scale that approximately exceeds 7 billion yen as of 2005. A robot that is currently drawing attention as a non-industrial type of robot is the so-called "partner robot." Specifically, the partner robot is a next-generation robot that assists people in making their lives more pleasant by assuming tasks for the purpose of realizing entertainment and security for the general household, and supporting daily living in general. I will present more details on partner robots at a later point, but for now I would like to point out that according to the "Report on the Round Table Conference on the Vision for Next-Generation Robots"[4] released by the Ministry of Economy, Trade and Industry in April 2004, the market size for next generation robots is projected to be worth about 7.2 trillion yen in 2025. Considering that the current robot market size is around

700 billion yen, this would mean that a considerably large increase is anticipated to occur in the next 20 years.

In addition, in the same report, "the three issues that next-generation robots could help resolve" were stated to be as follows; low-birth rates and the aging of society (retention of the labor force), security (security countermeasures to protect against disasters), and convenience and leisure (creation of free time). When a researcher involved in robot development searches for a possible direction a research program could take, they will necessarily run into relevant scholarly papers. However, referring to reports that are published by public offices such as the one mentioned above will also prove resourceful.

In the 2006 report issued by the Ministry of Economy, Trade and Industry's Society for the Study of Robotic Policies,[3] you can find points that reflect on robot-related projects that had been carried out to date. Specifically, the report states that it was regrettable that conventional robot-related projects to date had been focused on R&D without linking themselves to market needs in any meaningful way. It goes on to further state that a balance must be struck between market preparation and technological development. Interestingly, the same report also points out that industrial robots had formerly had the same problems as the ones faced by the current service-oriented robots. These problems are as follows:

1) As is often the case with seed-type products, development geared toward the realization of an application was necessary.
2) Application-specific development of features and performance enhancements were necessary.
3) A great deal of time and effort was required for reducing the time between failures and for enhancing durability.

The industrial robot projects have overcome these problems to evolve into an extremely large market, and the lessons that can be learned from their successes are certainly to be indispensable for the development of next-generation robots. Naturally, it goes without saying that the lessons to be learned from successful precedents are vital for not only robots, but for all other products as well.

8.1.4   *Technology and Japan's competitive advantage required for the development of robots*

If you regard the robot as a "computer capable of motion," the technical expertise necessary for its development will need to cover the subjects of mechanical engineering and computer science. In *The Society for the Study of Robotic Policies Report*,[3] drive-related technology, sensor technology, battery technology, materials technology, communications technology, and software technology are mentioned as elemental technologies that are necessary for developing robots (see Figure 8-3). It can be said that we have to combine these wide-ranging technologies to develop robots.

Strategies for the Creation of New Industries,[5] which was released by the Ministry of Economy, Trade and Industry in 2004, states that the existence of this country's advanced components industrial clusters is a large advantage for realizing the progress of the robotics industry.

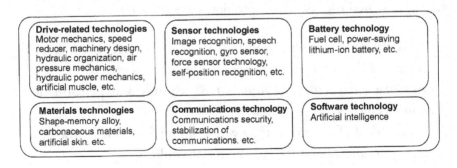

Figure 8-3:   Elemental Technologies Necessary for the Development of Robots
Source: Ministry of Economy, Trade and Industry's Society for the Study of Robotic Policies, *The Society for the Study of Robotic Policies Report*, May 2006.

In the same report, it is also stated that the reason why the liquid-crystal display industry can be found to be concentrated in Japan, Korea, and Taiwan is because the industry is strongly dependent on Japan's manufacturing industry, such as the materials industry, which excels in synthesizing special materials, and the functional components industry, which excels in precision microprocessing. Similarly, Japan is expected to play a pivotal role in the robotics industry with its superior manufacturing technology.

8.2 Robots That Pursue Function

As mentioned previously, historically speaking, the industrial robot is the original robot (see Figure 8-4). In the 1960s, robot operations became popular in automotive assembly processes and largely contributed to improving productivity. Even as of today, industrial robots still account for a principal part of all robots and were developed and improved by robot makers such as Kawasaki Unimate, Yaskawa Electric Corporation, and FANUC. However, their origin lies in Joseph F. Engelberger's Unimation.

Engelberger created a robot called the Unimate by essentially using a method known as "playback." The playback method established the teaching process, which instructed the manipulator to

The industrial robot typically demonstrates its strengths in welding, handling, assembling, cutting, polishing, and coating.

Figure 8-4: Industrial Robot

assume the position and posture it should take beforehand and then make it reproduce them (playback) subsequently. To make a manipulator assume various postures, it was necessary to specify the three-dimensional positions and posture angles of the fingers and find out what angle each joint of the manipulator should take to assume the specified positions and postures. In other words, it was necessary to resolve the issue of inverse kinematics in real time. While this is not difficult to accomplish at present, at the time, they were not able to formularize and had no procedures to solve the problem. So, at a time when computers were not developed, the playback process, in effect, had made it possible to carry out minimum calculations and thereby make practical application a reality.

In the case of Japan, success was assured by not only realizing technological progress for the robot alone, but by attaching much importance to the environmental arrangement of use and thereby technically improving the usability of robots. One consequence of this policy was the fact that hydraulic robots became electric robots.

In the following section, I will introduce robots that are intended for demonstrating superhuman functions within certain specialized environments.

8.2.1 *Significance of maintaining the external environment*

Figure 8-5 shows the roles of industrial robots in society.

All of them are robots that specialize in restricted environments. While robots are used in various sectors, general-purpose robots that can be adopted for two fields, such as agriculture and construction, are currently rare.

For example, if we examine disaster-relief robots (see Figure 8-6), we can see that its form is designed to allow infiltration into small and narrow spaces. It moves not with wheels, but with a caterpillar track, making it possible to move over unstable grounds as well. It is also equipped with a camera to detect people and a communication

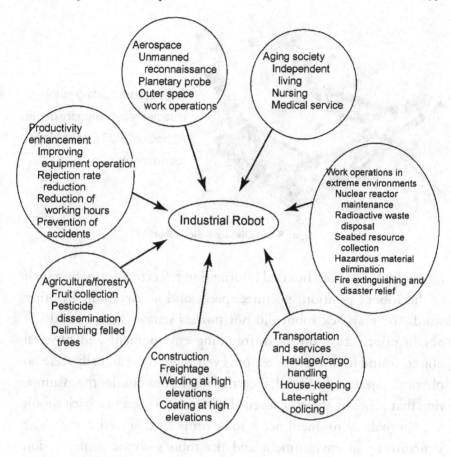

Figure 8-5: The Roles of the Industrial Robot in Society

facility to instantly report on the results of its detection. You can clearly see that these functions are geared towards fulfilling the purpose of disaster relief. By defining the intended tasks, robots that have appeared in recent years have started to become capable of carrying out those difficult tasks that are beyond the capability of humans to carry out.

Then what is the difference between the current robot and the playback robot, which was the first robot to be created? From a technical standpoint, it can be seen that the playback robot had extremely limited functions. For example, the playback robot made use of only

A robot participating in the disaster relief category of the RoboCup 2005 Osaka world tournament.

Figure 8-6:   Disaster-Relief Robot

internal information. Internal information refers to information such as the robot's position, posture, speed, and acceleration. In other words the playback robot did not possess sensors that could let it obtain information on its surrounding environment and physical objects found in it. For this reason, even when there actually were no physical objects to be found, it carried out its tasks under the assumption that physical objects existed. Therefore, to use a playback robot, the external environment needs to be properly designed as well. The structure of an environment and the robot's sensor configuration need to be predetermined in accordance with the applicable external environment. To this day, the playback robot continues to be a major force in the manufacturing process and developing robots with designs that take the environment into consideration remains important today as well.

8.2.2   *Second-generation robots that recognize environments*

Figure 8-7 shows the process of developing robots. While the playback robot only had internal sensors, the production line around 1980 began to see the appearance of robots equipped with power and visual sensors. In other words, they were second-generation robots,

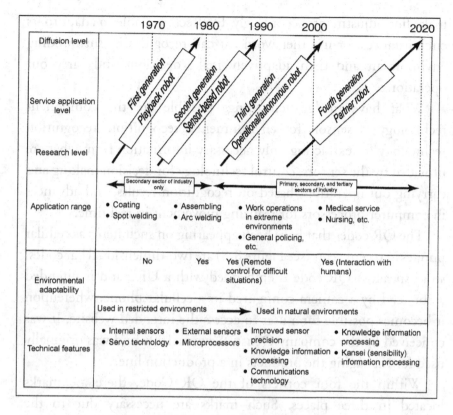

	1970	1980	1990	2000	2020
Diffusion level					
Service application level	First generation Playback robot	Second generation Sensor-based robot	Third generation Operational/autonomous robot		Fourth generation Partner robot
Research level					
Application range	Secondary sector of industry only		Primary, secondary, and tertiary sectors of industry		
	• Coating • Spot welding	• Assembling • Arc welding	• Work operations in extreme environments • General policing, etc.	• Medical service • Nursing, etc.	
Environmental adaptability	No	Yes	Yes (Remote control for difficult situations)	Yes (Interaction with humans)	
	Used in restricted environments ⟶ Used in natural environments				
Technical features	• Internal sensors • Servo technology	• External sensors • Microprocessors	• Improved sensor precision • Knowledge information processing • Communications technology	• Knowledge information processing • Kansei (sensibility) information processing	

Figure 8-7: The Progress of Robot Development

which were robots that could judge their surrounding environment and determine how best to move the body. In effect, they made use of knowledge databases, and they could be given instructions that used a robot language, and dynamic position control was made possible with these models as well. Dynamic position control takes robot dynamics into consideration and realizes the control of the arm. For example, in the case of spot welding, it would be appropriate to specify the place precisely beforehand, but in the case of arc welding, since physical objects could slip out of position or become deformed by heat, if the robot only carried out movements that had been specified beforehand, then it will fail in its task. When a second-generation robot carries out arc welding, it can detect weld lines and make fine adjustments accordingly. In effect, it is able to adapt to its circumstances, or in other words, it can recognize its surrounding environment and then adaptively make decisions and carry out operations.

What have made such things possible are the component technology of sensors for environmental recognition, recognition technology for extracting only necessary information from what are provided by the sensors, control technology for decision making and carrying out operations based on recognition results, and advances in computer processors for realizing movement in real time.

The QR codes that have been appearing on such items as cellular phones in recent years (see Figure 8-8) are two-dimensional bar codes, so to speak. A QR code is embedded with a URL and is intended to be read by a camera configured in a cellular phone, whereupon it becomes possible for a user to access the intended website. It was conceived by the company Denso Wave in 1994 and was originally used for managing the products in a production line.

Within the four corners of the QR Code, there are marks located in three places. Such marks are necessary due to the

The QR code has come into widespread, everyday use in recent years. It conveys encoded information to devices, which read the information by detecting marks located in its corners.

Figure 8-8:   QR Code

limitations of current recognition technology. For example, humans can understand that a whole apple and a partially eaten apple are both apples, but such a grasp is not easy for the robot. However, if the robot is presented with marks such as those found in a QR code, it will be able to recognize the apple like a human with some level of precision, even if the placement of the apple is positionally askew. Within such a prepared environment, robots have become capable of recognizing their surroundings and subsequently carrying out tasks.

8.2.3 *From pre-arranged environments to natural environments*

The first-generation playback robots were merely repetitive machines whose movements were made possible by internal sensors and a servomechanism. While these robots demonstrated redundancy and flexibility to a certain extent, they did not change the fact that they were merely being repetitive. As for second-generation sensor-based robots, it should be noted that they could be effectively used in pre-arranged environments such as those found in factories, but they become useless when customized environmental arrangements are not made for them. However, when the scope of robot usage goes beyond manufacturing industries, the demand arises for them to carry out tasks under relatively inferior circumstances, which are not pre-arranged. For example, since it is dangerous for humans to enter inside the furnace of a nuclear power station, it is favorable for robots to carry out tasks there. But even though its interior structure may be roughly known in advance, it is an area whose environment cannot be designed and optimized for a robot. Therefore the development of robots that could play an active role in not only pre-arranged environments but also in natural environments is necessary.

Third-generation robots fall into either of the following two categories; those that understand the environment and operate autonomously and those that receive commands from humans.

1) *Autonomous robots*

NASA's Mars exploration robot, Rover, used lasers to recognize its periphery and secure a map of the environment within a probabilistic framework. Consequently, it moved with the aid of visual sensors based on this map. In other words, by modeling the outside world with a peripheral environmental map, the robot could carry out proper judgments even in natural environments.

The "grand challenge" for the US's Defense Advanced Research Projects Agency (DARPA) is the unmanned robotic automobile race. In 2005, the race was carried out in the Mojave Desert in the US, and Stanford University's robotic car, Stanley, won the championship by covering a distance of 131.6 miles in 6 hours and 53 minutes (see Figure 8-9). Stanley detects passable roads using cameras and lasers and plans a model route. The relative positional relationships with obstacles found in the periphery are determined through cameras and lasers, while its own position is recognized through GPS use.

2) *Operational robots*

The Hybrid Assistive Limb (HAL) is a robot that functions as a robotic suit and was developed by Sankai Group of the University of Tsukuba. A person who wears this robotic suit could augment their physical capabilities. Since humans manipulate HAL's movements, it can operate in environments that are not pre-arranged. This type of robotic suit is expected to be used in the nursing sector, which will become increasingly vital from now on.

The surgery robot, Da Vinci, is a robot that is operated by a surgeon through remote control. The placement of a human organ varies

Stanford University's unmanned car robot.

Figure 8-9: DARPA Grand Challenge

subtly by the person, making it difficult for a robot to autonomously carry out surgical tasks. However, if we can accurately communicate images of a patient and the tactile feedback of inserting a scalpel, surgical tasks can be carried out from remote locations. Tactile feedback refers to such elements as the weight and the feel a person perceives when holding a cup and is also known as haptic information. The doctor operates the robot based on the communicated images and haptic information. To realize actual use, accurate detection of haptic information and real-time communication are necessary.

To operate robots in natural environments, technology that allows accurate recognition of the environment is crucial. For environmental recognition, superior sensors are necessary and there are sensors available today that surpass the capabilities of the fives senses such as cameras equipped with the telephoto lens. However, for the moment, there are apparently no sensors that can surpass the subtle sense of touch of humans.

Let us now compare robots with humans (Figure 8-10). While sensors that surpass human capabilities exist, knowledge information processing technology and sensory information processing technology are still in need of a breakthrough to match the level of the

Humans	Robots
Intelligence	Intelligent information processing/Sensibility information processing
Arms/hands	Manipulators/robotic hands
Muscles	Motors
Feet	Wheels/crawlers/4 footed/2 footed
Senses	External sensors (sense of sight, sense of touch, sense of force, sense of hearing) Internal sensors (gyros)
Energy	Battery

Figure 8-10:   Comparisons between Humans and Robots

human brain. Third-generation robots that operate autonomously in natural environments will be demanded to not only process information from sensors accurately, but also to carry out complex decision-making based on the inputs of information obtained through the sensors. In other words, they will be demanded to demonstrate a level of intelligence that is on par with the level of intelligence of humans. It may be said that the deepening of the knowledge information processing technology and sensory information processing technology will tie into the further progress of third-generation robots.

8.2.4   *The role of information search in robot development*

The robot has evolved into an agent for carrying out human work. To search for information that can prove useful in developing such robots, observing humans is advisable.

Norbert Wiener carried out thorough observations of human actions and proposed the concept of "feedback" in a theory of motion he had deduced from his observations. Having noted the way humans and machines take action by acquiring information from the environment, he realized that there have to be underlying principles common to both entities or that both organisms and machines could be thought to share common principles. One such principle he proposed was the principle of feedback.

For example, let us consider the act of driving a car. All drivers gauge the distance between their car and the one ahead of them and step on the accelerator or brake pedal accordingly. If the distance between the cars shortens, the driver will step on the brake pedal, and if applying too much brake leads to the lengthening of the distance between the cars, the driver will step on the accelerator pedal. In effect, a flow of cause and effect is creating a loop — as a result of the output of a system, the environment changes, and when the environment changes, the input into the system changes, and when the input into the system changes, the system's output changes. This is the phenomenon known as feedback.

Wiener emphasized the fact that humans are constantly acting in response to their observations of the world around them, which are, in essence, information that are fed back to them from the world around them. Additionally, he asserted that it was the same for machines as well. In his book titled *Cybernetics*, it is written that you can examine principles of organisms through machine analogies and that if you acquire principles of organisms, then you will also be able to design machines, which will have functions of organisms based on those principles.

The act of observing and studying humans, and applying their mechanisms to the field of engineering for the purpose of realizing practical use can yield more fruits than just feedback. For example, the senses of sight and hearing are cases in point. If you register letters or faces into a knowledge base, a machine will be able to distinguish them, although not to the advanced degree of humans. Specifically, the machine is making comparisons with data stored in the knowledge database and humans are thought to be carrying out a similar form of information processing.

8.3   Robots That Take Intelligence into Consideration

Thus far, I have introduced robots that pursue functionality. For such robots, there has been progress made toward turning them into autonomous machines that would allow them to adapt to their surrounding environments. Along with this progress, there has been progress made in recognition and artificial intelligence technologies. The inheritors of this direction will be partner robots that will be able to interact with humans. Here, I would like to introduce the subject of these partner robots, which are fourth-generation robots, and R&D cases concerning the robotic brain.

8.3.1   *The brain and the computer*

It is said that the human brain carries out the following three mental activities; intellect, emotion, and volition.[6] Most of the research to date has been aimed at the intellect part of mental activities. The intellect is further classified roughly into knowledge and intelligence. Regarding knowledge, there is knowledge that is postnatal and deliberately learned and there is knowledge that is not deliberately studied but nevertheless acquired without one's knowing. The former can be procured for computers as a knowledge database, and with the progress of knowledge engineering, there are databases with an abundant amount of embedded knowledge in them at present. The form of knowledge most suitable for a computer is simple memory, and this will last almost indefinitely, once the computer stores it. In these present times when computers have made significant progress, the faculty of memory is viewed as a mechanical faculty and its value is beginning to wane.

As for understanding how knowledge is acquired naturally, there is still much work to be done. Common-sense knowledge, such as the fact that "an apple is something you eat," cannot be configured into a conventional database because of the need to understand the statement at a conceptual level and because of the fact that there are many exceptions. These matters are presently at the R&D stage. For example, let us consider human speech. Children aged three to four have a limited vocabulary but can nevertheless talk in their own special way. On the other hand, a robot can have a stored memory of a much larger vocabulary than a child's vocabulary, but making it converse will prove to be difficult, even if it is made to converse at the level of a child's proficiency.

In recent years, an approach that carries out natural speech patterns is being studied as a possible solution to this problem. This is based on a probabilistic approach called the Bayesian network approach and it is also a technique used in searches conducted by the Internet search engine, Google. Specifically, it involves expressing connections between words in terms of probability and learning them from past experiences.

Additionally, even if a computer were in possession of much knowledge, the computer would be receiving that knowledge from humans. In other words, the knowledge would not be something that the computer would actively secure on its own. With regard to actively acquiring knowledge, most of the current machines do not have such a faculty. In the fields of machine learning such as artificial intelligence, knowledge engineering, and neurocomputing, the concept of self-learning is discussed. However, I believe it could be said that as far as the process of humans teaching machines is concerned, it is still in a developing phase essentially.

Then how about intelligence? Among the different types of intelligence, the computer is adept in the area of handling logical reasoning. For example, humans pale in comparison to the computing power of current computers when carrying out such tasks as factorization, but when it comes to giving computers the faculty to consider or create new ideas, we are at present clueless, not even having a clear methodology to address the issue.

In recent years, in addition to researching the concept of "intellect" in robots, research into the concept of "emotions" in robots has also started. For example, Sony's robot, AIBO, expresses joy through its movements. But it cannot be said that the robot itself is actually experiencing this emotion. Strictly speaking, it is humans who perceive that to be the case. While I would be very hard pressed to reply to the question of whether there would be any sense in reproducing emotions themselves in a machine, to make a robot naturally interact with humans, it would be necessary to have the robot experience emotions, as that would make humans have an emotional response as well.

Additionally, there is the field of Kansei engineering (sense engineering), where experts are attempting to have computers and robots understand the fuzzy, "somehow or other" line of human reasoning. For example, images evoked by the name of the actor "Takuya Kimura" will vary by the person perceiving the name. Some people may think he is cool, while others may associate the name with music and among these people, there may be those who associate the name with outdoor sports, such as surfing and fishing. Similarly, the interpretation of quantity indicated in the phrase "a little" found in the expression "add a little salt" would also vary by the individual. It is thought that for robots to spread through society, understanding such individualistic variations is necessary.

As for "volition," if the question of whether it is necessary for robots is also asked, I am inclined to make an argument similar to the one for "emotions." Additionally, it can be said that "volition" emerges in association with "emotion." Sony's product titled "CoCoon" pioneered a feature that can be seen in hard-disk recorders available today, and this feature is that of a machine proposing programs to users by learning what they like to watch. Although the only thing the machine is actually doing is mechanistically following the dictates of pre-programmed evaluations, it is as if the system inside the machine is exhibiting its own "volition" or intent, establishing a more intimate relationship with the human user in the process. It can be said that the times are changing from an On Demand era, when people acquire what they desire instantly, to a For Demand era, when machines propose what people desire.

8.3.2 *The approach of making machines having "intellect"*

In the previous section, we made comparisons between humans and computers from the viewpoints of intellect, emotion, and volition. Here, I will discuss approaches concerned with giving computers intelligence.

The first approach is artificial intelligence. This involves the prior creation of knowledge regarding a particular world and forming behavioral models based on this knowledge. These models can be said to be patterned after the cognitive models of humans.

The second approach is an extension of object-oriented programming, which is a form of programming that is currently prevalent in software technology. This involves seeing whether more "emergent" movements can be developed by increasing the autonomy of multiple objects and promoting competitive and cooperative reactions among them. This is an approach that is related to "the complex system" concept, which was popular during the latter half of the 1980s through the first half of the 1990s.

The final third approach involves giving rise to high-level behaviors through the accumulation of low-level behaviors. When humans instinctively carry out behaviors to evade danger, such behaviors are often simple in nature and do not involve the use of the brain. For example, the action taken to avoid danger arising from sensing heat at your fingertips is not complex and does not involve the brain's faculty of making judgments. It is a rather much lower level, reflexive, cervical response. So this idea is one that proposes developing high-level behaviors that approach intelligence by promoting the accumulation of the kind of low-level behaviors just described.

Since the second and third approaches are believed to closely resemble each other in that one is dependent on the cooperation between agents while the other is dependent on the cooperation between low-level behaviors, they can be considered to be one and the same. However, since the types of contextual knowledge they use differ, I have treated them as distinctively different from each other. The knowledge of the former can be defined as a set of rules that a person can arrange in the mind and write down, but the knowledge of the latter is information that comes more from hardware.

As an example of the third approach, there is what is known as "Subsumption Architecture," which was proposed by Rodney Brooks, a professor at the Massachusetts Institute of Technology (MIT) in the US. This concept involved the attempt of creating a robot that successfully moved through spaces strewn with many obstacles. With the AI approach, movement begins after forming an action plan through inputting data such as the positions of all obstacles. However, this would cause accidents whenever the positions of the obstacles changed after formulating the plan. In response to this situation, Professor Brooks created "Genghis," a walking robot. Specifically, this robot was able to avoid obstacles with a relatively simple set of rules, such as "if the place where the forefoot is placed is angled in an X sort of way, then move the other foot in a Y sort of way."

The fact that the creation of an intelligently behaving robot was made possible through the application of a simple set of rules made waves at the time. Currently, this architecture is apparently adopted as basic technology for autonomous robots, such as Sony's "AIBO."

Now let us turn to the second approach's competition and collaboration between agents, which is the extension of object-oriented programming. Object-orientation in software development does not focus attention on the procedures of a program, but takes up the challenge of creating proper orders through placing a key emphasis on objects, which are units that contain procedures within themselves.

In this concept, the object was formerly viewed as something static, but the agent model is a model that views the object as something dynamic with a higher level of autonomy. The concept of the agent became topical after the US firm, General Magic, introduced the programming language known as "Telescript" along with the concept of "mobile communication." The agent supports human activities by acting autonomously and coordinately over a network. For example, a travel-agency agent can be created and a user can convey to this agent what type of trip they would like to have under a certain budget range. This travel agent will then compete against, cooperate with, or exchange information with agents of other travel agencies or airline companies and bring the results of those interactions to the user. This can be considered to be an approach for creating a software robot.

8.3.3 *Partner robots*

In recent years, the need has been rising for robots that could play an active role in assisting humans in their day-to-day living. Such robots include nursing and housemaid robots, but their practical application is not simple by any means. For example, let us consider the creation of a robot that could fetch the remote controller for a television set found in a household. How will it know the place where the remote controller can be found? How should it proceed to this place while avoiding obstacles along the way?

Sony's QRIO, Honda's ASIMO, and NEC's PaPeRo were intended to be such a robot and even Mitsubishi Heavy Industries and Toyota were involved in their development. PaPeRo can distinguish the faces of up to ten people through image recognition and also recognize approximately 650 words through voice recognition (see Figure 8-11). Additionally, its level of intimacy varies by the individual and its way of interacting changes accordingly. Additionally, it autonomously takes walks across a room and connects to the Internet to obtain information and convey the news and weather reports.

In the case of partner robots, friendliness with humans is a point of concern. This includes technical elements such as the ability to naturally interact, but such elements as gestures and outward appearance can also be considered to be vital factors. Additionally, the fact that these robots have names is indicative of the importance of realizing a sense of familiarity.

Sony's AIBO pursues this familiarity or friendliness by being "a robot that learns movements." While the AIBO can carry out adorable movements with its preloaded basic movement program, by having it learn new movements, it can be made to carry out movements with even further variations. This learning feature is helping to make the interaction between robots and humans pleasurable. AIBO's version of the Three Laws of Robotics is slightly humorous:[7]

1) A robot must not harm a human being. Fleeing from a human who is attempting to harm it is permitted, but it must not launch a counterattack.
2) A robot as a rule must direct care and love to a human, but it may also occasionally assume a defiant attitude.
3) A robot as a rule must patiently listen to the idle complaints of humans, but it may also turn nasty sometimes.

While safety is obviously important, the apparent trait of a defiant attitude and the tendency to "turn nasty" make the robot seem alive. Essentially, with partner robots, not only are their level of

Switch for detecting pats on the head	Recognizes its head being patted
CCD cameras	Using the CCD cameras embedded in each of its two eyes, PaPeRo walks while avoiding objects, spots a person and approaches them by measuring the distance to them, chases people, and registers and distinguishes faces.
LED	The LED configured in the mouth and cheeks gives PaPeRo facial expressions. The LED in the ear indicates that the robot is listening to a person's voice and the LED in the eyes indicates that the robot is seeing a person. The LED in the eyes flash green when the robot is searching for someone, stays green when the robot finds the person, and turns orange when it finds the face of the person.
Microphones that detect the direction of a sound source	There are a total of three microphones installed. One at the front, and one each to the sides. The robot estimates the direction of a sound by figuring out the differences in the times it takes the sound to reach each of the microphones. In so doing, the robot faces the direction from where the sound came.
Microphone for voice recognition	One directional microphone is installed in the head. Since PaPeRo speaks to a person by facing the person through image recognition, the microphone is naturally pointed toward the person as well. For voice recognition, the robot uses NEC's Smart Voice technology.
Speaker	PaPeRo plays words and music through stereo speakers.
Ultrasonic sensors	There are a total of five of these installed. Three at the front and two at the back. While PaPeRo moves, it avoids objects by processing the images captured by the CCD cameras. However, to avoid colliding into objects that are located in the robot's blind spot or those that jump into view suddenly, the robot uses ultrasonic sensors as well to measure the distance to objects.
Bump sensor	This sensor helps the robot to detect bumps in its path ahead to avoid falling.
Hoist sensor	This sensor detects the act of being lifted.
Wireless modem	PaPeRo can wirelessly access the Internet and wirelessly receive commands for actions and behaviors from an external PC, on which those commands can be created.
Wheels	A total of three wheels. Two front wheels and one rear wheel. Two motors drive the two front wheels. The maximum traveling speed is 20 cm per second.

		Action			
		Detection of a figure's orientation	Planning the path to reach targeted person	Obstacle evasion/ locomotion	Interaction with targeted person
Hardware	CCD cameras	O	O	O	
	Ultrasonic sensors		O	O	
	Microphones that detect the direction of a sound source	O			
	Bump sensor			O	
	Wheels			O	
	LDE				O
	Speakers				O
	Head pat/swat switch				O
	Voice recognition microphone				O
	Head (motor-activated)				O

Figure 8-11: PaPeRo's Hardware Configuration (top) and Examples of the Hardware Used in a Single Motion
Source: NEC Robot Research Website.

functionality considered to be important, but also their level of affability. This is their defining characteristic.

To realize widespread use of partner robots that can help human beings lead richer lives, it would be necessary to improve their performance. Toward this end, it would be necessary to make strides in all the technological elements raised in Figure 8-10. Japan's all-encompassing and highly advanced technological capabilities can prove to be extremely fruitful in the development of partner robots.

8.4   Development of a Robot at the Global Cutting Edge

In this last section of the chapter, I would like to discuss the development of Honda's ASIMO, which is a world-class, state-of-the-art robot.

ASIMO is a humanoid robot developed by Honda and it stands approximately 130 cm tall and weighs approximately 54 kg. ASIMO has the physical appearance of an astronaut clad in a space suit worn when carrying out outboard activities.

Walking just like a human being by using two feet, its gait is extremely smooth. Naturally, it gives the impression that its gait is somewhat more or less different from a human being's normal gait, but for the most part, it does not strike you as being odd. With the new ASIMO model released in 2005, the normal walking speed was 2.7 km per hour and the straight-line running speed reached 6.0 km per hour. Considering that by 2004 the straight line running speed was 3.0 km per hour, you can see that a drastic evolution had taken place (see Figure 8-12).

Honda began the development of a humanoid robot in 1986 and began developing ASIMO only after undergoing R&D for ten types of robots. The early seven types (the E-Series: models ranging from E0 through E6) aimed to realize smooth bipedal motion and did not have a head and arms. While the early E0 models succeeded in walking by having their two feet step forward in turns, every step had taken about five seconds to complete. In effect, they were carrying out what is known as static locomotion, which involves placing the center of gravity at the sole of the foot. Subsequently, with the E2 model, the robot succeeded in achieving a speed of 1.2 km per hour,

Height	130 cm
Width	45 cm
Weight	54 kg
Walking speed	When walking normally: 0~2.7 km/h When running in a straight line: 6.0 km/h
Grip force	0.3 kg (using one hand) 1.0 kg (using both hands)
Actuator	Servo-motor+harmonic decelerator+electric unit
Control unit	Walk/motion control unit Wireless communication unit Image processing unit
Head sensor	Vision sensor IC communications card used in combination with the optical sensor
Hand sensor	Force sensor
Body sensors	Floor surface sensor Ultrasonic sensor Gyro accelerator sensor
Foot sensor	Torque sensor
Operation unit	Notebook PC Handheld unit

Figure 8-12: Major Specifications of ASIMO
Source: Honda Motor Website.

and then with the E5 model, the robot went on to succeed in realizing a steady bipedal motion across stairs and even slopes.

The development of robots with legs only ended with the E6 model, and from 1993 onwards the focus shifted to the P Series, which was comprised of models that had a head and arms. With the release of the P2 model in 1996, the world's first autonomous bipedal humanoid robot was realized, and with the P3 model released in September 1997, miniaturization was attempted and the height had shrunken down to 160 cm.

Subsequently, ASIMO debuted in 2000. While its outward appearance has not changed that much since this time, as mentioned previously, in terms of walking speed, smoothness of motion, and collaborative attitude toward humans, the robot has shown considerable progress.

There may be those who question why Honda, an automobile maker, had begun development of a humanoid robot in the first place. Apparently, this is because Honda currently claims itself to be "*a mobility company* that is interested in anything that moves." In actuality, Honda is not only carrying out R&D for cars and motorcycles, but also for such means of transportation as small aircrafts. However, among the innumerable "things that move" in this world, why did the company choose to undertake the R&D for a humanoid robot capable of carrying out bipedal motion?

At the keynote lecture of the "Exhibition of Virtual Reality for Industrial Use" held in 2002, the company's representative Mr. Kazuo Hirai spoke on the particulars of how robot development began. In his explanation he used the example of "dimensions" and pointed out that second-dimension mobility was about developing cars equipped with a high-level of intelligence so as to be able to carry out unmanned and unattended operations. Second-dimension mobility was also about developing the power fuel cell, which could become the next-generation powerplant. Third-dimension mobility was about developing the "small aircraft" for the purpose of carrying out fundamental research for the "flying car." Finally, fourth-dimension mobility for Honda was about the development of an entity that could make movements on behalf of humans — in other words, the humanoid bipedal walking robot.

Apparently, this fourth-dimension alludes to the daily living circumstances of human beings. In other words, in such circumstances, there may be staircases that are difficult to access with existing means of mobility and what Honda is aiming to realize is the development of an entity that has human or even superhuman capabilities that can be applied in such daily living circumstances.

When the second dimension is correlated with automobiles and the third dimension with aircrafts, the correlation of the fourth dimension with the daily living circumstances of human beings seems to be a considerable leap, especially for engineers, who may be uncomfortable with the use of the concept of dimensions in this way to begin with, since they are aware of the fact that it has a fixed definition in the field of natural science.

The concept of dimensions may just be an afterthought and it may be just that the company was simply considering the circumstances or environments in which Honda's products were not applied or were not moving, as it were. However, in any case, in the present day and age when humanoid robots are being actively developed, the idea of benefiting from smooth mobility within daily living circumstances is extremely common. However, in light of the fact that not many other corporations were pursuing the full-fledged development of a humanoid robot at the time, Honda's conception can be considered to be truly wonderful.

To realize bipedal walking, it has been said that the developers of ASIMO made observations of the movements of actual pedestrians as well as of animals at the zoo. For example, the placement of the leg joint seems to have been modeled after the configuration of the human skeleton.

During his keynote lecture at the "SEMICON Japan 2002" exhibition, Mr. Masato Hirose of Honda R&D's Fundamental Technology Research Center commented, "When we were busy developing, the management used to make frequent visits to the research laboratory to scold us. They used to say, 'If you shut yourselves in the laboratory, you won't be able to create anything. Get active!' When we were observing pedestrians (for the purpose of researching bipedal motion), we were questioned by the police and when we inquired a doctor on where anesthesia could be injected to disable walking in order to further our understanding of the mechanism of the foot's movement, we were scolded again. But thanks to such deeds, we were able to come up with 'turnaround ideas,' such as the application of rubber, which was thought to be too soft to be stable, and controls that took advantage of the act of actively falling to realize walking." It can certainly be said that this was exemplary of Honda's traditional attitude toward development, which comprises the following three principles — scene, object, and reality.

It should be noted here that referring to the movements of people and animals for the purpose of technological development is not limited to ASIMO. There are many other developments that do the same. This type of technology that is modeled after living things is known as biomimetics and is evident in various fields. For example, neural networks, which are applied in the field of machine learning, are modeled after the human brain.

As for ASIMO, since quality targets for its movement capabilities had been achieved with the model released in December 2005, Honda is now concentrating on the aspect of intelligence that can help realize natural communication with humans.

Akihito Sudo

Acknowledgments

In the course of writing this chapter, I received considerable support and encouragement from Mr. Norimasa Kobori, who conducts robot-related research at a Japanese company. I herewith extend my deep gratitude to him.

References

1. Japanese Industrial Standard JIS B 0134-1998.
2. Seiichi Shin, *Illustrations — Cutting Edge Car Electronics — The Robotization of High-Tech Automobiles*, Kogyo Chousa Kai (transl. Industrial Fact-Finding Committee), March 2006.

3. Ministry of Economy, Trade and Industry's Society for the Study of Robotic Policies, *The Society for the Study of Robotic Policies Report*, May 2006.
4. Ministry of Economy, Trade and Industry's Round Table Conference on the Vision for Next-Generation Robots, *Report on the Round Table Conference on the Vision for Next-Generation Robots*, April 2004.
5. Ministry of Economy, Trade and Industry, *Strategies for the Creation of New Industries*, May 2004.
6. Susumu Tachi, *Introduction to Robots*, Chikuma New Book, 2002.
7. Kazuhiro Fujiwara, Kazuko Tojima, Kazuo Kadota, *Life Textbook — Living with Robots*, Chikuma Shobo Publishing, July 2003.

Chapter 9

The Role of Communication and Management Inside and Outside Business Organizations When Manufacturing Accidents Occur — Case Examples of Carbon Monoxide Poisoning Accidents Committed by Company M and Company P

In the development phase of new products, quality control checks and safety evaluations are carried out repeatedly from various angles before they are introduced into the market. However, even with doubly sure quality control practices in place, product-related accidents occur. In this chapter, we will be examining cases of carbon monoxide poisoning accidents caused by household products and equipment and ascertain how corporations respond to such matters. In particular, we will be ascertaining the issues and reality of such matters from the viewpoints of "the implementation process for emergency responses" and "the dynamics of organizational PR."

9.1 Occurrences of Accidents Related to Goods for Home Use

Accidents caused by household products are occurring frequently. Familiar and everyday products that are essential to daily living are taking the lives of many consumers. With products that are traditionally associated with being easily fatal if misused, such as cars, medicines, and medical devices, strong caution is advised and under the supervision of the regulating authorities, strict safety standards have to be met in the designs of such products. Furthermore, in the event such products give rise to any accident, a company is demanded to submit a swift report. However, today, even household products that do not generally give the impression of being hazardous have been tainted with the possibility of causing serious physical harm to consumers. In recent years, the public had even been notified through various media to take precautions in the use of such products. Among the TV commercials, the impressive ones are those running a calm commentary while publicizing the dangers of the products of relevant corporations.

In this report, I would like to elaborate on the cases of two firms (Company M and Company P) to shed some light on the situation of repeating accidents caused by household products. Both of these companies share in common the fact that their products had caused death by poisoning due to the release of carbon monoxide gas from malfunctioning products. We will ascertain how these corporations responded as an organization to the emergency of accidents caused by their products and how they carried out crisis management measures to minimize damage (or in the event of not having been able to carry them out, we will inquire into the causes behind the inaction). In this way, we will ascertain the reality and issues of these matters from the viewpoints of "the implementation process for emergency responses" and "the dynamics of organizational PR."

This report does not end with the ascertainment of crisis management methods carried out by the concerned companies after the occurrence of their respective accidents. Specifically, it does not attempt to qualitatively and quantitatively measure whether their organizational behavior processes that helped them carry out a series of emergency response systems were strictly valid in society's judgment or not. Instead, you should understand this report to be placing an emphasis on ascertaining the ethics involved in the response the concerned parties should carry out whenever the emergency of a product-related accident occurs. In particular the report will focus on gaining an understanding in how the concerned companies responded in emergency situations and in the organizational attitudes and climate that gave rise to their particular responses as organizations. With these things in mind, I would then like to consider the ideal shape and implementation of an organizational design that could help a company to respond on a functional level even at times of an emergency involving business-related accidents that are mainly due to accidents caused by products.

This book treats information searching for the development of new products as a main objective as well. For developing new products, you should search for information related to the type of product the market will receive and furthermore promote a business plan that is in line with an appropriate financial strategy. Additionally, after having introduced a developed product into the market, an advertising strategy for promoting sales will become necessary. Various types of information searches will become necessary in the product development and sales promotion phases.

To put it differently, this report should be understood as an investigation into how to best organize and release information on products that have been searched and collected whenever an accident occurs. In the course of developing a product, it is desirable to make effective use of information acquired for each development phase. In particular, if information on the aspects of a product undergoing the phase of fundamental development is adequately publicized to users, any potential harm to people and objects can be effectively kept in check.

9.2   Crisis Management in the Cases of Company M and Company P

9.2.1   *Crisis management of Company M*

1)   *Summary of the accidents and the causes behind them*

The concerned business received from the Ministry of Economy, Trade and Industry an emergency interim order based on Article 82 of the Consumer Appliances Security Law and expressed its intention to carry out a cost-free recall and exchange program for designated sold components of 25 models of the Forced Draught Balanced Flue type (FF type) oil heater and flat radiant oil heater, which were manufactured from 1985 through 1992. They also expressed that the program was to be carried out for the purpose of securing the safety of the consumers who had bought the products. It was reported on April 20, 2005 that three incidents of carbon monoxide poisoning had occurred. The cause was attributed to the use of an FF-type oil heater, whose safety aspect had been suspect. One person had died as a result, while several others had been hospitalized (including people who were discharged and were recovering, receiving check-ups, and people who had been discharged the next day). The poisoning was said to have been chiefly brought about by a crack that had developed in the secondary air hose made of heat-resisting rubber that supplies air into the combustion chamber of the concerned heater. The crack was said to have been caused by deterioration over time.

2)   *Organizational response*

The concerned company went on to set up an emergency market task force for FF models and reported on December 19, 2005 the progress of emergency countermeasures they had put into place for protecting against risks associated with FF-type oil heaters and flat radiant oil heaters. The following points describe the concerned company's typical post-accident responses, which were found in their news release issued on the same day.

Reexamination advisory for owners of already serviced products

In this advisory, as an emergency safety measure, the company addresses all owners of the products that had already been serviced. Effective from December 8 of the same year, for those who wish to hand over the product, the company reports that it will accept them at a cost of 50,000 yen per unit. For those who wish to continue using the product, the company reports that it will once again replace faulty air hoses with revamped ones while also distributing and installing partial combustion devices.

Complete report on activities aimed at arousing caution in consumers

The measures carried out under the supervision of regional task forces set up in cities and districts were large scale. In this document, Company M reports on having all the employees of its group companies pay visits to nationwide kerosene purchasing routes to carry out a roller strategy that would help them gain an understanding of the buyers of the concerned products and to carry out poster placements and flyer distribution. During December 13 through 16 of the same year, the number of personnel committed to the roller strategy amounted to 6,500 and it did not stop at households but extended to boarding houses, private homes providing lodging for travelers, and country inns as well.

The flyers were distributed to residents by all employees of Company M's group companies and additionally were bundled into the packaging of the company's other products. Furthermore, they were distributed at mass retailers, specialty stores, and showrooms of the company. Even pass-along circulation activities that took place in municipalities were large scale. Additionally, notices ran on top web pages of major Internet providers such as DION, OCN, and So-net.

Progress report on notification activities carried out through the mass media

Newspaper announcements ran in 62 papers nationwide for several days starting from December 4. From December 8–9, an announcement was made by the President in an ad titled "An apology and an announcement." It was 15 columns long. In addition, all advertising on TV (spot commercials and sponsored program commercials) and sponsored radio program commercials were replaced with "An announcement and a request." Additionally, 45 million newspaper inserts were distributed from December 13 through 14 nationwide.

Report on subsequent activities planned

The company expressed their intent to continue their announcement activities with the aid of the mass media. These activities included announcements made through newspapers, TV commercials titled "An announcement and a request," continued distribution of newspaper inserts, placements of announcements in city magazines, and announcements made via other magazines. In addition, the company expressed their intent to carry out mailings of flyers by inspectors of electric meters, announcements to foreign residents, announcements through TV commercials, and mailings of leaflets as enclosures in credit card bills.

After December 20, the recall and repair (or buy back) work based on the number of units found in the customer list was coming to an end, so the company expressed that its recall effort was now going to focus on those products that were difficult to discover and recall.

3)   *Investigation*

Reporting of support progress as occasion demands/complete disclosure

The characteristic aspect found in the acts carried out by the company in this accident was its swiftness in supporting the recall and repair (or buy back) of the product in question after the occurrence of the accident. Additionally, another characteristic was that the company had appropriately reported the progress of the support situation over its corporate website. Since December 5, 2005, I was able to confirm at least nine postings mainly related to the implementation of emergency countermeasures, the results of the accident research, and the situation of current countermeasures.

The particulars of the countermeasures were very detailed, and under the category titled "Stock numbers of the targeted products and their existing quantity," not only were the stock numbers and the quantity of existing units disclosed, but so were the products' manufacture periods. Regarding the cases of products that did not lead to accidents but had dislocated air hoses despite having been inspected and repaired in the course of a second inspection, the company established a "listing for cases of dislocated air hoses" and meticulously disclosed each location where an accident had occurred, stock number, repair history, the content of notices from users (smells of kerosene, fails to ignite, etc.), causes, disposal details, and the date when disposal was completed. There were disclosures of even more particulars.

These series of disclosures obviously cannot be thought of as mere formalities carried out to fulfill legal obligations. They can be instead understood as voluntary and proactive acts aimed at realizing sincere communication with society. Additionally, the series of these disclosures had the effect of showing parties within and outside the organization that the company was pursuing the right course of action in an emergency situation brought about by the occurrence of an accident.

In 1982, Johnson & Johnson's medical product Tylenol was found to have been illegally contaminated with cyanide. It was the so-called Tylenol scare. The company carried out an active information disclosure campaign immediately after the incident occurred. They carried out simultaneous satellite broadcasts to 30 cities, set up an exclusive toll-free hotline (136,000 inquiries made in eleven days after the incident occurred), ran front-page newspaper ads, and carried out TV broadcasts (exposure frequency of 2.5 viewings per household for 85% of the households in the US). The number of news reports that addressed the company's support information and notification of caution is said to have amounted to more than 125,000.

As a result, by December of the same year in which the incident had occurred, Tylenol sales were restored to its pre-incident level of 80%. It is believed that the company's success in restoring faith in Tylenol at an early stage is attributable to its corporate stance that sincerely prioritized "being responsible to consumers," which is the company's corporate philosophy.

The emergency recall measures carried out and the PR setup established by the concerned company in response to the crisis situation brought about by its products bear a resemblance to Johnson & Johnson's responses to this Tylenol incident.

Organizational risk communication that takes emergencies into account

The features apparently shared in common by all corporate scandals are deficient information analysis, negative attitude toward disclosures, passive support, and the unwillingness to make amends or even face the problems by clarifying responsibility for the scandal or accident in question. However, such drawbacks were not evident in the case of the concerned company. Rather, it can be said that the company had behaved proactively as an organization. In fact, it should be further noted that the company, prior to experiencing the accident, had already built a consensus regarding the organizational response it should make when an emergency strikes. This means that the company had been conscious of its organizational emergency response measures since its normal times and had been putting them into practice since then as well.

The attitude in recent years of the company towards business ethics began with the establishment in 1992 of the "corporate behavioral criteria," but in 1998 they had revised this to reflect their aim to (1) promote business ethics by thoroughly putting their management philosophy into practice, and (2) deal with value standards demanded by the new orientation of the times regarding the environment, human rights, and information. Since then, the company's legal department began to earnestly take measures towards pursuing ethical business practices, and by December 2000, the head of the legal department and all executives in charge of risk management were held in charge of ethical business practices. At the same time, the Business Ethics Room of the Legal Headquarters was also established.

The Corporate Behavioral Criteria clearly indicates the direction to be aimed by the organization as a whole and its sentences characteristically begin with the expression, "We will."[1] In the section titled Safety for Six Products found in its first Chapter, the following items are expressed with clarity: (1) prioritization of safety, (2) provision of information, and (3) responses to make when an accident occurs. These items are understood to have been put into practice as the general will of the company, as were the contents of the preceding section titled "three organizational responses." The traditional organizational behavior guidelines of the company remained clearly valid.

9.2.2　Crisis management of Company P

1)　*Summary of the accidents and the causes behind them*

Due to a series of accidents caused by vented-type instantaneous water heaters, Company P received a mandate from the Ministry of Economy, Trade and Industry to recall these products. The company subsequently went on to offer support for free inspections, collections, and replacements. The control boxes, which were placed in these products to prevent impartial combustion, had damaged easily and since they had been shoddily reconfigured, they had caused carbon monoxide poisoning accidents that had led to the deaths of many people.

2)   *Organizational response*

In the case of Company P, there was the impression that their response was initially unclear after the product-related accident had taken place, making them appear distrustful. In the case of Company M, at a specific point in time, they had made full disclosure of their progress in dealing with their crisis situation over their website. In the case of Company P, however, regarding their response after the occurrence of the accident and their PR activities, you were only able to come to know about them through newspapers for the most part. What follows below is an account of this company's response after the occurrence of the accident based on information acquired from newspapers.

On July 28, 2006, the company received a mandate from the Ministry of Economy, Trade and Industry to recall their products and the next day, a press conference was held at the headquarters of the company. They appeared to have taken the mandate from the ministry very seriously, but did not acknowledge that the seven models targeted for recall were defective products. In fact, they commented that there was a difference of opinion. At this point, the company did not recognize that they were fundamentally responsible for the accidents caused by their product. Up to the point this press conference was held, the company had been going ahead with product recalls, inspections and repairs in parallel. While the company had made arrangements to allow inspections, collections, and repairs of the concerned products by having its employees pay visits within a few days to users who had requested inspections, the number of units that had been replaced with new ones stopped short at 7,734 as of

August 23. The remaining 10,000 units had been inspected, but they were allowed to be temporarily used until they were to be replaced with new models.

Additionally, like Company M, this company warned users of the possible dangers associated with their certain products through the use of various media. Specifically, in addition to using newspaper and television ads, they carried out leaflet distributions to households using gas supplies, sent out direct mail to users, and announced free inspections via their corporate website. In effect, they addressed the risk of the frequent occurrence of accidents and announced their intent to carry out free replacements for consumers.

In addition to carrying out emergency support for users to restrain the spread of accidents, the company carried out a drastic structural reorganization. They also revealed that they would be setting up a third-party committee comprised of outsider experts to gain advice on organizational conduct.

3)   *Investigation*

The unprepared and dysfunctional state of the PR setup

Firstly, there was the impression that Company P was stumbling since the press conference after the accidents took place. It did not have a PR department before experiencing the concerned accidents. As a result, their support for news coverage on the accidents did not advance smoothly. Even competitors who ran smaller operations than Company P had PR departments of their own.

At the press conference held at the company after the accidents took place, the company did not acknowledge that the products targeted for recall were defective. Additionally, they once again asserted that the products in question were not defective at the press conference held two days later. However, they did not present any data or research findings that backed their assertion, making their credibility thin. While the company had completely denied that any of its employees were responsible for any shoddy modifications, at this press conference, they revised their official stance to "We cannot state definitely that our employees were not involved in the modifications in every case." The basic function of information gathering was not working. Under such circumstances, even if PR functions were working properly, society's confidence in the company cannot be retained.

The decision was reached to establish a new post that would be in charge of managing and collecting information on the problems associated with the products. It should be noted here that the company had started to reinforce their setup for managing accident-related information for the first time in this way only after the concerned accidents had taken place. The current Gas Act stipulates that the duty to report any accidents related to gas appliances rests with not the maker of the appliance, but with the gas supplier. In the case of the carbon monoxide poisoning accidents associated with Company P, on top of the fact that there were omissions in the report from the gas supplier, the information on the accidents that Company P had grasped had not been submitted to the Ministry of Economy, Trade and Industry. This state of affairs, it has been pointed out, had led to the further flaring up of the accidents. However, the PR department is a department that should be in charge of collecting various sets of information in the course of promoting a company's business activities. Such sets of information include "project development information," "product information," "business promotion information," and "financial information." Consequently, in the event a company becomes involved in a scandal or an accident, the department is there to see to it that relevant information based on these collected data are dispatched. The decisive factor in why the post-accident press coverage did not proceed smoothly can be found here.

Originally, there is the general impression that the function of PR is geared toward corporate advertising and brand image. In other words, it is generally associated with the sales promotion of products that are going to be introduced into the market (or have already been introduced into the market). However, on a fundamental level, PR should be understood for what its initials stand for — public relations. PR is the ideal method for facilitating interactive communication between a company and the public, and in the event any inappropriate incident related to the company's business activities surfaces based on information and indications from outside the company, PR should prove to help in promoting reforms and revisions as necessary.

If the company had made full use of general PR functions (such as reporting the details and causes of the accidents, and the progress of the support situation) and if it were aware of PR's original purpose, it is believed that the company would have been able to control and minimize the damage to itself, and additionally, it is believed that the post-accident news coverage facilitated at public venues would have proceeded smoothly.

Organizational insubstantiality (dysfunctional information transmission)

The concerned company was a family concern and its organizational structure was inadequate. They did not have any monitoring functions that could help them make objective decisions concerning business activities and they were not running their organizational operations in an adequate and correct manner.

Firstly, the company's ability to size up situations and make decisions at the managerial level was insubstantial. There is testimony claiming, "A meeting of the board of directors was like the President's one-man-show." The meeting was not a place for gaining approval for large-scale business developments by carrying out discussions to arrive at objective and appropriate conclusions backed by detailed market research. Nor was it a place to engage in discussions on the company's role in society or to discuss middle to long-term business strategies. The carbon monoxide poisoning accidents caused by the concerned products became a topic of discussion at board meetings but there were no drastic countermeasures adopted subsequently, and the problem ended up being neglected. Furthermore, despite the fact that it had become necessary to urgently submit reports and proposals from the scenes of the accidents to high-level departments and the management, these types of information remained at the level of the scenes.

Even though there were internal rules, the decision to report or not report on product-related accidents to the President rested with the quality control division manager. Regarding one accident case, this same manager declared, "I did not report it on the grounds of the understanding that shoddy modifications are a problem separate from the problem of quality." However, at a later time, the manager explained that this case, along with others, "should have been reported." Even though no critical defect of the concerned product could be recognized at this point in time, there was no evidence of the company showing solidarity in the cause of preventing the recurrence of these accidents and uncovering their root cause. The organization's information transmission mechanism, which should have been functioning, was in effect malfunctioning.

Additionally, at the level below the quality control department, which is the level of the scene where the actual work took place, basic principles of ethics relating to repair work had not been cultivated. A former employee of a service office of the company says that at the time of his entry into the firm, "A senior colleague taught me how to carry out shoddy modifications as a means to make do when required components were lacking." Additionally, this method for making shoddy modifications was known to repairmen of contracted service shops and repair agents affiliated with the gas companies. However, when modifying in this way, it was thought to be common sense to inform the user of the dangers involved and the need to ventilate, and make swift repairs again once the required components were procured.

Some have stated that they had made modifications for a countless number of times over several years until an internal memo prohibiting shoddy modifications was issued in January 1992. If the modifications in question were meant to serve as temporary, stopgap measures to protect users from some form of imminent danger, then those modifications, even if they were shoddy, could be considered in the end to have been measures that had taken the safety of the users into account. However, if they were indeed temporary emergency measures, then it should have been necessary to follow through with supplementary work. This would have been critical. Nevertheless, because the work remained inadequate, a catastrophe had been brought about.

In the above sections, I discussed how Company M and Company P responded as an organization to the crisis of accidents being caused by their respective products and how they carried out measures to minimize damage. In other words, I discussed how the two firms carried out crisis management (or if they were not able to carry it out, then I discussed why that was the case). From this point onward, I would like to take those cases into account and add my considerations on the "implementation process of emergency responses" and the "ideal organizational design" that could help realize this process. The concept concerned with the ideal organizational design explained in the following section is not limited to the function of preventing product-related accidents and the function of realizing disaster reduction, but also encompasses the idea of corporate crisis prevention. It also should be understood as a management system for minimizing damage.

9.3   Risk and Crisis Management in Business Organizations

9.3.1   *Thoughts on risk management that should apply throughout an entire organization*

Pure risks are material or immaterial elements that can cause damage to people and materials in the course of running business operations. In business organizations these days, it is said that gaps in awareness exist for this concept between on-site workers, administrators, and top management executives (the decision makers).

In general, the work front personnel (especially the engineers who carry out work at places that are close to production processes) are conscious of the issues of "safety and reliability" on a daily basis and are also highly conscious of the importance of a healthy organizational climate in the sphere of their own business activities.

In the production field, it is likely that revalidations of safety management processes based on reviews of the production process are being repeatedly carried out. Additionally, engineers are not only conscious of product development, but of also safety management measures that need to be put into place after products have been distributed into the market. Meanwhile, at the administrator and top management levels, it has been pointed out that awareness for managing "safety and reliability" issues at present is not as strong as evidenced at the work front level.

In the case of Company M, crisis management measures were recognized in common by everyone in the company, ranging from top management executives to work front workers. These measures would help them carry out safety management and respond to product-related accidents whenever they occurred. On the other hand, in the case of Company P, due to the fact that there were gaps in awareness for risk management between the top management and work front levels, awareness for "safety management" at the work front level was low, just as it was at the top management level as well.

The need for systematically treating the subject of risk management (protection against disasters and reducing disasters — henceforth referred to as RM) as an important part of the theoretical lineage of business administration can be validated by just taking a broad view of the theoretical lineage of the present business administration theory. From the postwar period through the time the industrial structure of the heavy industries was formed around the 1970s, business administration in Japan experienced a time of comprehensively reconstructing German business economics, the US theory of business administration, and also Japanese management practices, which had been traditionally studied. It is thought that the theory of business administration in Japan after the latter half of the 1980s was strongly influenced by the American theory of business administration, which is premised on the construction of methods rooted in scientific observations, measurements, and proofs. The present form of the Japanese theory reflects this influence. In covering RM for this report, the fields that should be emphasized are management engineering, business management theory, and organization theory, which are fields than can prove helpful in implementing product design and safety management. These fields strongly bear the characteristics of American business administration theory in particular.

While the fields of management engineering, business management, and organization theory each deal with the study of risk, they vary in terms of critical thinking processes, the events they cover, and the methods they construct to solve problems. In the case study of Company P mentioned above, it is believed that the escalation of damage had occurred because the company experienced a combination of product-engineering problems, management theory problems, and organization theory problems. Drawing lessons from this case study, it is thought that it is necessary to tie each of these disciplines that had developed on their own into one field that can serve as a field specializing in the study of pure risks surrounding the business organization. Consequently, there will be a demand for the rise of new analytical structures and, based on such structures, new management system designs for the corporate organization.

9.3.2 *System architecture guidelines/efficacy evaluations*

Now, based on the awareness of the issues mentioned above, I would like to consider how to best apply RM ideas to organizational design — ideas that could be applied as methodologies across the board of all the fields of business administration. In my judgment, towards this end, the Ministry of Economy, Trade and Industry's "JISQ 2001 Guidelines for Building a Risk Management System" is recommendable (see Figure 9-1).

These are guidelines that have been conceived for making RM function as a system without being limited by the scale and form of an organizational entity. In Figure 9-1, the categories titled "risk analysis," "risk evaluation," and "RM target setting" are relevant to the fields of management engineering and business management theory. In the field of management engineering these days, it is often the case that scenario analyses are carried out for every accident model, and in the case of analyzing the probability of occurrences, quantitative considerations are added by applying databases of accident information, accident statistics, and failure rate data.

Additionally, in terms of Figure 9-1's system as a whole (system construction, cultivation of people, construction of the RM framework, creation and implementation of programs), ideas of business management theory [the fields of labor management and personnel management administration (human resources)] are reflected. Additionally, it is believed that it would be ideal to construct a system based on the ideas of this business management theory and have it fit into the framework of the strategic thinking of organization theory.

With this RM system, every department, administrator, and top management executive in a business organization must be conscious

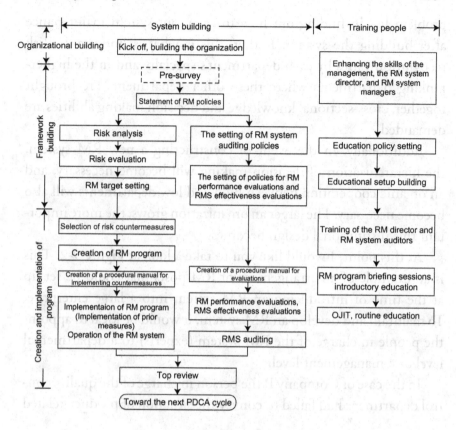

Figure 9-1: Risk Management System

Source: Toshimasa Suzuki & RM Consortium 21's *The One-Stop Guide to Understanding Everything About Risk Management*, Nikkan Kogyo Shimbun, 2002, p. 71, Figure 3-8 (The flow of RM system building for organizations incorporating it for the first time).

of safety management objectives shared in common and must constantly make assessments of their validity[1] and continue to reexamine the PDCA cycle (Plan-Do-Check-Act cycle). However, the

---

[1]This is the so-called cost-benefit analysis and it advocates the implementation of a measure once its benefits have been calculated and the probability of a risk materializing and the consequent damage levels arising after its implementation are deemed to be at acceptable levels. For details, refer to pp. 123–124 of the *Risk Management Guide,* authored by the Engineering Policy Research Section of the General Security Research Center of the Mitsubishi Research Institute. It was published by the Japan Standards Association in 2000.

problem lies in finding out how to carry out system maintenance after building the system. Rather, this is what is important. Risk recognition varies by each department's specialty and in the higher-ranking departments where these other departments are brought together, cross-sectional knowledge and decision making abilities are demanded.

Additionally, in the event of constructing a new RM system, the hierarchization of decision-making will become necessary, and an organic cooperation between high and low departments will also become necessary. The larger an organization grows, the more important this institutional design becomes.

At this point, I would like you to take a look at Figure 9-2. This is an example of an arrangement of RM posts that could be set up at the time of introducing an RM system into a large enterprise. To maintain and develop an RM system, it would be ideal to appoint the people in charge of the RM system (experts) to a departmental level or a management level.

In the case of Company P, the person in charge of the quality control department had failed to convey the situation of product-related

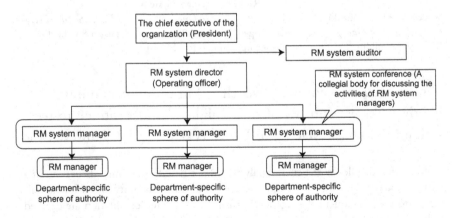

Figure 9-2: The Setup of RM System Building and Maintenance for Large Enterprises
Source: Same source as Figure 9-1, p. 79, Figure 3-13 (The setup of RM system building and maintenance for large enterprises (an example)).

accidents to senior-level executives because the person himself did not realize the magnitude of the events. If this person in charge had been carrying out his duties and appropriately reporting to senior level executives as someone in charge of an RM system that would have made it possible to recognize comprehensive risk management, the further flaring up of the accidents would have been avoided. The task of heading an RM system should ideally be carried out at the level of the department where authority has been transferred. It would then become possible to comprehensively collect and analyze information for resolving problems and negotiate with overseas departments and upper-level management. Additionally, it would become possible to carry out integrated decision-making at the high-ranking managerial level by incorporating policies proposed by lower level personnel. As a result, it would become possible for the organization as a whole to reorganize and develop the RM system.

9.3.3 *Stages of crisis management*

When considering production activities and various business activities of corporations, you will begin to see that there are various factors that serve to make the continuation of such activities difficult. In particular, the occurrences of man-made accidents and incidents, which are caused by an organization's internal factors, tend to be sudden and unexpected, making it difficult to predict the scale of damage that may arise. To minimize human and economic damage after a disaster strikes, you will need to properly design a crisis management plan beforehand and share the same views, system design, and behavioral guidelines regarding crisis management throughout the entire organization. Here, I would like to discuss the guidelines for constructing a corporate crisis management plan, which is a post-disaster response.

At this point, I would like you to take a look at Figure 9-3. This figure indicates management strategies for pre-disaster "disaster prevention measures" (risk management) and post-disaster "disaster

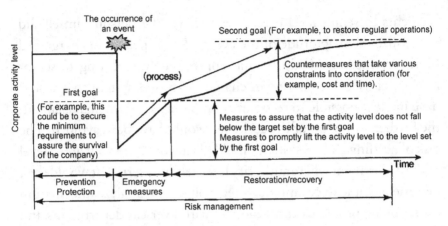

Figure 9-3: The Phases of Risk Management
Source: Same source as Figure 9-1, p. 117, Figure 3-37 (The phases of risk management).

reduction measures" (crisis management) *vis-à-vis* accidents that beset corporations. In general, the figure should be understood to be showing the "stages of risk management" that comprise the concepts of the former and latter.

I would like you to pay particular attention to "emergency measures" and "the restoration and recovery" process (everything to the right of "occurrence of event" in the figure). These are put into place after a disaster strikes and are grounded in the concept of crisis management. At the stage of "emergency measures," disaster has already struck and the survival of the corporation and the safety of consumers using the products in question must be maintained. An "urgent" form of management is demanded to minimize physical damages that include damage to humans and to economic elements. Since the product-related accidents considered in this chapter are assumed to be fatal, this form of management needs to be all the more emphasized.

Additionally, at the stage of "restoration and recovery," which follows the implementation of emergency responses, it is necessary to secure minimum conditions to maintain the continued survival of the corporation. Subsequently, the company should now aim to bring manufacturing functions and general administrative functions back to their ordinary, pre-crisis levels, taking into account the cost and time invested for putting restoration measures into effect. In the case of Company P, a cost of more than 20 billion yen to cover for inspections of models associated with a series of accidents had to be defrayed. Additionally, due to the fact that these accidents had resulted in many fatalities, the company also had to consider compensating the aggrieved parties. Indeed, they had to shoulder a vast burden of expenses.

Additionally, what the company must be particularly cautious about is being blamed for collateral damages. Responses to any moves that may bring about such an outcome must be carried out with scrupulousness. Since the damage to the image of related products may occur and contribute to a decrease in sales, a reexamination of the production plan must be taken into consideration as well. Additionally, it will be necessary for the organization as a whole to deepen its normal recognition of the business structures of the related departments. If you experience a crisis that directly involves your own department, you must confirm how the damage extension system is assumed to work.

9.3.4 *Implementation process of crisis management*

So how should we build and implement the process of crisis management mentioned above? At this point, I would like you to look at Figure 9-4. This figure shows a timeline of the sequence of events to be implemented when a company is confronted with a crisis situation, beginning with the first report received after an accident or incident takes place. The formation of a group for responding to an emergency situation at an early stage, and seeing to it that the mechanism of the task force's responses function smoothly will become extremely crucial. With Company M, these series of responses were carried out very swiftly and are believed to have functioned effectively.

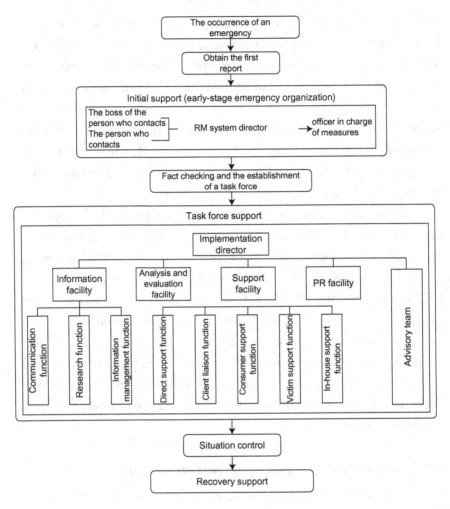

Figure 9-4:   Support Chart
Source: Same source as Figure 9-1, p. 171, Figure 4-5 (Support chart).

What becomes important after obtaining the first report is the formation of the "initial emergency responder group." What is key here is to have the person in charge of the risk management system (or the RM System Chief as specified in the figure) also become the person in charge for carrying out the measures. It is preferable for this role to be assumed by an executive officer. This is because such a person tends to have abundant knowledge of past crisis situations and also tends to be an expert in making responses for disaster reduction. Additionally, such a person can provide a very high-level of analytical and decision-making skills backed by rich experience and also offer the ability to adeptly develop a chain of command. When confronted with a crisis situation, this figure will take central command for the measures to be implemented and helm the task force.

The next important thing to achieve is substantial support for disaster reduction through the formation of a task force. As for the facilities of the task force, it is advisable to set up the following ones under the supervision of a person in charge of implementation — "information facility," "analytical assessment facility," "response facility," "PR facility," and an "advisory team facility." These facilities should be set up as independent operations. They must effectively be linked to each other through a mutually cooperative communication process.

With the "information facility," personnel will be entrusted with the task of carrying out centralized information management to assure that the situation is grasped without any discrepancies. Toward this end, the personnel will repeatedly carry out thorough research regarding the crisis situation and collect relevant information. In the case of Company P, inconsistencies in their official announcements began to surface at press conferences. We cannot therefore avoid judging that this facility had been particularly weak in Company P's case. With the "analytical assessment facility," analytical assessments are carried out on the basis of information provided by the "information facility." With the "response facility," the results of the "information facility" and the "analytical assessment facility" are used as inputs in determining the in-house behavioral criteria and subsequently actions are carried out to get the situation under control.

The "information facility," "analytical assessment facility," and "response facility" need to be structured so that one cycle of their work process is reached when the stage of emergency or the follow-ing restoration/recovery stage is reached. This cycle is similar to the PDCA cycle. The actions taken by the organization to take control of a situation must be conveyed as social announcements to stake-holders through the "PR facility." It will be important to continue reporting on how well a situation is under control and on what problems and issues remain, even if a deadlock has been reached.

9.4   Conclusion

At present, international guidelines for ethical standards of corpo-rate behavior are in the process of being formed. This movement is recognized as an attempt at forming guidelines for sound corporate conduct and for implementing appropriate actions. It is deemed nec-essary that this movement be repeated — or to put it differently, the practice of international business behavioral guidelines is still under-going development[4] and has many issues yet to resolve. Regarding the thinking behind corporate governance, which contemplates the sound and adequate ways a corporate organization can function, in the general rules of the Organisation for Economic Co-operation and Development (OECD) that were set forth in 1999, the phrase "important information" was used in relation to an explanation on the kinds of corporate information that should be accessed. However, in the revised general rules (new general rules) set forth in 2004, the expression was changed to "sufficient and reliable information on a timely and regular basis."

In recent years, in socially-responsible corporations, where valu-able traditional theories and experiences are seen to be thriving, cor-porate governance has made strides.[5] For this reason, it is advisable to be open to learning about attitudes and approaches from such corporations. In particular, the response made by Company M to deal with their accidents are sure to become classic examples of crisis management, along with Company S's response to the "fan heater accident" in 1985.

So what will be important from now on regarding corporate responses to the occurrence of accidents? The answer is believed to be the compilation and classification of the patterns of organizational conduct. If such work progresses, general principles of the best organizational behaviors can be imaged to a certain extent. Consequently, deceptive responses such as concealing or falsifying accident-related information are thought to decrease as well.

What is necessary for this task is the active disclosure of "a detailed accident analysis report." In the event a corporation causes an accident, it is obligated to create a detailed analytical report on the accident under the direction of the regulating authorities. However, these materials tend not to be actively disclosed to third parties. Insurance companies and consultancies that investigate accidents also do not show such reports to third parties. This is because they have a legally binding agreement with their client companies to keep such information confidential.

From now on, it is hoped that the corporation responsible for causing an accident will play a key role in disclosing the accident analysis report. While it is understandable that no one wishes to actively disclose their past mistakes, to prevent similar accidents from occurring again, it is necessary to pinpoint the fundamental causes behind an accident and inspect the patterns of the factors triggering it. Toward this end, the task of compiling "detailed reports" on similar accidents and the task of classifying accidents based on these materials become urgent requirements. Additionally, it is believed that the fruits of classifying accidents can be shared throughout society and largely contribute toward realizing disaster protection and reduction.

Atsushi Tsujimoto

References

1. Junnichi Mizuo, *The Business Ethics of Self-Governance*, Chikura Publishing Company, 2003, pp. 82–83.
2. Takashi Inoue, *Introduction to Public Relations*, PHP Institute, 2003, p. 5.
3. Japan Corporate Governance Forum, *OECD Corporate Governance — Analysis and Evaluation of Revised OECD Principles*, Akashi Shoten, 2006, p. 151.
4. Ros Oakley, Ian Buckland, What if Business as Usual Won't Work?, Adrian Henriques, Julie Richardson (editors), *The Triple Bottom Line: Does It All Add Up? — Assessing the Sustainability of Business and CSR*, EARTHSCAN, 2004, p. 131.
5. Rute Abreu, Fatima David, Corporate Social Responsibility: Exploration Inside Experience and Practice at European Level, David Crowther, Lez Rayman-Bacchus (editors), *Perspective on Corporate Social Responsibility*, Ashgate, 2004, p. 130.
6. Company M website, *Related Press Releases* (see 15 August 2006 release).
7. Company P website (see 15 August 2006).
8. Atsushi Tsujimoto, *Crisis Management — Guidelines for Building Its System and Evaluating Its Effectiveness*, Ohmsha, 2006, Vol. 93, No. 8.
9. Atsushi Tsujimoto, *Crisis Management — Its Organizational Communication Process and Guidelines for Management Building*, Ohmsha, 2006, Vol. 93, No. 9.
10. Yomiuri Online (http://www.yomiuri.co.jp/) (see 25 August 2006).
11. Asahi.com (http://www.asahi.com/) (see 25 August 2006).
12. *The Tylenol Story* (http://www.tylenol.jp/story.html) (see 25 March 2006).

Afterword

The demands made on authoring a work revolving around the introduction of case studies and precedents are considerable. However, the process of carrying out such work is rarely disclosed. This is because doing so will risk threatening a corporation's market predominance gained through the use of its very own intellectual assets. However, among the several cases introduced in the latter half of this book, the particulars of how certain product development and business development projects had led to successful outcomes are exposed in detail and without any hesitation. Even the field of Kansei Engineering (Sense Engineering), which has been attracting attention in recent years, has been concretely covered in the chapter titled, "Robot Development Case Examples — The Intelligential and Functional Approaches."

Additionally, in this book, needless to say, you could find accounts of methodologies that are essential to planning and implementing project management measures. Such methodologies include "strategy planning and research and development management," which form the basis of a management strategy, and "planning, selecting, and rating research and development projects." These methods are lasting and will continue to remain valid even when times change.

Business administration is said to be a discipline that is explored within the framework of empirical science. It is a discipline that empirically extracts meaningful phenomenon on a precedent-specific basis and aims to reclaim as many scientific premises as possible so as to be able to replicate measures drawn from those premises. Toward this end, the practitioner of the discipline must gain a cumulative knowledge of case studies through a foundation that realizes mutually beneficial cooperation between the businessman and the researcher and sublimate that knowledge into a theoretical system. It is a gradual, cumulative process of contributing to the knowledge that has been resolutely built up and crystallized by tenacious forerunners. It also has a theoretical framework that requires perspectives from both the businessman and researcher for its smooth succession.

I am glad that this book is testimony to the fact that wonderful results can be achieved through the establishment of a strong relationship of mutual trust and cooperation between businessmen and researchers.

The earlier book, Akira Ishikawa's *The Q&A Primer to Information Searching for Developing New Products and New Businesses*, was the genesis for this book and its first edition was published in 1988. While this book showed information search techniques for developing new products and new businesses, drastic revisions were necessary regarding such points as the "new systematization and strategization of information" and the "methods of gathering information and the prerequisites of such methods that should be considered." This is because these management strategies and their approaches needed to be updated to reflect the development and elaboration of both internal and external network structures of corporations. However, as we went through discussions for the revisions, we began to unexpectedly see new directions for the development of new products and new businesses.

With the progress of the communalization strategy of information (knowledge management), which is associated with the creation of databases and networks for corporate information, and with the rapid progress of electronic commerce that accompanied the creation of networks for connecting with external transaction firms and consumers, the distribution of information associated with the commercial activities of the IT age has seen remarkable progress. The new "policies and approaches" necessary for corporations to effectively support these new socioeconomic systems are being explored by many scholars and researchers and the fruits of their work are being revealed little by little. However, the approach attempted in this book is believed to be a completely original approach. It is one that involves studying policies and precedents of developing new products and new businesses through searching a pool of information found within an organization and outside of it. With this approach, it is believed you can find clues that could lead you to the discovery of creative solutions that can be applied toward the cultivation of a new product and new business development mindset and toward the development of an information management system.

Various people contributed to the preparation of this book. They included people who play an active role at the forefront of marketing, people who are involved in the management of R&D projects, proprietors of venture companies, and management consultants. To these people, I would like to express my deep gratitude for taking the time off from their busy schedules during the height of the summer season to contribute to this project.

Additionally, I would also like to offer my sincere gratitude to all the people who endeavored to offer their advice and encouragement. Although I cannot name them all here, I would like to say that their input proved to be extremely valuable in the publication of this book.

Atsushi Tsujimoto
September 2006

About the Authors

Akira Ishikawa (Introduction, Chapter 5)*

Professor Emeritus at Aoyama Gakuin University. Senior Research Fellow at the University of Texas ICC Institute. Awarded a Ph.D. in Business Management from the Graduate School of Business Administration of the University of Texas. Completed postdoctoral studies at MIT. Fields of expertise include management science, management accounting, crisis management, research and development management, and accounting and finance for contents businesses. Principal book: *Theory of Strategic Budgetary Control*, Dobunkan, 1993. Thesis: Understanding Intellectual Capital and the Modeling Approach to Intellectual Capital Management, *Aoyama Management Review*, 2003. Over 70 publications comprise translations or works in which the author has written or edited. Over 400 theses published. Further details of the author can be found at http://www.brainsbank.net/ishikawa.

Junpei Nakagawa (Chapter 2)

Associate Professor at the Business Administration Department of Komazawa University. Acquired units for a Ph.D. degree in Economics from the Graduate School of The University of Tokyo. Fields of expertise are institutional economics and organizational theory. Principal book: *Institutions and Organizations* (co-author, editor: Tokutaro Shibata), Sakurai Shoten Publishing, 2007. Thesis: Rethinking the Technostructure Theory, *Annual Report of the Society of Economic Sociology*, No. 23, September 2001, etc.

Hiromichi Yasuoka (Chapter 3)

Senior consultant at the Financial Business Consulting Department of the Nomura Research Institute. Awarded an M.S. in Science and Engineering from the Graduate School of Keio University. Awarded a D.B.A. from Newport University in California, USA. After leaving NRI, started up a new e-business at SQUARE (currently SQUARE ENIX). Engaged in business consulting at Arthur Anderson (currently Bearing Point). Joined NRI again to consult on creating CRM marketing strategies and on operational reforms. Principal books: *Enterprise Currencies of 2010 — The Point Economy of the Googlezon Age* (co-author) and *Enterprise Currency Marketing* (co-author), Toyo Keizai Shinposha, etc.

Tetsuro Saisho (Chapter 4)

Associate Professor at the College of Economics, Kanto Gakuin University. Awarded an M.B.A. in International Politics, Economics and Business from the Graduate School of Aoyama Gakuin University. Awarded a Ph.D. in Science and Engineering from the Graduate School of Chuo University. Fields of expertise are information systems, information security, management information, and corporate strategy. Principal book: *Installation and Deployment of Information Security Management*, Kanto Gakuin University Publishing Society, 2006. Thesis: Changes in the Environment Surrounding Corporations and System Risk Management, *Japan Society of Security Management Magazine*, Vol. 19, No. 1, pp. 25–43, September 2005, etc. Recipient of the 12th Japan Information-Culturology Society Award in 2006.

Hideto Maeda (Chapter 6)

Senior Brand Manager at the Functional Tea Group of the Brand Marketing Department of Coca-Cola Japan. Awarded an M.S. in Medicine from the Graduate School of Keio University. Entrusted with the development of skin care products for countries in Asia (including Japan) and in Europe at the Skin Beauty Care Product Group of the R&D Department of Procter and Gamble Far East Inc. Joined the Business Knowledge Department of Coca-Cola Japan in 2001 and since then has been handling a wide range of tasks, ranging from the construction of consumer models to searching for new materials and branding.

Yoshisuke Yamakawa (Chapter 7)

Representative Chairman of the Board of ALBERT Inc. Graduated from the Materials Chemistry Department of the Engineering Department of Yokohama National University. After engaging in development and product planning at the Recording Medium Business Unit of TDK Corporation, moved to Maruman Co., Ltd., and consecutively held the positions of Marketing Manager and Executive Director at the company's Consumer Electronics Business Unit. Established M&C Corporation in 1995 and took office as the firm's Chief Executive Officer. In 2000, established Interscope Inc., and in July 2005, established ALBERT Inc.

Akihito Sudo (Chapter 8)

Enrolled in the later stage of the Ph.D. curriculum of the Interdisciplinary Graduate School of Science and Engineering of the Tokyo Institute of Technology. Awarded a B.S. in Physics and an M.E. in Pure and Applied Physics from Waseda University. Former employee of Nomura Research Institute. Field of expertise is information engineering (the fundamental technology of artificial intelligence in particular). Thesis: Associative Memory for Online Learning in Noisy Environments Using SOINN, *Information Technology Letters*, pp. 189–192, 2007 (co-author). Recipient of the Funai Best Paper Award.

Atsushi Tsujimoto (Chapter 9)*

Assistant Professor at the Interfaculty Initiative in Information Studies at the University of Tokyo. Acquired units for a Ph.D. degree from the Graduate School of Humanities and Sociology of the University of Tokyo in September 2006. Fields of expertise are informational organization theory (fundamental informatics, http://www.digital-narcis.org/) and risk management. Principal book: *Risk Management 99* (co-author), Shumpusha Publishing, 2006. Thesis: Fire Hazards That Impact the Environment and Risk Management — Reorganizing the Communication Process in Organizations Handling Hazardous Materials (Young Investigator Excellence Award 2006), *Crisis Management Review*, No. 14, pp. 43–50, March 2006, etc.

(*Editor)

Index

313

person-to-person word of mouth, 128
personal computers, 10
personal information management system, 3
personal life, 3
personnel training, ix
peta, 2
phases of risk management, 298
photo collage, 175
photocharacterizations, 138
picosecond, 2
pithecanthropus, 1
playback robot, 245
potential customers, 104
practical use stage, 103
practical-use research, 127
pre-adjustments, 117
preventive medicine, 172
principal companies, 44
private enterprise, 10
process innovation, 27
product and service attributes, 44
product architecture, 22
product development, 106, 107, 144
product innovations, 27
product life cycle, 43, 116
product recommendation website, x
product strategy, 144
product structure (product line), 114
product's life cycle (PLC), 33
production management/process control, 9
production-to-order, 18
Productivity Dilemma, 27
productivity evaluations of meetings, 12
productization research, 139
products, 106, 107
profit per unit cost, 146
profitability, 29, 74
proto-man, 1
proximity searches, 99
psychological factor, 216
pure risks, 292

qi, 181, 182
QRIO, 267
quantitative expressions, 91
Quartz wristwatches, 148
questionnaire-based filtering, 200
Q&A format, vii

ratio of new product sales to old product sales, 145
rationalization strategy, 112
Ready to Drink (RTD), 155, 156
recycling rate, 147
reframe, 157
regression analyses, 173
relational structure, 91
relative margin, 116
relaxation of regulations, 3
relevance rate, 97
research and development, viii
research fellowships, vi
resource-based theory, 31
resource-poor nation, v
response time, 98
responsiveness to technical requirements, 146
revised key-needs method, 60
risk aversion ratio, 147
risk management personnel, x
Risk Management System, 294–296
robot, 243, 244
robot development case, x
Rogers, Everett, 227
rolls, 99
rule-based filtering, 200
R&D, viii, 127
R&D alliances, viii, 37
R&D budget, 31
R&D budgetary control, 145
R&D department, viii
R&D expenditures, 17
R&D information, 86, 102, 108, 109, 112, 114, 115, 119, 123
R&D management, 127
R&D programs, 13
R&D projects, 8, 13
R&D risk, 86

Santorini, 2
Science Council of Japan, vi
Scientific and Cultural Organization (UNESCO), 143
scope and depth, 97
security, 238
security concerns, 101
security system, 119